KU-473-793

■ Unionists, Loyalists, and Conflict Transformation in Northern Ireland

STUDIES IN STRATEGIC PEACEBUILDING

SERIES EDITORS
R. Scott Appleby, John Paul Lederach, and Daniel Philpott
The Joan B. Kroc Institute for International Peace Studies
University of Notre Dame

STRATEGIES OF PEACE
Transforming Conflict in a Violent World
Edited by Daniel Philpott and Gerard F. Powers

UNIONISTS, LOYALISTS, AND CONFLICT TRANSFORMATION
IN NORTHERN IRELAND
Lee A. Smithey

Unionists, Loyalists, and Conflict Transformation in Northern Ireland

Lee A. Smithey

OXFORD
UNIVERSITY PRESS

OXFORD
UNIVERSITY PRESS

Oxford University Press, Inc., publishes works that further
Oxford University's objective of excellence
in research, scholarship, and education.

Oxford   New York
Auckland   Cape Town   Dar es Salaam   Hong Kong   Karachi
Kuala Lumpur   Madrid   Melbourne   Mexico City   Nairobi
New Delhi   Shanghai   Taipei   Toronto

With offices in
Argentina   Austria   Brazil   Chile   Czech Republic   France   Greece
Guatemala   Hungary   Italy   Japan   Poland   Portugal   Singapore
South Korea   Switzerland   Thailand   Turkey   Ukraine   Vietnam

Copyright © 2011 by Oxford University Press, Inc.

Published by Oxford University Press, Inc.
198 Madison Avenue, New York, New York 10016

www.oup.com

Oxford is a registered trademark of Oxford University Press.

All rights reserved. No part of this publication may be reproduced,
stored in a retrieval system, or transmitted, in any form or by any means,
electronic, mechanical, photocopying, recording, or otherwise,
without the prior permission of Oxford University Press.

Library of Congress Cataloging-in-Publication Data
Smithey, Lee A.
Unionists, loyalists, and conflict transformation in
Northern Ireland / Lee A. Smithey.
p. cm.—(Studies in strategic peacebuilding)
ISBN 978-0-19-539587-7 (hardcover: alk. paper)
1. Northern Ireland—Politics and government.
2. Protestants—Northern Ireland—Politics and government.
3. Protestants—Northern Ireland—Attitudes.
4. Protestantism—Northern Ireland.
5. Religion and politics—Northern Ireland.
6. Orange Order.
7. Unionism (Irish Politics)
8. Peace-Building—Northern Ireland.   I. Title.
DA990.U46S 587 2011
941.60824—dc22   2010046864

9 8 7 6 5 4 3 2 1

Printed in the United States of America
on acid-free paper

To my family, Judith, Alison, and Zeb, who made this book possible with their patience and care.

■ ACKNOWLEDGMENTS

I want to express my deep appreciation for the enduring support of my wife, Judith, and our children, Alison and Zeb. Our parents and families have also, as always, played important roles in encouraging us. Several institutions facilitated this research. My colleagues and students in the Department of Sociology and Anthropology, the Program in Peace and Conflict Studies, and Swarthmore College's Northern Ireland Semester have been immensely supportive. I would like to thank Dr. Dominic Bryan and the Institute for Irish Studies at Queen's University of Belfast for providing an institutional home in 2007. The staff in the Political Collection of the Linenhall Library provided important archival support, and ARK's publicly available datasets, the Northern Ireland Life and Times Survey and the Young Life and Times Survey, feature at several points in this book. I am grateful to the editors of the Studies in Strategic Peacebuilding series for the opportunity to participate and for the important contributions they have each made to this field. My editors at Oxford University Press have shepherded this project with great efficiency and patience. Jennifer Keltran at Kelsey Transcripts provided friendly, professional, and timely transcription services. Anne Holzman crafted the book's index with care and enthusiasm.

Funding by Swarthmore College, the Northern Ireland Community Relations Council (CRC), and the James Michener family enabled me to conduct necessary fieldwork. Duncan Morrow and Paul Jordan at the CRC were helpful in administering financial support and providing valuable contacts and guidance. The views and expressions of opinion contained in this research do not necessarily reflect those held by the Northern Ireland Community Relations Council or other funders.

I owe a debt of gratitude to many people for their encouragement, intellectual engagement, and feedback. They include Mark Hammond, Lester Kurtz, Nadine Kolowrat, Gareth Higgins, Anne Kane, Marc Ross, Dominic Bryan, John Brewer, Joe Liechty, Eric Kaufmann, Brian Kennaway, Joy Charlton, Gregory Maney, Pat Coy, Dan Mears, Alex McClung, Mike Demand, Webster Younce, Dave Magee, and Tom Dee. My students and fellow writers, Reina Chano, Samia Abbass, and Maurice Weeks, inspired me with their enthusiasm for Northern Ireland. Colleagues at the Solomon Asch Center for the Study of Ethnopolitical Conflict at Bryn Mawr College stimulated my thinking on many of the topics covered within these pages, and I have appreciated opportunities to share my findings with them.

This book was only possible with the assistance of many contacts across Northern Ireland. I would like to extend special thanks to the Grand Orange Lodge of Ireland and the staff and congregation at the East Belfast Mission. In the interest of protecting identities and with the assurance that I could not possibly name all who so kindly shared their thoughts and insight, I want to express my deep gratitude en masse. Similarly, I could not list all of the friends and family, in both the United States and Northern Ireland, who have supported and encouraged us, but I will venture to name Fiona Clark, Mark and Jude Hammond, Mark McCleary, Jayne McConkey, Pádraig Ó Tuama, and all branches of the Dark family. Trevor Henderson planted a very early seed or two in my mind that have germinated into this book. I am sure there are many others I will soon regret not acknowledging. If I were allowed the space, I could detail a multitude of kindnesses and important leads. Even so, the arguments presented in this work and any errors are my own.

CONTENTS

■ ABBREVIATIONS

ACE   Action for Community Employment, government-funded employment scheme

AOH   Ancient Order of Hibernians, an Irish Catholic fraternal organization

BACS   Ballymacarrett Arts and Cultural Society

BBC   British Broadcasting Corporation

B/GFA   Belfast/Good Friday Agreement

CDRG   Community Development Review Group

CRC   Community Relations Council (Northern Ireland)

CTG   Cultural Traditions Group

CTI   Conflict Transformation Initiative (UPRG/UDA)

DCAL   Department of Culture, Arts, and Leisure (Northern Ireland)

DELNI   Department for Employment and Learning Northern Ireland

DUP   Democratic Unionist Party

EBHCS   East Belfast Historical and Cultural Society

EBM   East Belfast Mission

EU   European Union

GAA   Gaelic Athletic Association

GOLI   Grand Orange Lodge of Ireland, the central body of the Orange Order in Ireland, a Protestant unionist fraternal organization

IFI   International Fund for Ireland, a development and reconciliation fund established by the United Kingdom, United States, Australia, Canada, New Zealand, and Australia

INLA   Irish National Liberation Army, a republican paramilitary

IRA   Irish Republican Army (Provisional), a republican paramilitary

LOL   Loyal Orange Lodge, precedes the number and follows the name of individual Orange lodges

LVF   Loyalist Volunteer Force, a loyalist paramilitary

MLA   Member of the Legislative Assembly

MP   Member of Parliament

NICRA   Northern Ireland Civil Rights Association

NICVA   Northern Ireland Council for Voluntary Action

NIHE   Northern Ireland Housing Executive

NILTS   Northern Ireland Life and Times Survey

NIO   Northern Ireland Office, the United Kingdom department responsible for Northern Ireland affairs

NUPRG   New Ulster Political Research Group, an advisory group to the Ulster Defence Association

OPW   Office of Public Works (Republic of Ireland)

PCROs   peace and conflict resolution organizations

PSNI	Police Service of Northern Ireland, established in 2001
PUL	Protestant/unionist/loyalist
PULSE	Protestant Unionist Loyalist Social Education, an Internet loyalist radio station and networking site
PUP	Progressive Unionist Party, a loyalist political party with links to the Ulster Volunteer Force
RTE	Raidió Teilifís Éireann, public broadcasting agency in the Republic of Ireland
RUC	Royal Ulster Constabulary, the police service established in 2001 that preceded the Police Service of Northern Ireland
SDLP	Social Democratic and Labour Party, a nationalist political party
TUAS	Tactical Use of Armed Struggle, a republican conflict strategy
UDA	Ulster Defence Association, a loyalist paramilitary
UDP	Ulster Democratic Party, a loyalist political party with links to the Ulster Defence Association
UDR	Ulster Defence Regiment, a local part-time Army regiment merged with the Royal Irish Rangers in 1992
UFF	Ulster Freedom Fighters, a loyalist paramilitary organization
UK	United Kingdom
UPRG	Ulster Political Research Group, an advisory group to the Ulster Defence Association
U.S.	United States of America
USHC	Ulster-Scots Heritage Council
UUP	Ulster Unionist Party
UVF	Ulster Volunteer Force, a loyalist paramilitary
WBACS	West Belfast Athletic and Cultural Society
YCV	Young Citizens Volunteers, militant loyalist youth organization associated with the Ulster Volunteer Force
YLTS	Young Life and Times Survey

■ Unionists, Loyalists, and Conflict Transformation
in Northern Ireland

1 Introduction

But if we grant that symbolic systems are social products that contribute to making the world, that they do not simply mirror social relations but help constitute them, then one can, within limits, transform the world by transforming its representation.
—Pierre Bourdieu (Bourdieu and Wacquant 1992:14)

In 2005, as we drove through Portadown, a primarily Protestant Northern Ireland town, a friend and colleague who lives there pointed out a mural[1] and said simply, "There's King Rat." The mural featured a portrait of a man with close-cropped hair and a goatee flanked by garlands of poppies and orange lilies. Banners over and beneath the portrait read, "In honour of Grenadier William 'Billy' Wright LVF." Below, two masked gunmen wearing spats and white belts brandished automatic weapons and gazed up at the visage of Wright. Between them, a scroll displayed a verse from the New Testament of the Bible: "Greater love hath no man than this, that a man lay down his life for his friends — John 15:13" (see figures 1.1 and 1.2).

The mural on the Brownstown Road valorized a contentious figure who not only threatened Catholics but was a lightning rod for divisions within loyalist paramilitary organizations.[2] Wright was a notorious dissident loyalist paramilitary leader who was ousted from the Ulster Volunteer Force (UVF) and formed the Loyalist Volunteer Force (LVF) in 1997 after his organization allegedly killed a Catholic taxi driver, Michael McGoldrick. In December 1997, Wright was assassinated in the Maze prison by fellow prisoners who were members of the republican Irish National Liberation Army (INLA). Like many murals, Wright's could conjure fear, mistrust, grief, triumph, or honor, depending on the viewer's own experience and perspective.

On a return visit to Portadown only two years later, I found that the mural had been replaced with a commemorative tribute to the famous footballer[3] George Best, one of Europe's all-time best players who hailed from East Belfast. This time, the banners on the mural were blue and simply read, "George Best 1946–2005" above the logo of the Irish Football Association.[4] This clear and intentional change in public symbols on the Brownstown Road has become common in Protestant, unionist, and loyalist (PUL) communities across Northern Ireland as initiatives are undertaken to alter familiar symbols and practices including flags, parades, and bonfires as part of a cultural transformation in the region.

In a commemorative garden a short distance from the mural, at the center of a flagstone patio sat a large polished granite stone with the inscription: "In memory of all victims of conflict." In the background, at the rear corners of the patio, sat

LIVERPOOL JOHN MOORES UNIVERSITY
LEARNING SERVICES

Figure 1.1 A mural honoring Billy Wright, a founder of the Loyalist Volunteer Force (LVF), photographed June 29, 2005.

two small tablets, each inscribed: "In loving memory of" alongside several individuals' names. One held the names of Billy Wright and another LVF member; the other listed four UVF members. Each stone bore the familiar loyalist commemorative phrase, "At the going down of the sun and in the morning we will remember them," from Laurence Binyon's poem, "For the Fallen" (see figures 1.3 and 1.4).

I had the opportunity to interview Gareth and Daniel, two men involved with a local community organization that helped organize the mural redesign and commemorative garden.[5] Gareth pointed out that the garden was carefully arranged so that the larger stone could be read by passersby on the sidewalk or the road while the smaller tablets were intentionally inclined upward so that they could only be read by people who entered the garden and walked to its back corners. The arrangement of the garden diminishes the prominence of the kinds of violent images and references that had dominated the original Billy Wright mural nearby. However, according to Gareth, the design of the mural and garden projects involved a difficult, months-long process of consultations, and while the removal of the Wright mural brought tears of grief to some eyes during the unveiling, others expressed

Figure 1.2 A mural honoring Billy Wright was replaced with a mural celebrating George Best. Brownstown Road, Portadown, photographed January 20, 2007.

their appreciation and a sense of liberation. He described the thought that went into the design of the garden:

> The symbolic nature of those two constituencies [LVF and UVF] sharing the same space as a reflective space, I think, was a considerable achievement locally. But, we were very conscious we didn't want that space to become a shrine for paramilitarism.... We then secured a huge bit of Mourne granite, and we said, "We want to rein this back into being a community space," and there is a huge stone right in the middle that a blind man can see. Literally, "In loving memory of all victims of conflict," full stop. You can interpret that whatever way you want.

One must wonder whether everyone grieving a victim of the conflict would feel comfortable reflecting on their loss in a garden in the presence of the two smaller stones, but the change is nonetheless significant.

Such shifts in the symbolic landscape lead us to inquire about concomitant changes in the social psychological landscape of a region where ethnopolitical conflict has been perpetuated by both violence and prejudices. If the downward spiral of fear and retaliation that characterized thirty years of paramilitary and military violence accompanied a proliferation of antagonistic symbols and

Figure 1.3 Granite monuments to "all victims of conflict". Brownstown Road, Portadown, photographed January 20, 2007.

rituals, what accounts for a widespread, if incomplete, trend in the opposite direction? How are such changes negotiated within and between polarized communities? Who is involved in the mitigation of polarizing cultural expressions and why? What does the process look like, and what does it tell us about the potential to transform intractable conflict? Those are the questions we will explore.

Collective identities and the ritual and symbolic actions that shape and maintain them are recursively related with one another, and much of this book concerns itself with the renovation of public displays of Protestant unionist and loyalist identity. By redesigning bonfires and murals (such as, the Wright-Best mural in Portadown) or choreographing Orange and loyalist band parades in ways that mitigate some of their most offensive facets, unionist and loyalist activists introduce new values carefully reconciled with long-held understandings of their collective identities. The result is a softening of a politically charged symbolic landscape and a reconsideration of polarized ethnopolitical identities. In some cases, symbols can become shared across the ethnopolitical divide. In other cases, the process of adopting new symbols and practices or shaping collective memories through the construction of historical narratives can open opportunities for cross-community dialogue.

Figure 1.4 Granite monument to Loyalist Volunteer Force (LVF) paramilitaries. Brownstown Road, Portadown, photographed January 20, 2007.

This is not a post-conflict process but rather a continuation of conflict by other means. Conflict in Northern Ireland has long been contested by many means: political, economic, cultural, and military. The central story of the peace process has been a long shift away from violent and coercive methods toward persuasive and political ones, and we might do well to adopt Brewer's (2010) nomenclature of "post-violent society" while acknowledging (as Brewer does) that political and sectarian violence does not necessarily end neatly when political negotiations get under way (Brewer 2010:16–28, 32–33). The conflict is, instead, in a state of transition. Such shifts are not merely the product of strategic calculations, though they may be shaped by pragmatism. They are imagined, debated, and adopted by people with collective identities that have been catalyzed in threatening, unjust, and often violent circumstances. Indeed, ethnic and political identities have become closely linked to calculuses of winning and losing. This is not to say that identities or strategies are monolithic. New strategies can be and have been introduced, but unless or until they align, or are made to align, with collective identities, they are unlikely to be fully adopted. How even the most ideologically committed organizations come to mitigate or replace violent or offensive activities warrants our attention as well as the ways in which collective identities and community relations change in tandem.

Although I have chosen to focus on the Protestant community, a study such as, this could be productively undertaken within Catholic and nationalist organizations and communities. Republican leaders in Sinn Féin, the largest political party within the republican movement, have carefully reframed republicanism since they rediscovered the potential of nonviolent action and then constitutional politics over the course of the hunger strike of 1981 (Shirlow and McGovern 1998). Protestants are arguably facing equal if not greater challenges in adapting to new political and economic circumstances. Many of the institutions around which Protestants, unionists, and loyalists historically rallied have been relinquished or suffer from decline. Working-class Protestants, especially, feel they need new organizing skills, a shared sense of confidence, and more social capital to participate and benefit fully in the newly emerging Northern Ireland.

This book documents an emerging, if tenuous, process in which prominent conservative unionist and loyalist organizations, such as, the Orange Order[6] and other voluntary organizations, are seeking to cultivate political and social capital by abandoning practices that are seen as sectarian or offensive and engaging more proactively in public relations. These are unfamiliar strategies for Protestants who have tended to feel that change is a harbinger of defeat. Thus, the process of internal transformation is a slow and contentious one as leaders work to introduce new policies and practices while continuing to hew to deeply held beliefs about themselves, the conflict, and their role in it.

Brewer and Higgins (1998) identify three domains in which sectarianism and division have been perpetuated in Northern Ireland: *ideas, individual behavior,* and *social structure*.[7] The prominence of each domain can vary across a range of social situations, such as, class divides, but each reinforces the others in an extensive system of division and inequality. Prejudices and stereotypes reflect power differentials in the social structure and underpin destructive individual behavior in the forms of discrimination, intimidation, and violence (pp. 2, 183).

The structural contexts in which conflict transformation occurs are important, and much strong scholarship on Northern Ireland tracks the shifting interacting political, economic, and demographic contours that influence the trajectory of the region's conflict. Thus, chapter 3 will present essential historical and political background information that is essential for interpreting an ever-important microsociological context. In this book, I focus on ideas (cultural schemata and identities) and behavior (political and cultural collective action), asserting that conflict transformation involves both a shift from coercive means of engaging in conflict toward more persuasive ones as well as subjective redefinitions of in-groups and out-groups. Paradoxically, much of the critical work of transforming conflict and developing less polarized collective identities takes place *within* even the most conservative and traumatized communities and organizations, and we will consider the experience of Protestant/unionist/loyalist (PUL) activists and organizations in Northern Ireland where innovations in traditional cultural expressions contribute to reshaping the contours of unionist and loyalist identities.

For a sustainable peace to emerge, emotions, identities, and ideologies, as well as the rituals and cultural expressions that sustain them, must begin to accommodate one another. The process of replacing a culture of mistrust and fear with one of cooperation is a slow tenuous process, and contention across the ethnopolitical divide will continue. However, we can say that a conflict is in a state of transformation when fundamentally polarized in-group and out-group perceptions have begun to change, albeit slowly and incrementally. For more than twelve centuries, Ireland has been marked by legacies of invasion, colonialism, and conflict. With the wide-scale influx of English and Scottish settlers from the beginning of the seventeenth century and the subsequent rebellions and subjugation of the Gaelic Irish population, the stage was set for four centuries of conflict over the merits and injustice of British rule, even though the lines of contention never perfectly conformed to a religious divide between Catholics and Protestants. From the seventeenth century to World War II, economic interests, European geopolitics, and British concerns about the security of its western flank drove British policies with regard to Ireland. However, religious and ethnic divisions increasingly came to parallel political contention over issues such as, sovereignty and equality. The potent combination of divergent political agendas and ethnic and religious prejudice, or "sectarianism," has limited dialogue, creative problem solving, and compromise, leaving suspicion, fear, and often violence to feed on one another (Liechty 1995; Liechty and Clegg 2001).

Among cases such as, the former Yugoslavia, Cyprus, South Africa, Sri Lanka, and Israel/Palestine, in which core ethnopolitical identities have contributed to zero-sum mentalities, Northern Ireland has received considerable attention, especially with regard to "the Troubles," the period of armed conflict among paramilitaries and state security forces that is usually considered to span the period from 1968 to 1998. The conflict produced over 3,700 deaths and ten times as many injuries between 1969 and 2001 (Smyth and Hamilton 2003:18–19). Thankfully, Northern Ireland has also become remarkable for its ongoing political peace process. Negotiations between the British government and the paramilitary Irish Republican Army (IRA) as well as between John Hume, the leader of the nationalist Social Democratic and Labour Party (SDLP) and Gerry Adams, the leader of the republican political party, Sinn Féin, developed into more than two decades of political negotiations involving the British and Irish governments, local parties, and international intermediaries.[8]

As the paramilitary cease-fires have remained relatively stable since 1994, and political negotiations have continued despite intermittent suspensions of the power sharing Northern Ireland Assembly[9] that was established under the terms of the 1998 Belfast or Good Friday Agreement (B/GFA), the prospects of a return to widespread violence have diminished, and the future of politics has increasingly become a question of when political institutions will stabilize. Backdoor political negotiations and all-party talks have led to a political peace process that, at the time of writing, features a legislative power sharing arrangement in the form of the Northern Ireland Assembly, led by Sinn Féin and the Democratic Unionist Party (DUP), formerly the most diametrically opposed parties. After having been suspended several times, the resurrection of the Northern Ireland Assembly in 2006 was followed by an executive partnership in 2007 between firebrand Free Presbyterian Church founder and staunch unionist politician, Ian Paisley, and Martin McGuinness, who served as Officer Commanding of the Provisional IRA in Derry in the 1970s. The friendly relationship between the new first minister and deputy first minister astonished even the savviest pundits.

Northern Ireland's peace process and power sharing government have rightly become celebrated examples of patient and painstaking peacemaking underpinned by decades of largely unsung grassroots work by peace and conflict resolution organizations (PCROs). Yet, the challenge of grassroots peacebuilding remains (Cochrane and Dunn 2002; Fitzduff 2002; Gidron, Katz, and Hasenfeld 2002).[10] Significant structural and psychological barriers persist, not to mention the relative fragility of the political process. We should celebrate the tremendous progress that has been made in ending one of the world's longest running violent conflicts while acknowledging that the collective psychological and emotional wounds that need healing must continue to be addressed as all involved build a vibrant and cooperative democracy.

Polarized ethnopolitical identities remain among the most significant obstacles to building a healthy multicultural civil society in Northern Ireland and elsewhere around the world. Subjective interpretations of the conflict and intercommunity and intracommunity relations among Protestants and Catholics are all subject to change, and yet, they are not easily changed, especially while the trauma of thirty years of recent violent conflict remains fresh. However, subjective dimensions of the conflict have been shifting in ways that have made space for much of the political progress to date and have in turn been facilitated by political developments, such as, the cease-fires and power sharing governance.

How political change takes place in the context of the paradoxical malleability and tenacity of ethnopolitical identities deserves attention (Hayes 1990:4). A sustainable peace depends on the ability of even the most ideologically committed organizations and individuals to develop new interpretations of themselves and adversaries that make space for dialogue, cooperation, and coexistence. By delving into the contemporary experience of Protestants involved with unionist and loyalist organizations and activities, we find an uncharted and difficult process of renegotiating the past, present, and future that is central to contemporary peacebuilding in Northern Ireland. This volume explores those subterranean cultural and social psychological processes that accompany the more visible headline-making developments in the political sphere.

In subsequent chapters, we will examine how charged ethnopolitical symbols and rituals among unionists and loyalists, such as, Orange parades, murals, music, dancing, and historical activities, influence and facilitate the construction of ethnopolitical identity. Among Protestants who have long felt "under siege," redesigning murals to replace images of masked gunmen with local historical figures and World War I battle scenes in France and Belgium and working with the Northern Ireland Tourist Board to attract visitors to annual Orange parades signal a shift from their former defensive orientation. It is important to note that innovations in traditional cultural expressions are not attempts at reconciliation. They continue to communicate narratives of a distinctive Protestant experience and thus inscribe difference, but they constitute a reorientation, an interest in enhancing Protestants' abilities to engage effectively in discourse and debate. The overall effect is to soften social psychological boundaries and make dialogue and relationship building across the ethnopolitical divide more likely. The results may seem modest, but they reflect the depth of division that has made intractable conflict so difficult to manage in Northern Ireland.

▪ INTRACTABLE ETHNOPOLITICAL CONFLICT

Intractable ethnopolitical conflict, of which Northern Ireland has been considered a primary case, has proven a prominent and growing global social problem over the past century and can be found at the root of most ongoing major violent conflicts and wars in recent decades (Scherrer 2008). Social scientists have struggled to conceptualize the powerful forces that can be generated when major political disputes parallel lines of ethnic and racial division. Symbolic expressions of ethnic identity and political ideology represent and reproduce psychocultural schemata in which groups find ontological security and through which organizations build consensus and mobilize for (sometimes violent) political action. Conflict over human rights, inequality, and sovereignty within disputed borders all take place within what Marc Ross (2009) has called contested "symbolic landscapes" in which collective senses of identity among warring or contending populations can become magnified and mutually polarized, providing fertile ground for fear, dehumanization, violence, and a downward spiral of retaliation and division.

Intractable ethnopolitical conflicts, which Mats Friberg and John Paul Lederach refer to as "identity conflicts," are so tenacious in large part because they are driven by deeply psychological and emotional forces converging with large-scale structural forces (Lederach 1997:8). At the individual level, victims of bombings, assassinations, and punishment attacks struggle with the trauma that accompanies the brutalization of a neighbor or loved one. At group or community level, intimidation and fear encourage defensive attitudes, stereotyping, and racism or sectarianism as cultural schemata are constructed that interpret and legitimize the grievances and aspirations of each community, and in many cases, valorize those who have taken up arms in the name of communal defense (Liechty 1995:15; Brewer and Higgins 1998).

In extreme conflict situations, adversaries' identities can become defined such that they are mutually opposed to one another, indivisible and nonnegotiable. They become inseparable from the conflict that comes to be understood in zero-sum terms of "us" and "them." Using this calculus, any gain by one side amounts to an unacceptable loss by the other side. Each group feels as if its very existence is under threat, and each responds defensively, further modifying their own interpretive schemata to distinguish their opponents from themselves in even more stark terms, justifying more extreme action against opponents (Tajfel 1981; Waddell and Cairns 1986; Kriesberg, Northrup, and Thorson 1989; Northrup 1997; Brewer and Higgins 1998; Coy and Woehrle 2000).

Such conflicts become "intractable" in part because the vicious cycle involving identity and violence becomes almost seamless. As Terrell Northrup (1992) points out, a cultural "collusion" can develop between adversaries in ethnic conflict. By defining themselves and each other primarily in terms of their mutual antagonism, they collude with each other in perpetuating the psychological bases for destructive conflict. Political struggles, such as, those in Northern Ireland, Israel and Palestine, Rwanda, and the former Yugoslavia, that have centered around core group identities are known to be particularly contentious and susceptible to intractability (Cairns 1994; Kriesberg 1998b; Northrup 1989).

Identity plays such a crucial role in these conflicts because shared schemata for perceiving and making sense of the world direct ethnic groups to interpret their actions and those of their opponents in ways that protect in-group ontological security (Kriesberg 2007:55–56, 157–58). Ross (2001) calls these schemata "psychocultural interpretations" or "the shared, deeply rooted worldviews that help groups make sense of daily life and provide psychologically meaningful accounts of a group's relationship with other groups, their actions and motives" (p. 189). Worldviews that become widely shared as "collective identities" are constructed and continually reconstructed from origin myths, historical narratives, commentary on contemporary states of affairs, and teleological visions (Brewer and Higgins 1998).

Ethnopolitical conflict features closely related symbolic and social dimensions. Narratives that shape collective identities may compel people to collective action, sometimes to violence. Participation in conflict shapes the way groups perceive themselves and their opponents and how they express collective identities. Rituals and the public display of symbols organize perceptions and call people to solidarity by celebrating in-group narratives and values and casting others in adversarial roles. They stake claims to rights and preferred political arrangements and demonstrate a collective will. Symbolic displays can themselves become central issues of contention, perpetuating conflict. Irish language signs and band parades, for example, are often said to mark out territory in Northern Ireland in exclusive ways.

Polarized communal identities are constructed and reconstructed on a daily basis over long periods of time, sometimes spectacularly (through intimidation and direct attacks) or symbolically (public rituals, flags, and emblems), and sometimes in quite mundane ways (what newspaper one buys, where one shops, or where one attends school) Hamilton, Hansson, Bell, and Toucas 2008. Each becomes invested with emotional value, and one of the greatest challenges in addressing intractable conflict in divided societies lies in slowing and reversing a vicious and yet, often subtle cycle of out-group prejudice, dehumanization, coercion, and fear. To the extent that opponents in an ethnopolitical conflict situation ignore, condone, or openly advocate exploitation over another group, those parties will heighten the boundaries between them by intensifying distinctions and casting blame. Inter-group boundaries can become so rigid and others vilified and dehumanized to such an extent that group members become more likely to sanction, overlook, or employ the use of lethal force, fueling a cycle of fear, retribution, and division.

In intractable conflicts, according to social identity theorists, natural tendencies to create in-group and out-group distinctions become heightened as each group feels under threat and rallies around increasingly defensive collective identities seeking to maintain ontological security. It is worth noting, however, that the construction of in-group and out-group identities is part and parcel of social life. Cognitive psychologists assert that all people have a limited capacity for processing stimuli from the world around them. They simplify the world through social schemata, stereotypes, or ideologies, thus meeting a need for ontological coherence (Tajfel 1982; Cairns 1994). They are also compelled to maintain a positive sense of self-worth, self-efficacy, and self-authenticity (Melucci 1995; Gecas 2000). The combination of these drives produces solidarity and in-group cohesion, while comparison with out-groups facilitates the process. Two leading scholars of social identity theory, Henri Tajfel and John C. Turner, (1986) have derived the following theoretical principles:

Individuals strive to achieve or to maintain positive social identity.

Positive social identity is based largely on favorable comparisons that can be made between the in-group and some relevant out-groups: the in-group must be perceived as positively differentiated or distinct from the relevant out-groups.

When social identity is unsatisfactory, individuals will strive either to leave their existing group and join some more positively distinct group and/or to make their existing group more positively distinct (p. 16).

Unfortunately, in deeply divided societies in which groups have come to fear one another, the option of leaving one's own group is often limited, either because social solidarity costs are too high, or there simply are not other groups readily available to which one can switch.

As Ed Cairns (1994), a psychologist at the University of Ulster in Northern Ireland, has put it, "What I hope Social Identity Theory will do is influence people to see the conflict as a form of behavior which is determined by essentially normal psychological processes, but normal psychological processes which are operating in exceptional circumstances" (p. 14). Those circumstances include a long history of colonialism, resistance, discrimination, open conflict, and in many cases poverty. Political struggles of this sort that involve core group identities have proven particularly contentious and susceptible to intractability (Kriesberg, Northrup, and Thorson 1989; Northrup 1989; Cairns 1994; Kriesberg 1998b; Weiner 1998; Crocker, Hampson, and Aall 2005). Once destructive conflict is under way, a range of factors can cause the conflict to deepen. These include groupthink, organizational inertia, specialized vested interests, miscommunications, coercive strategies, changes in organizational makeup, and external intervention (Kriesberg 2007:155–81). The institutionalization of conflict parallels the polarization of ethnopolitical identities contributing to a vicious cycle of conflict escalation.

Ethnopolitical Division in Northern Ireland

A range of political, religious, and ethnic traditions in Northern Ireland tend to align broadly into Protestant/unionist/loyalist and Catholic/nationalist/republican blocs that maintain incompatible views on the history and sovereignty of six of the nine counties that make up the region called Ulster.[11] Over centuries of conflict in Ireland, especially since the late eighteenth century, and more recently over the course of the "Troubles," from approximately 1968 to 1998, Northern Ireland has become a deeply divided society in which Protestants and Catholics have been pushed and pulled into segregated public and cultural spheres. Often, division and segregation have been the direct result of British colonialism, unionist rule through the middle of the twentieth century, paramilitary intimidation, and radical political movements. Protestants and Catholics have also routinely segregated themselves in education, housing, sports, and arts, to name a few domains. Motivating factors include fear, anger, habit, familiarity, and tradition, and while a great deal of attention is paid to the working-class communities in which paramilitarism and the state's counter-terrorism efforts have been focused, ethnopolitical division is subtly perpetuated throughout society (Liechty and Clegg 2001:107–10).

Over a decade after the signing of the Belfast/Good Friday Agreement,[12] Northern Ireland remains significantly divided despite continuing progress in developing a pluralist agenda (Hughes, Donnelly, Robinson, and Dowds 2003; MacGinty, Muldoon, and Ferguson 2007). The consultation paper *A Shared Future* (2003) published by the Office of the First Minister and Deputy First Minister outlines concerns over ongoing ethnopolitical division.

- In order to achieve this vision we must deal with the very deep and painful divisions in our society that have been exacerbated by more than 30 years of conflict. Some progress has been made, but there is clear evidence that deep divisions remain.

- Violence at interfaces between communities continues to affect lives, property, businesses and public services.
- Whilst levels of tolerance and respect for diversity within the Protestant and Catholic Communities had been improving, there is evidence that they have decreased recently.
- Housing has become more segregated over the last 20 years. More than 70% of Housing Executive Estates are more than 90% Protestant or more than 90% Roman Catholic.
- Around 95% of children still attend separated schools. Despite evidence that more parents would prefer this option, there has only been a small increase in the number of children attending integrated schools.
- There are high levels of racial prejudice in Northern Ireland and the situation has recently become worse. The rate of racial incidents here is estimated at 16.4 per 1000 non-white population, compared to 12.65 per 1000 in England and Wales.
- There is little change in the extent of inter-community friendship patterns.
- In some urban areas further divisions are emerging within local communities. This is linked to paramilitary influence, especially at interfaces.
- People's lives continue to be shaped by community division. Research suggests that, in some areas, community division plays a large part in the choices that people make about where they work, and how they use leisure facilities and public services.
- Northern Ireland remains a deeply segregated society with little indication of progress towards becoming more tolerant or inclusive. (pp. 1–2)

As Stephen Farry (2006), a former general secretary of the Alliance Party, has declared in a United States Institute for Peace Special Report on Northern Ireland, "Peace has come at the price of reconciliation" (p. 27).

Survey research indicates that despite progress in consociational political arrangements, social attitudes remain significantly polarized. More worryingly, young people's attitudes tend to be less favorable to integration than adults', especially among Protestant youth (McAuley 2004a; Leonard 2008; Hayes and McAllister 2009). According to the Northern Ireland Life and Times Survey (NILTS),[13] the decade leading up to and immediately following the signing of the Belfast/Good Friday Agreement (1989–1999) witnessed a general improvement in adults' attitudes about community relations, especially among Catholic respondents. However, between 1996 and 1999, both Protestants (17 percent to 26 percent) and Catholics (11 percent to 18 percent) increasingly reported wishing to live in neighborhoods populated by only people of their own religious background, essentially returning to 1989 levels.[14] The same trend held for preferred workplace arrangements, though more Catholic adults (57 percent rising to 72 percent) came to prefer integrated schools in contrast to fewer Protestant adults (65 percent declining to 57 percent), a trend that fluctuated between Protestants and Catholics until 2003 when Protestants began to more consistently prefer mixed religion schools (ARK 1998–2008; Hughes and Donnelly 2003:652–53; Hayes and McAllister 2009).

Census data for 2001 show that 66 percent of the population in Northern Ireland live in areas that are more than 99 percent Protestant or more than 99 percent Catholic (up from 63 percent at the 1991 census; Brown 2002; Shirlow 2003). The 2003 Young Life and Times (YLT) survey of 16-year-olds in Northern Ireland reports that living in segregated areas significantly diminishes the likelihood of having friends from the other religious community (Devine and Schubotz 2004:2–3),[15] and research by Peter Shirlow (2003) indicates that 68 percent of 18- to 25-year-olds in neighborhoods in Belfast separated by "peace lines" have never had a meaningful conversation with anyone from the other (Protestant/Catholic) community.

Attitudes about mixing tend to be more stable than attitudes about community relations (Schubotz and Devine 2009:4), and among adult respondents who participated in the Northern Ireland Social Attitudes and NILTS surveys, Hughes et al. (2003) have noted a growing pessimism about the state of community relations since the Belfast/Good Friday Agreement was signed, especially among Protestants. By 2001, the percentage believing relations between Protestants and Catholics "are better now than five years ago" had returned to nearly 1994 levels (before Republican and Loyalist paramilitaries declared cease-fires) of just below 30 percent. The same was true for Protestants' predictions of the state of community relations in five years' time.

As of 2003, the YLT survey indicated that youth attitudes about community relations were ambiguous. Large minorities of respondents reported "favourable" attitudes toward the other community (38 percent for Protestants; 45 percent for Catholic), and larger percentages were more likely to say they felt "neither favourable nor unfavourable" toward the other community (49 percent for Protestants and 43 percent for Catholics). Just over half reported that they often or sometimes socialized with people from a different religious background. Levels of geographical segregation seemed more severe than youths' attitudes, but national identities remained important for three out of five YLT respondents (Devine and Schubotz 2004; Muldoon, Trew, Todd, Rougier, and McLaughlin 2007). From 2003 to 2007, 16-year-olds in the YLT have been significantly and consistently less open than NILTS adults to religious mixing in neighborhoods, workplaces, and schools. In 2007, just under 50 percent of youth (Protestant and Catholic) supported integrated educational settings, with Catholics more reticent than Protestants (Schubotz and Devine 2009).

The picture with regard to community relations has improved but continues to signal fundamental divisions. By 2008, in the wake of renewed devolution, the percentage of adult respondents reporting they felt relations were better than five years ago had more than doubled from 2001 to 65 percent. Preferences for mixed religion neighborhoods rose to 83 percent, preferences for mixed educational settings rose to 70 percent, and preferences for mixed religion workplaces rose to 94 percent. In each of these domains, percentages fell between 2 percent and 8 percent in 2009 for adults, and while youths' attitudes tracked adults' on improvements in community relations, they continued to lag on integration concerns by 17 percent to 20 percent (ARK 2008a,b; ARK 2009a,b). NILTS results indicate rising optimism among adults, but the potential for polarization remains, especially considering youth preferences to maintain structural divides along traditional ethnonational lines.

Though this study focuses on adults, it delves into the social landscape where deeply socialized identities, political fears, and their expressions meet new structural circumstances and inspire strategizing and innovation. To capture the deeply held beliefs and ideas that constitute communal identities and buttress prejudices and stereotypes and to document the strategic thinking and activities through which identity transformation occurs, it can be necessary to focus on one community or set of organizations on one side of an ethnopolitical divide instead of undertaking cross-community research. In this case, I have focused on Protestants, often on working-class Protestants, who, either by virtue of their organizational affiliation or the areas in which they live and work, endorse, advocate, or are familiar with unionist and loyalist ideology and identity, which I refer to as "grassroots unionism"; McAuley (1997) refers to this domain of unionism as "community unionism" or "communitarian unionism" (p. 159).

In focusing on a range of distinctly Protestant and unionist or loyalist organizations and communities in this project, I adopt Liechty and Clegg's (2001) "chastened 'two-traditions' logic," which recognizes considerable religious, political, and economic diversity across Northern Ireland but also acknowledges an unavoidable and prominent religious and national divide between Protestants and Catholics (p. 36; Muldoon et al. 2007). In describing the divide, Eyben, Morrow, and Wilson (1997) said, "Churches, sports, political parties, central policy makers, law and order, local government, community sector, business all reflect, and sometimes contribute to the division of people in Northern Ireland into two major identity groups. Sometimes, the fault line appears dormant; at other times it lies wide open and raw. Whatever its state, it is always present" (p. 1). At the same time, identity change is a central theme of this book, and it is dangerous to generalize and overlook diversity within the Catholic and Protestant population (Rolston 1998; Nic Craith 2002). This is perhaps especially true for Protestants, among whom one finds considerable class divisions, a disjointed organizational infrastructure, and denominational divisions. I will endeavor to represent the complexity of intracommunity networks and worldviews (cf. Shirlow and McGovern 1997b), but I will also address experiences that are commonly shared among many Protestants, whether they prefer to define themselves as Protestants, unionists, or loyalists, and thus I will often refer to the Protestant/unionist/loyalist (PUL) population or community. That said, the data collected for this project lean toward working-class and traditional organizations and "hard to reach" communities where one finds strong Orange, loyalist, or unionist in-group identification.

■ PROTESTANTS, UNIONISTS, LOYALISTS, AND ETHNOPOLITICAL IDENTIFICATION

Since the partition of Northern Ireland in 1921 and throughout the Troubles, Protestants have depended on political ascendancy and the strategic and political interests of British governments to protect, both militarily and economically, what Protestants have considered a necessary refuge in Ulster. The proroguing of the unionist controlled Stormont government that presided over Northern Ireland affairs from partition of the island in 1921 (separating Northern Ireland from the southern Irish Free State) until the imposition of Direct Rule from London in 1972 was a bitter pill for many unionists. However, it was preferable to the alternative of a wholesale British withdrawal, the potential of a civil war, and the prospects of becoming absorbed into a united Ireland (Walker 2004:195–96). During thirty years of the Troubles, most Protestant unionists' attentions were turned to maintaining strategic pressure on British governments through political maneuvering at Westminster and supporting the police and military, and in some cases, paramilitary forces.

Today, Direct Rule has ended, including the long-anticipated devolution of justice and policing powers; the principle of the consent of the majority has been enshrined in political agreements, and the responsibilities of government have been devolved to a power sharing executive at Stormont. Many of the circumstances on which unionists and loyalists based their assumptions about life in Northern Ireland have changed significantly. Under devolution, the concepts of civil society and politics take on greater significance, and many Protestants find themselves in a position for which they were not fully prepared. In the absence of normal politics, and with the exception of moments of crisis, there has been little development of an infrastructure of voluntary grassroots organizations. Under the threat of republicanism, unionist politicians wielded significant political capital in the halls of Westminster, but relatively little working social capital has developed among Protestant organizations.

Often, Protestant communities in need of resources, such as, jobs and housing, are not sufficiently empowered to advocate for and make full use of government programs. Research by Blackbourn and Rekawek (2007) argues that the social and economic dividends of peace have been pursued more aggressively in Catholic communities than Protestant ones (pp. 80–81). A sense of British identity remains strong among Protestants, and the union would appear politically secure for the foreseeable future, but the quality of that future now rests in their ability to organize and navigate a new and changing political landscape.

In the introduction to their edited book on Protestants, unionists, and loyalists, Peter Shirlow and Mark McGovern (1997a) express the importance of forging a new shared vision for relations on the island of Ireland: "In overall terms the crisis facing Ireland, North and South, Catholic and Protestant, Nationalist and Unionist, is to reconceptualise who 'the People' are in order to achieve a new social and political consensus" (p. 9). Since the publication of their book, a young and contested political dispensation has developed through the negotiation of the Belfast/ Good Friday Agreement and more recently through the reestablishment of the Northern Ireland Assembly via a remarkable coalition of Sinn Féin and the DUP, who were previously the most opposed among the large political parties. The "social consensus" that Shirlow and McGovern propose is less clear, however. Lingering sectarianism and polarized identities, while showing signs of improvement, constitute a vexing backdrop to the end of the Troubles and the establishment of power sharing governance.

■ CONFLICT TRANSFORMATION
   IN NORTHERN IRELAND

If polarized and entrenched identities contribute to intractable conflict, the transformation of those identities into ones with less defensive and more inclusive orientations should occupy a central place in peacebuilding models. Constructivist models offer a framework for understanding the opportunities for and limits to identity change and the important role that symbols and cultural activities play in mediating identity change, and chapter 2 addresses the central role of identity formation in conflict transformation.

Three themes shape the analysis of conflict transformation among Protestant unionists and loyalists that follows: capacity building, cultural innovation, and pragmatic motivations. Cultural entrepreneurship figures prominently, but it is important to pay attention to the strategic imperatives that motivate cultural innovation and the organizational changes that contribute to the empowerment of alienated Protestants.

Capacity building

Material conditions, the capacity to organize in pursuit of collective interests, and how a community perceives itself and its neighbors are closely related. Each feeds into the level of security or insecurity that influences whether various segments of unionism and loyalism are able and prepared to participate fully in planning for the future and the transformation of conflict in Northern Ireland. If fear, uncertainty, and inequality lie at the root of ethnopolitical conflict, conflict transformation involves the development of resources that empower polarized groups to engage nonviolently as equals and then acknowledge and take advantage of their interdependence (Eyben, Morrow, and Wilson 1997; Mac Ginty and du Toit 2007:29). Those resources may be political, economic, or cultural, and it is worth noting that the distribution of resources within the Protestant population is not uniform. Middle-class Protestants have been able to avoid the worst of the violence of the Troubles and have tended to maintain a comfortable distance from local politics, influencing policy through professional organizations that lobbied

Direct Rule ministries. Historically, unionists have looked at relatively poorer economic conditions in the Republic of Ireland and argued that a united Ireland would mean being absorbed into an inferior economy without British subsidy and would inevitably sacrifice quality of life. Middle-class unionists were no exception, and they oriented themselves toward Britain to pursue their business interests and send their children to university (Coulter 1997).

Working-class Protestants, with fortunes closely tied to manufacturing bases that predominated in Northern Ireland, have seen the union as inextricably linked with Ulster's industrial successes but have suffered from declines in industrial production and its replacement by service and technology industries. Economic and social problems including unemployment, low educational attainment, and substance abuse plague working-class Protestant communities. The trauma of the Troubles remains a fresh memory for adults and still echoes today in interface tensions and outbreaks of violence that perpetuate a sense of alienation, both from neighboring Catholic communities, which Protestants have watched advance economically and politically, and from the Protestant middle class, by which they feel abandoned (Blackbourn and Rekawek 2007). They therefore draw on whatever sense of security their collective identity as British citizens affords, insisting that their loyalty and service to the union, especially in terms of military service, amounts to political capital. However, they are simultaneously unsure or even skeptical about the value of that capital, as British governments have signaled their willingness to see Northern Ireland leave the union under the right conditions of popular consent (Coulter 1997:116). Undermining insecurity remains a fundamental task for improving community relations (Mac Ginty and du Toit 2007).

In her typology of approaches to community relations work, Mari Fitzduff (1991) refers to "contextual community relations work" as activities, such as, community development, building trusted and accessible security forces, encouraging pluralist or mixed environments to encourage contact, targeting social need, and training in critical thinking, that are necessary to create a suitable environment for improvements in community relations. Unfortunately, the fields of community relations and community development have often been disconnected from one another, and yet, both are fundamental to the prospects for sustainable peace (Eyben, Morrow, and Wilson 1997). This research takes up the challenge of assessing the extent to which and the ways in which organizations within the Protestant/unionist/loyalist (PUL) population are seeking to adapt themselves to new political circumstances by building social and cultural capital and organizing capacity.

Cultural innovation and collective identities

In some cases, community development work parallels a kind of local single-identity work that involves modifying cultural expressions and undertaking historical education projects. To the extent that historical and cultural identity work helps to diminish a sense of uncertainty, builds confidence, enables cross-community cooperation, and develops organizing skills that allow grassroots organizations to advocate effectively for collective interests, it might be considered part of conflict transformation, though we should also consider the countervailing trends that act as obstacles to such a process.

Modifying public expressions of collective identity, such as, parades and bonfires, that have traditionally been seen as triumphalist, cannot simply be programmed or made policy within an organization or community. The adoption of new schemata is never a wholesale proposition. New ideas are smuggled into group discourse in the very rituals and practices that sustain the continuity of collective identities. Change, even heresy, is never far from tradition. Often symbolic rituals, such as, bonfires and parades, can become sites at which somewhat unorthodox group members, out of devotion to a tradition or institution, seek to influence the discourse and dispositions of fellow participants. Symbols closely associated with authority and tradition retain their power even when they are appropriated and modified (within limits) to express new ideas and new iterations of collective identity (Kurtz 1983; Smithey and Young 2010).

Collective action and collective identity are thus closely related and mutually recursive; a change in one signals or requires a change in the other. To the extent that loyalists begin to emphasize publicly features of their identity that are not defensive or expressions of mistrust or antipathy toward Catholics and nationalists, they signal a new orientation across the political and ethnic divide. They aim to maintain in-group solidarity and ontological security through these practices, but as they adopt new forms that are less exclusive, they incrementally lower the salience of sectarian and ethnopolitical boundaries that have helped fuel conflict in Ireland and thus participate in conflict transformation.

Pragmatics and public relations

Attempts to reorient collective identities are influenced by groups' perceptions of their adversaries and other influential social actors and are deeply implicated with the ways in which they present themselves to those parties. Cultural traditions projects attempt to shore up communal solidarity and improve community esteem and confidence, but they also reframe collective identity in ways that are more widely palatable to the general public, funders, and other sources of local and international support. Thus, there is a pragmatic dimension in which unionists and loyalists use cultural activities in the pursuit of political, social, and economic goals. Protestant interviewees often speak of their cultural traditions work in comparison with the successes that republicans have enjoyed in their own transition to politics, community organizing, and international public relations. Increasingly, Protestant organizations in Northern Ireland are undertaking to build capacity for social change by developing community organizing and public relations skills.

Yet, decisions to emphasize particular features of group history or beliefs are not merely strategic. Leaders may not simply dictate core identities to members. Modifications must be negotiated by individuals and groups, sometimes leading to conflict internally, but the benefits to the group's political or social capital may incentivize such attempts to reframe group identity. This often takes the form of public relations work, media management, and the modification of public expressions of identity.

■ OVERVIEW OF THE BOOK

Unionists and loyalists have not abandoned their objections to nationalism, and they often continue to frame their agendas in relation to the real or imagined threat of a return to republican violence and restrictions on their cultural expressions. In this sense, ethnopolitical conflict in Northern Ireland continues but in ways that open possibilities for cooperation and constructive competition. Conflict is thereby transformed from the inside out among partisans, many of whom once prioritized paramilitary or military violence. In 1995, after the IRA committed itself to a cease-fire, Gerry Adams, the president of Sinn Féin, famously declared, "They haven't gone away, you know," to the disgust of Protestants across Northern Ireland. (Many unionists still question whether the IRA has gone away if its Army Council continues to exist.) Portadown's District Orange Master, Daryl Hewitt, echoed the line after his Orange lodge's leadership met with Adams to discuss their dispute with nationalist Garvaghy Road residents (2008). Neither has gone away, but they have not stayed the same either.

The rest of this book examines a contested process by which self-described unionists and loyalists navigate a contested social psychological landscape where identity and action are inseparably intertwined. As we discuss in chapter 2, conflict transformation involves changes in the way conflict is carried out. The political peace process, a form of sophisticated conflict management, has constructed an arena in which even the most militant parties believe they can pursue their core interests. Support for political parties remains one way of signaling collective identity, but as we will see in subsequent chapters, rituals and other symbolic activities offer another arena in which many unionists and loyalists are active and in which we find an intentional shift toward developing the arts of persuasion.

Chapter 3 details the development of the peace process and the political circumstances in which unionists and loyalists find themselves. Chapters 4, 5, and 6 follow symbolic and ritualistic expressions of ethnopolitical identity through activities that are often associated with tradition or heritage, such as, murals, bonfires, parades, reenactments, and amateur historical pursuits. In each case, unionists and loyalists have been modifying some of their most cherished activities to expand their appeal within their own communities and further afield. Such modifications are important because they both reflect and require that they can be justified within the frames of the collective identities they represent and thus become part of the slow iterative process of identity transformation as well.

The process is not purely endogenous to unionist and loyalist communities and organizations, though it must be said that that is where much of the action of conflict transformation occurs. As we discuss in chapter 6, sea changes in the political sphere have forced unionists and loyalists into reconsidering their positions and their futures. Some have resolved that they must develop a new political influence that is not purely associated with British patronage. The development of public relations skills is not surprisingly applied first to their most public expressions of identity. Moreover, the state has incentivized the mitigation of cultural expressions of identity, which fits into the consociational model embodied in the Belfast/Good Friday Agreement. Thus, while much of the process of conflict transformation detailed in the book revolves around culture, identity, and emotion, there are important pragmatic dimensions to consider as well. The concluding chapter summarizes the findings, anticipates the future of conflict transformation in Northern Ireland, and raises cautionary questions about the potential limits and pitfalls that unionists and loyalists might encounter and the ramifications for community relations.

■ Notes

1. Murals are large paintings, often found on the gable ends of houses that, historically, have displayed themes of ethnic identity and political ideology. During "the Troubles," thirty years of armed conflict since the late 1960s, murals often valorized paramilitaries and armed struggle.

2. Republican and loyalist paramilitaries are non-state armed organizations formed to challenge or defend British rule and unionism in Ireland, respectively.

3. European football is called soccer in the United States.

4. Best had died only five months after my original visit to Wright's mural, which was redesigned and unveiled in May 2006. He had played for both Manchester United and Northern Ireland, and the mural portrayed him twice, once in his red Manchester uniform and again wearing his green Northern Ireland gear.

5. Extensive interviews were conducted within grassroots unionist organizations and communities. Excerpts of these interviews appear throughout the book. All interviewees were assigned pseudonyms.

6. The Orange Order is one of several all-male fraternal organizations that dedicate themselves to the preservation of the Protestant faith and British sovereignty in Ireland. The Orange Order is the best known, though others (some closely affiliated with the Orange Order) include the Apprentice Boys of Derry, the Independent Orange Order, the Royal Black Preceptory, and the Royal Arch Purple. On July 12 each year, the Orange Order celebrates the victory in 1698 of King William III's victory over the Jacobite forces of James II at the Battle of the Boyne. The Twelfth celebrations are preceded on the Eleventh Night by celebrations and the burning of large bonfires in Protestant communities across Northern Ireland. Tricolour flags of the Republic of Ireland and other nationalist or republican symbols are often burned with the bonfires.

7. Ruane and Todd's (1996) approach to conflict transformation similarly calls for action at cultural, structural, and relational levels (pp. 306–15).

8. The distinctions between unionism and loyalism or nationalism and republicanism are often not clear, and usage is contested, changing from context to context, but I offer a

brief explanation here for readers uninitiated in Northern Ireland politics. In its broadest sense, nationalism refers to the universe of political positions that advocate a united Ireland. More specifically, "nationalist" refers to those people, primarily Catholic, whose political goals emphasize civil equality for all and redressing decades of discrimination against Catholics. Many nationalists value Gaelic culture and a united Ireland and prefer constitutional means of pursuing their political goals. "Republicans" are nationalists, often working class, who insist on equality and a united Ireland but have been willing to use both violent and institutional political means. The paramilitary Provisional Irish Republican Army (IRA) and the political party Sinn Féin are the most prominent organizations within the republican movement.

Broadly, "unionism" refers to a commitment to Northern Ireland's remaining part of the United Kingdom. In its particular sense, unionism refers to a stance institutionalized in political parties supported primarily by Protestants (e.g., the Ulster Unionist Party and the Democratic Unionist Party) that focuses on Northern Ireland's membership in the United Kingdom and British identity (Miller 1978; Hennessey 1996; Ruane and Todd 1996). "Loyalism" refers to an ideology or cultural stance held by many Protestants, usually working class, who insist on Northern Ireland's remaining part of the United Kingdom while also defending Protestant culture and identity. Loyalists' cultural commitments may include Protestant evangelicalism and a contractual or covenantal view of their relationship to the British crown (Whyte 1990; Brewer and Higgins 1998). Like republicanism, the term "loyalism" also often refers to support for paramilitary organizations, such as, the Ulster Defence Association (UDA) and the Ulster Volunteer Force (UVF).

9. The Northern Ireland Assembly is the elected legislative body established by the 1998 Belfast or Good Friday Agreement (B/GFA).

10. "Peacebuilding" is often used to refer to initiatives that aim to transform attitudes and build capacity in civil society while "peacemaking" usually refers to attempts to encourage dialogue and negotiations among political figures or individuals with political influence. "Peacekeeping" is a form of conflict management that includes the capacity to keep opponents from attacking one another (Galtung 1975:224; Ryan 1995).

11. Northern Ireland consists of six of the traditional nine counties of Ulster. Donegal, Monaghan, and Cavan remain in the Republic of Ireland.

12. After protracted negotiations, the Belfast/Good Friday Agreement established a power-sharing assembly in Northern Ireland. It was signed by major political parties on April 10, 1998, and it was endorsed in subsequent referenda in both the north and south.

13. The Northern Ireland Life and Times Survey is an annual omnibus survey conducted by Access Resource Knowledge Northern Ireland (ARK) and co-sponsored by Queen's University and the University of Ulster.

14. Research by Ian Shuttleworth and Chris Lloyd (2006) using 2001 census data, however, indicates that levels of actual segregation have probably remained the same throughout the 1990s, findings that moderate but do not extinguish concerns about levels of division between Catholics and Protestants.

15. Forty-seven percent of youth respondents living in primarily Catholic areas had no Protestant friends, and the corresponding rate for Protestants was 34 percent.

2 Ethnic Identity Change and Conflict Transformation

A man who cannot change his mind cannot change anything.
—George Bernard Shaw

What wound did ever heal but by degrees?
—William Shakespeare, *Othello*

Over the course of the twentieth century, Northern Ireland has suffered from increasingly polarized ethnic and political identities that have contributed to and been exacerbated by violent conflict, especially over the course of the Troubles. Political negotiations are essential to the transformation of ethnopolitical conflict, but they are inevitably tied to grassroots community relations. Political leaders' abilities to make compromises and embrace new initiatives are enabled or limited by the legitimacy and authority they derive from their constituencies, which may fear their traditions and sense of identity are under threat. David, who has sponsored community development work in loyalist working-class East Belfast, characterized the challenge for Northern Ireland in an interview:

> I think my worry always about this peace process is if you do end up building a benign apartheid, there's nothing to say that in ten or fifteen years the thing cannot begin all over again. You know, there are big questions. How do you heal memories? How do you get people to engage genuinely? There are lots of models out there. But what is genuine engagement? What does that mean? And, how do you stop people when the doors are closed, the curtains are closed, telling stories, passing pain, hatred, and sectarianism down to another generation?

The persistence of mutually polarized identities remains an important concern with which practitioners and scholars continue to wrestle. If the cultural and psychological underpinnings of division persist, they will challenge the sustainability of any agreed political arrangements, and thus we must assess the potential for identity change.

Ethnicity and the formation of ethnic identities have featured prominently in discussions of intractable conflict as conflicts between groups with mutually exclusive core-identities exhibit an intensity that defies compromise. As the sociologist George Simmel ([1908] 1971) has pointed out, fighting for a cause or "supra-individual claims" can contribute to intense conflict as people subordinate their individual interests and "personality" to a perceived collective good.

Cross-cutting similarities and a sense of shared humanity are excluded from the shrinking frames of reference that define a conflict. The substantive interests underlying disputes are replaced with "noble" commitments to ideological positions often suffused with ethnicity (p. 87). Ethnic identities become synonymous with the "cause" of "the people." Consequently, understanding what constitutes ethnicity and how ethnic boundaries are formed is important when considering how they might become more malleable, porous, and less likely to be paired with violence.

■ ETHNIC IDENTITY AND IDENTITY CHANGE

Primordialists or foundationalists have attributed the durability and resilience of ethnic solidarity to the generational transmission of emotionally charged kinship bonds. One is, in a sense, born into one's ethnic identity, which is sustained by the deeply emotional and perennial perception of "descent-linkages" or "felt kinship ties" buttressed by race, language, region, religion, and custom (Geertz 1963; Connor 1994; Ruane and Todd 2004:211). Primordialists emphasize the depth of ties developed through biological connections to family and early childhood socialization within communities (Eller and Coughlin 1993; Grosby 1994).

By contrast, constructivism, inspired by Fredrik Barth's (1969) work, holds that ethnic identity derives from categories constantly reconstructed through boundary-setting processes that produce a sense of social cohesion and historical integrity. Identities are considered reflections of boundaries that are performed and shaped through narratives and discourses. Categories of identification or boundaries supersede groups, or put another way, groups are an *effect* of the *processes* of people identifying with one category or another. Jenkins' (2008) "basic anthropological model" of ethnicity concisely summarizes the constructivist approach:

> Ethnicity is a matter of "cultural" differentiation (bearing in mind that identity is always a dialectic between similarity and difference);
>
> Ethnicity is a matter of shared meanings –"culture" – but it is also produced and reproduced during interaction;
>
> Ethnicity is no more fixed than the way of life of which it is a part, or the situations in which it is produced and reproduced; and
>
> Ethnicity is both collective and individual, externalized in social interaction and the categorization of others, and internalized in personal self-identification. (p. 14)

Constructivists have focused on the *process* of perceiving and attributing difference, and while their approach could anticipate the potential for considerable fluctuation in collective identities, they have been primarily interested in the construction and maintenance of prominent ethnic identities.

In recent years, however, sociologists and anthropologists have begun to adopt what Todd (2005) calls a "soft constructivist" approach that problematizes the prevailing focus on neatly defined analytical categories and "emphasizes the fluctuating, relational, and situational quality of self-definitions which are constructed in social practice and interaction, not in depth psychology" (p. 432). Similarly, Wimmer (2008) addresses "varying degrees of boundedness" (pp. 976, 980; see also Ross 2001). Growing interest in peace and reconciliation processes and the accelerating rate at which ethnic groups are encountering one another in a globalizing world has inspired models that accommodate identity change and the reconstruction of identity categories. These "soft constructivist" approaches expand the "construction" in constructivism.

Four theoretical developments in particular have opened doors for examining identity change and the transformation of conflict. First, we can conceive of identity as shifting and subject to incremental change as individuals and groups experiment with new identifications and boundary frames. Ethnic categories are not discrete or always mutually exclusive. The result of experimentation is, according to Todd, "a slowly changing 'cultural substratum' which may underlie more radical category change" (Todd 2004:6). There is often more change within categories than across categories. The contours and permeability of ethnic boundaries are not rigid and vary from situation to situation across dimensions of political salience, insularity, levels of cultural differentiation, and stability or vulnerability to redefinition (Wimmer 2005:59; Todd et al. 2006:329; 2008:976–85). Ethnic boundaries can shift by contracting, expanding, blurring, changing salience in relation to other boundaries (inversion), or through subversion by individuals who are able to cross them (Todd et al. 2006:329–333; Wimmer 2008:986–90). Identity change can be precipitated by significant social and political change, requiring psychocultural work in reconciling new circumstances and power relations with old identity categories (Todd 2004:10–23). Much of this book is concerned with the ways in which both identity categories and the practices that reflect and reinscribe identity are modulated in response to social and political change while also contributing to it.

Second, approaches drawing on Piere Bourdieu's work on field theory and *habitus* account for both the significant influence of identity in shaping social action and the intervening pressures and incentives to adapt to shifting structural opportunities or threats (Todd 2004:5–6; Wimmer 2005:56). In "field theoretic" models, ethnic boundaries are established and change on a contested social field in which individuals and groups pursue their interests. Bourdieu and Wacquant (1992) have situated social action within an inherently conflicted field of rules that define the parameters of what is possible and yet, provide space for innovation (p. 17). Players interact with others in jointly structured spheres of engagement for which participants have been socialized and to which they are drawn by virtue of their socialization and experience. The field is structured by power relations in which players utilize various forms of capital in a perpetual process of maintaining or subverting the configuration of capital (pp. 98, 108–9). Some individuals command economic resources while others may possess cultural resources, such as, prestige or authority, that allow them to exert influence on others and shape the way encounters occur. The rules governing the interaction and the usefulness of various forms of capital have been internalized (even in early childhood) by participants as *habitus*, sets of dispositions providing participants an unconscious "sense of the game" or a "practical sense" of how to proceed (p. 120).

Institutions, such as, the state, use their resources to encourage some ethnic categorizations and discourage others. Local entrepreneurs can challenge official strategies through alternative discourses, though one often finds considerable contention over which ethnic narratives and practices are emphasized, even among those who share ethnic categories (Wimmer 2008:990–1001). In the final analysis, ethnic boundaries are a product of the multiplex interactions of a range of individuals, organizations, and institutions whose relative positions of power can be in flux.

Actors are not, however, free to innovate, shed, or adopt ethnic identifications willy-nilly. In Bourdieu's social field, they act under the fundamental influence of their habitus. Similarly, where cultural differences are firmly established, embodied, or routinized, it becomes difficult for individuals or groups to alter identifications drastically (Wimmer 2005:58–60). Strategic interests may drive many boundary-setting processes, but the cognitive functions that ethnic identities fulfill in ordering and making sense of the world remain important. Once an investment has been made in ethnic identification, identity takes on a value of its own with which individuals find it hard to part.

Third, the content, the texts, objects, and activities through which ethnic boundaries are constructed are increasingly considered a significant component of ethnic identity construction. Barth's constructivism prioritized distinctions between identity categories. The means by which boundaries were established were of less importance. Differences between categories of identity are fundamental to the very concept of identity, and Barth's call to appreciate the simple power of difference is prudent. Nearly any object or activity can serve as a marker of distinction around which people establish in-group and out-group categories, but we should not overlook the emotion of perceiving a common experience with others, of sharing elaborate codes. The signaling of difference and similarity through symbols and practices can range from "telling" one's identification through markers such as, language, clothing, and behavior to the "thick" construction of worldviews through which people interpret social action around them and from which they derive emotional satisfaction (Todd et al. 2006:324, 328).

The narratives that communicate values and assumptions, the "stuff" by which categories are constituted, are subject to change. Similarly, the diverse ways in which ethnic symbols are created, reproduced, and consumed are important and subject to modification (Jenkins 2008:172). Radical change is unlikely, especially during times of threat and crisis, but gradual and incremental redefinition of one's experiences and identifications happens (Todd, O'Keefe, Rougier, and Bottos 2006:335–38). Modest changes in myths, images, slogans, narratives, and long-established cultural practices and policies open the potential for a broad and graduated range of options for change within categories. Accumulating changes alter the character of categories. Each object or activity does the work of inscribing difference and weaving a meaningful narrative in its own way. Because they work together, and as each is open to adaptation and innovation, each holds the potential for incrementally shaping the fabric of an ethnic category. In this sense, the "cultural stuff" matters.

Not all articulations of similarity and difference are equal. Some are more participative and ritualistic, private or public, subtle or overt, iconic, and canonic. Within a repertoire of cultural expressions, variations exist that determine the valence, so to speak, of ethnic categories, the extent or *degree* to which they overlap or exclude and repel one another. Images that convey threats or sectarian doctrines or that assign divine favor to one group rather than another differ from expressions that celebrate cultural differences or that incorporate shared symbols.[1]

Fourth, if the cultural stuff matters, those who sponsor, authorize, choreograph, and participate in it also matter. Activists, community leaders, clergy, and others in positions of local authority organize or promote the work of expressing what it means to identify with an ethnic category. Pamphlets, books, and opinion-editorials are written and published; events are planned; public art is commissioned; and memorials are constructed. Each of these cases, and many more we could list, aim to contribute to a multifaceted and contested, but recognizable, "imagined community" (Anderson 1991). This is not, however, a simple and straightforward process. One rarely finds a monolithic or universally agreed conception of the "community." The psychocultural landscape is dotted with official and unofficial myths. Various actors share many of the same narratives and practices that tap into collective memory, each seeking to contribute to and draw on understandings of shared history and values. Thus, we do well to focus on what Mitch Berbrier (2000) calls "ethnicity in the making" and heed his call to "[follow] the agents of ethnicity through society" as they go about both sustaining and experimenting with collective identity and its expression (p. 69).

The work of such agents is important because the symbolic displays they develop both reflect and contribute to the formation of collective identities that in turn influence choices about future actions. This is, after all, the central point of a constructivist approach: a shared sense of identity is constructed when it is signaled and articulated to others in simple mundane ways in daily life and in the kind of elaborate and strategic ways that are addressed in this book. Somewhere in the cycle of action and identity formation, change takes place, both in the kinds of actions in which representative organizations engage and the construction of meaning and identity. In many cases, experimentation with a new conflict strategy or a new twist on a familiar tradition can trigger a reassessment of collective identity. Movement toward persuasive conflict methods, toward a more constructive stance, can provoke a redefinition of collective identity. The process is a controversial one, as even those who share ethnic identification make contending claims and compete to make their agenda or ideology more widely accepted.

The work of externalizing and enacting collective identity is also fascinating because it is both constrained and creative, posing a perpetual challenge for those who undertake it. Though constructivists emphasize the need for the constant renewal of ethnicity, there are significant constraints on the work of constructing ethnicity. Since ethnic identity is a shared concept, ethnicity work has meaning only when it is recognized as such by those who participate in it and consume it, resonating to the symbols that signify group identity. In this way, they maintain standards of categorization, reinvesting them with legitimacy and cueing that legitimacy to one another. This is what happens when people participate in or even simply attend cultural events. A sense of continuity is affirmed, and what we might consider an economy of cultural value is established. The psychological need for group membership creates an incentive or a shared expectation that the fundamental core of shared understandings and the symbols that represent them will remain consistent.

Consequently, agents of ethnic work must operate within the social psychological boundaries of those who identify with the set of categories that make up ethnic identity. Innovation is possible but limited. The range of possibilities is constrained, requiring what Jeffrey Alexander (2004) calls *cultural pragmatics*, in which careful attention is paid to the performance of ritual events (Smithey and Kurtz 2003; Smithey and Young 2010).

> The goal of secular performances, whether on stage or in society, remains the same as the ambition of sacred ritual. They stand or fall on their ability to produce psychological identification and cultural extension. The aim is to create, via skillful and affecting performance, the emotional connection of audience with actor and text and thereby to create the conditions for projecting cultural meaning from performance to audience. To the extent these two conditions have been achieved, one can say that the elements of performance have become fused. (Alexander 2004:547)

Authentic performances that achieve cathexis are able to condense and "fuse" common cultural references through careful choreography in such a way that actors and audiences co-participate in the construction of a shared reality.

There are nonetheless opportunities for the introduction of novel twists and modifications that can be incorporated into pragmatic performances. The performances must, on balance, pass the approval of the relevant audiences, but they can take on new tones and introduce new ideas into public discourse. In terms of ethnic identity construction, this latitude for experimentation introduces agency and makes possible the "moment of intentionality" in which agents of ethnic work choose to introduce new elements of performance or emphasize some ideas and practices over others (Bourdieu, cited in Todd 2005:433). As expressions of shared identity begin to take on new qualities, raise contradictions, and become incorporated and approved by ethnic audiences, they redefine the boundaries of identity. Who "we" are is fundamentally influenced by the actions we undertake or approve and their justification, which puts those who organize symbolic actions in an influential position.

Together, these theoretical arguments emphasize the *construction* of ethnic identities and contribute to a model that incorporates identity change while also accounting for limits on such change. Cultural entrepreneurs who undertake ethnic identity work through symbolic action are constrained by structural circumstances, strategic imperatives within fields of contention, and the social psychological needs of their communities. Nonetheless, there is room for change as well.

■ CONFLICT TRANSFORMATION AND CONSTRUCTIVE CONFLICT

I have argued that incremental changes in ethnic identity are possible or are often introduced through incremental changes in collective action, especially in symbolic and ritual displays. I also asserted that insecurity hardens ethnic identities and allegedly intractable ethnopolitical conflicts represent the apex of this phenomenon. How ethnic identities become less polarized in the midst of the aftermath of violent conflict is the golden ring for those who want to identify the potentials for sustainable peace. The first step in that pursuit is to understand that conflict, which we often associate with violence and coercion, continues after violence ends. It is carried on in political and symbolic struggles, which can be pursued with considerable ruthlessness and yet, have a distinctly different quality from armed struggle. Thus, we speak of transforming conflict on a continuum, ranging from violence and intimidation to other forms of conflict that require greater degrees of communication and even cooperation.

"Peace" is a term understandably held at arm's length by skeptics caught up in violent conflicts. By contrast, "conflict transformation" has the advantage of retaining the concept of conflict for those who, with good reason, find it difficult to jump directly from the difficult realities of intractable conflict to an ambiguous state of peace. Mari Fitzduff (2002) reminds us that "conflicts that are the length and depth of Northern Ireland do not end, but they can and do change" (p. xiii; Väyrynen 1991b; Wallensteen 1991; Galtung 1995:53–54). Indeed, from a sociological standpoint, conflict is an inescapable fact of social life. The renowned German sociologist, Max Weber ([1920] 1978), felt that conflict was part and parcel of social relations: "Even the most strictly pacific order can eliminate means of conflict and the objects of and impulses to conflict only partially" (p. 39). One of Weber's German contemporaries, Georg Simmel ([1908] 1971), took a similar approach when he claimed that conflict is ubiquitous, a "form of sociation" (p. 70). Conflict is a component of *all* relationships and regulates the balance of harmonious (e.g., loyalty, love) and discordant (e.g., hate, envy) forces within social relations. A certain balance of tensions in fact constitutes the character of a stable group

LIVERPOOL JOHN MOORES UNIVERSITY
LEARNING SERVICES

(pp. 70–72). The longevity of social relations is based on a "matrix of tensions" (p. 76), a balance of cohesive and repulsive forces. Opposition between actors can paradoxically serve as a sustaining force when those in relationship have the possibility of exerting their will and maintaining an individuality that constitutes a partner with which to be in relationship.

The social order itself is thus fashioned out of attractive and repulsive forces. As Simmel ([1908] 1971) puts it, "Society,... in order to attain a determinate shape, needs some quantitative ratio of harmony and disharmony, of association and competition, of favorable and unfavorable tendencies. But these discords are by no means mere sociological liabilities or negative instances" (p. 72). Simmel's and Lewis Coser's (1956) work is particularly relevant because both authors demonstrate that conflict is not uniformly dysfunctional, and groups can co-exist despite—or sometimes because of—conflict between them. Thus, impulses to eliminate conflict may be misplaced, but the quest to understand various *modes and outcomes* of conflict remains.

Conflict Methods Matter

The relationship between collective action in conflict situations and collective identities constitutes a central feature in the intractability of ethnopolitical conflicts. The experience of conflict depends largely on the methods opponents use, and changes in conflict strategies and methods influence opponents' mutually dependent collective identities. Intimidation, threat, and violence encourage fear, mistrust, and desperation and undermine communication and mutual problem solving. Nonviolent methods, by contrast, tend to be more communicative and provide opportunities for trust and relationships to develop.

A range of conflict methods exist, and they play a crucial role in the direction a conflict takes. According to Weber ([1920] 1978), "Conflict varies enormously according to the means employed, especially whether they are violent or peaceful, and to the ruthlessness with which they are used" (p. 42). Simmel argued in even greater detail that various methods have different effects on group relations. Violence polarizes groups, but less violent forms of conflict open the possibility for the development of solidarity between parties. "If, however, there is any consideration, any limit to violence, there already exists a socializing factor, even though only as the qualification of violence" ([1908] 1971:81). When groups engage in conflict without the use of violence or other destructive methods or even moderate the use of violence, the conflict has a greater potential to integrate opponents. In other cases, where relations are based on aversion and avoidance, conflict is more likely to eventually degenerate into violence when the occasion arises.

Since violence, coercion, and intimidation generate trauma and undermine trust that perpetuates further violent conflict, one of the central challenges of all peace initiatives is "the ending of violence" as John Brewer (2003) highlights in the title of his book on the subject. However, setting aside instances of unilateral military victory, and surrender, the ending of violence is not an end to conflict, but usually constitutes a transition from one mode of conflict to another. Fortunately, scholars of conflict have developed tools for the classification of conflict methods (Gamson 1968; Deutsch 1973; Boulding 1989; Kriesberg 1998a; Weiner 1998; Deutsch and Coleman 2000).[2]

Louis Kriesberg (1998a) offers a particularly useful model in which he distinguishes between three types of inducements: *coercion, persuasion,* and *reward,* which represent a continuum of conflict strategies.[3] He contends that nonviolent strategies, such as, persuasion and reward, are more likely to produce "constructive" outcomes while coercion promotes "destructive" outcomes (cf. Coy and Woehrle 2000).[4] Methods that impose sanctions on adversaries tend to encourage self-perpetuating conflicts, often leading to intractable spirals of violence.[5] Like Simmel, Kriesberg (2007:268) maintains that conflicts may be considered constructive when they result in mutual benefits and facilitate future relationships between adversaries, conflicts that Simmel ([1908] 1971) refers to as "integrative" (p. 74).

> Whether principled or pragmatic, some features of nonviolent strategies tend to foster constructively waged rather than destructively waged struggles. Certainly, the adversary tends to be less dehumanized by the process; and indeed, nonviolent action often appeals to the empathy and reasonableness of the adversary. It can even garner respect from the adversary. (Kriesberg 1998a:113)

In short, a move away from violence is a move, however tenuous, toward coexistence.

Thus, persuasion or "conversion" potentially paves the way for cooperation between opponents (Gandhi [1945] 1967; Sharp 1973:69; Bond 1992; Northrup 1997; Teixeira 1999).[6] In the empirical world, however, conflict styles are rarely pure, and persuasive methods can sometimes be used to coerce (e.g., when persuasion brings external pressure to bear on an opponent). Often, adversaries use combinations of coercive and nonviolent methods, just as some nationalist social movements, including those in Ireland, use both violent and nonviolent methods (Sharp 1973; Ackerman and Kruegler 1994; Kriesberg 1998a; Irvin 1999). However, with a reduction in coercion and violence, space is opened for dialogue, negotiation, and relationship building.

Students of nonviolent methods are already familiar with the relationship between nonviolent methods and cognitive phenomena. The objective of purely nonviolent methods of persuasion is not to induce an opponent via coercion or threat but to change the adversary's mind (cf. Gandhi [1945] 1967; Schelling 1976; Darby 1986). "Nonviolent struggle employs social power to 'work' through and affect human minds" (Bond 1992:55). Scholars studying nonviolent action argue that nonviolent methods may be successful through substantially limiting an opponent's options or *persuading and converting their collective will.* Thus, conversion, as Sharp (1973:69) calls it, has the potential of paving the way for greater cooperation and solidarity between opponents. Northrup (1997) asserts, "In fact, the process of nonviolent action can in itself become a source of identity transformation that has the potential for leading to powerful political change. Current identity theory has not yet, accounted for the contributions of such moves toward transformation, integration, and conciliation" (p. 241). This book takes up Northrup's challenge by examining the relationship between the adoption of less intimidating collective action strategies, including public symbolic displays and the reinterpretation of otherwise polarized collective identities.

Toward a Sociology of Nonviolent Persuasion

Persuasion and reward lack the destructive tendencies of coercion and violence. They require a more sophisticated engagement with adversaries based on communication and the kinds of empathic imagination that social theorists like Mead (1934) and Goffman (1959) have famously attributed to social relations. Persuasion in particular is communicative in that it appeals to shared cultural schemata and affords adversaries at least the parity of intellect and esteem that comes with being persuadable. Strategists use methods ranging from public statements to symbols and gestures to communicate persuasively. When a strategy employing persuasion is successful, the opponent or third parties willingly embrace the logic underlying the message (Kriesberg 2007:99). Persuasion changes perceptions by redefining the issues under dispute and the identities of people involved. Rewards utilize the will of opponents but rely on their pragmatic interests. Coercion and reward can be discursive like persuasion, but only persuasion is defined by an attempt to reframe a dispute such that the opponents or third parties decide to respond favorably because their goals, interests, and values require it under a new definition of the situation.

Participants in conflicts often send messages through formal statements or through the careful use of symbols that may be directed at opponents or third parties to the conflict (Smithey and Kurtz 2003). Gene Sharp (1973) has catalogued fifty-four methods for carrying out nonviolent protest and persuasion including "formal statements," "communications with a wider audience," "processions," and a category called "withdrawal and renunciation" that includes methods of avoidance, such as, walk-outs, silence, and turning one's back (pp. 109–82). The goal may be to persuade opponents and third parties that one's grievances are legitimate or to redefine the parameters of the conflict by emphasizing common interests and values. In each case, the development of persuasive tactics requires that a message be developed, which introduces an important subjective dimension. Each message constitutes a presentation of collective identity, thus contributing to in-group identity, and influences the construction of collective identity among out-groups, a crucial process in identity conflicts.

The persuasive actions groups take are not initiated from a cultural vacuum. Such tactics are intimately tied to value systems and memories that dictate what kind of action is considered acceptable or satisfying (Jasper 1997:237; Gecas 2000; Smithey

2009a). They must be seen to express a group's goals and values. Some strategies, while offering a strategic advantage, may not match well with a group's collective identity. Avoiding conflict with an opponent might offend a group's sense of honor. Similarly, an opponent's actions must be reconciled with the group's prevailing view of the opponent. For some, their opponents may "only understand violence," and negotiation or dialogue may be considered unethical or ineffective (Kriesberg 2007:16).

Collective memory contributes to the repertoire of tactics upon which any given group might call. Republican hunger strikes in Northern Ireland were couched in a practice of fasting in Brehon law called *destrain* in which a victim of injustice fasted outside the door of the offender until justice was done. The hunger strikers thus drew on a component of Irish identity and history to inspire contemporary political action (Aretxaga 1997). However, collective action is not limited to a pre-set repertoire. The formation of identity within conflict is contingent on the interaction of parties to the conflict.

■ COLLECTIVE IDENTITY AND COLLECTIVE INTERACTION

Earlier, I asserted that ethnic identity is both malleable and constructed in interaction, often stemming from experimental but strategic moves by cultural agents within ethnic communities. This "agent-centered approach" introduces interactivity into the construction and transformation of collective identities. They are not only shaped and made continuous by the expectations and social psychological needs of adherents, but they are also influenced by the construction and expression of competing identities (Berbrier 2000:69). The process is thus both agential and interactive, a perspective that aligns with work by theorists who advocate a "social ontology" that locates agency in the *interaction* between actors (Barnes 2000; King 2004:18; Sullivan and McCarthy 2004). Theorists such as, Barry Barnes (2000) and Anthony King (2004) situate agency within communication and interaction. They hold that social life is processual and that both continuity and change are the products of an ongoing "cascade" of communication, interpretation, response, and reaction through which people negotiate and enact a shared reality (King 2004:17–18). King argues that it is "shared understandings" that underpin social relations (pp. 59, 61). Similarly, Sullivan and McCarthy (2004) advocate a dialogical approach, drawing on Bakhtin to remind us that every human act is a response to a "felt other" (p. 295).

In short, there is always a reliance on the perceived response of the other to shape one's identity and actions. It is a highly intersubjective affair; only through interaction with others can an intelligible social narrative be constructed. Barnes (2000) calls this interdependency "accountability" (p. 74), which is similar to what Sullivan and McCarthy (2004) call "responsibility," a mutual necessity among people to contribute to a shared social reality (p. 296). A corollary to this proposition is that we are vulnerable or "susceptible" to one another, as Barnes (2000:68–70) puts it. We act as agents toward one another as we influence one another's actions and definitions of the situation.

Goffman's (1959, 1963) work is among the most notable on interaction. In his dramaturgical model, people interact according to shared but negotiable scripts. Individuals work to manage the impressions they project to their advantage, but there is also a pervasive drive to cooperate in the mutual production of social interaction. Parties to social interaction operate from senses of self that are multifaceted yet, coherent, and they need each other to maintain semipredictable roles in order to reliably respond to one another. Ultimately, participants' social selves (and collective identities at the group level) are developed through the accumulation of experiences within such social interactions. In short, identity is created through interaction as actors incorporate experience into identity.

The creation of identity through collective action, especially via symbolic ritual or moments of public dramatization, is well documented (Durkheim 1915; Kertzer 1988; Bryson and McCartney 1994; Loftus 1994; Buckley and Kenny 1995; Jarman 1997; Ross 2007). Collective identity guides action, but the process is not unidirectional. Action also reproduces collective identity (Bryson and McCartney 1994). Buckley and Kenney (1995) argue in their work on social drama in Northern Ireland that action of most any sort creates a moment in which the mental sense of self becomes tangible. "Identity is rooted in what people do" (p. 211). In explaining the relationship between identity and action, Buckley and Kenney apply Goffman's distinction between real and virtual identity. A "real" identity is one a person "really has" as opposed to the virtual identity the person presents to others. Virtual identities obtain reality or objectivity when they are mutually accepted in a negotiated relationship between participants in an interaction.

Furthermore, social interaction takes place within frames of meaning that contextualize encounters. For Buckley and Kenney, "operational frames" are unspoken and guide simple social action allowing people to negotiate common encounters, such as, a motorist slowing to allow a pedestrian to cross the street or a customer purchasing a product from a clerk. "Rhetorical frames" can be presented to another participant in an interaction "with the aim of changing his [or her] definition of a particular piece of reality" (p. 28). Public "dramatizations" ranging from a simple greeting to choreographed collective action can present rhetorical frames. The identities within the frame are then either accepted or rejected by other participants. "When one person presents himself [sic] to another, there are strong elements of both experiment and persuasion in the presentation" (Buckley and Kenny 1995:30). To the extent that rhetorical frameworks are roundly accepted, they become operational, and so it follows that "when a person acts he also defines himself." Or rather, he or she defines himself or herself if and when the rhetorical frame presented is accepted by others in the sphere of interaction. In that event, the virtual identity presented within the frame becomes to some extent real. Thus, people are co-creators with one another in the reconstruction of their identities.

Collective Identity and Collective Action Methods

Similarly, the methods groups employ while conducting conflict are central to the character of their relations and the construction of their interdependent identities. Public rituals or dramatizations (such as, parades) constitute moments in which collective rhetorical frames are presented and either accepted or rejected by participants and bystanders. Collective actions, especially those with high symbolic content, present definitions of the conflict situation that reflect and recreate collective identity. In conflicted relations, the dialectical relationship between identity formation and collective action methods becomes especially crucial because identities, and the values and principles they encompass, can inspire or limit the range of methods that a group deploys. The effectiveness of strategies will also depend, in part, on their perceived suitability for addressing opponents' and third parties' collective identities.

Furthermore, as Mach (1993) explains, *the character of relations* between groups (including their methods of interaction) influences the shape of their cultural models:

> The changes in the balance of power between the groups or in any fundamental aspects of these relations such as, increased or decreased degree of interdependence, changing legal or economic structure, influence the character of relations between people and transform their symbolic interactions which in turn introduce changes into interpretations of symbolic categories and into models of identity. The dynamic process of identification of action and interpretation consists in interdependence between the social world and its mental model with its intellectual and emotional content. This process constitutes the essence of the historical evolution of relations between various human groups. (p. 44)

Groups' models of the world, including stereotypes of others, are developed and refined within fluid and dynamic relations with others. Collective action tactics should be included in Mach's "fundamental aspects of relations" as they exemplify attempts to wield or create power. The ways in which groups conduct themselves in conflict situations reflect and influence the ways in which they perceive each other and vice versa, raising several important questions: How does variability in the types of collective actions employed in conflict influence the construction of identity on either side of a conflict? Must groups' cultural models of the world adapt to accommodate the tactics they use or that are used against them? Can the choreography of collective action events constitute discourse between parties in conflict and influence the mutual construction of their identities (Smithey and Kurtz 2003)?

Persuasion and Collective Identity

The relationship between collective identity and collective interaction is particularly important in the use of methods of persuasion. In a conflict situation, opponents attempt to make use of the other's frames to their own strategic advantage, often as a foil against which to sustain their own identity. The power of persuasion lies partially in the mutual dependence of each side's identity on the other. Crafting a message that transforms either oneself or the definition of the situation can compel opponents to alter their behavior in order to maintain the integrity of their own collective identity. For example, appropriating opponents' rhetoric may make it more difficult for the opponent to challenge one's actions (Smithey and Kurtz 2003; Woehrle, Coy, and Maney 2008).

In contrast to avoidance and coercion, persuasion is an attempt to communicate psychologically and emotionally powerful arguments to an opponent or third parties and induce them to willingly behave in a desired fashion. Persuasion can entail placing the opponent in a potentially awkward position of responding to a new definition of the conflict situation. By strategically presenting a virtual self, one can anticipate and diminish the attack of the opponent. For example, highlighting one's minority status can steal away opponents' charges of elitism.

Persuasive appeals that present new virtual identities can, at least temporarily however, force the protagonist group into the equally awkward position of assuming the new strategic guise. In the process, the group may modify its own collective identity by incorporating the new narrative. Strategically deploying a new virtual identity in this way can create in-group tension. The challenge lies in maintaining a stable sense of collective identity and yet, taking strategic advantage of persuasive methods at the same time.

Strategic persuasion is particularly pertinent to a discussion of conflict transformation because it can modify the premises on which opponents relate to one another. Persuasion requires the user to humanize adversaries. Opponents must be considered persuadable, and thus a measure of equality is injected into the relationship. A tension may arise between acknowledging the humanity of one's opponents and maintaining the usual distance from them, and consequently, some groups will struggle internally over the advantages offered by persuasive methods, the rhetorical frames presented by opponents, and the maintenance of their own ontological security.

In short, there is a considerable amount of cultural work that goes on as all parties try to reconcile their collective action methods and their understandings of the "other" with their own collective identities. The challenge for research lies in the difficulty of discovering the seams between identity and action. Collective action methods are deployed in discrete periods of time while identities are often developed over generations. Without extensive longitudinal data, one can be limited to an analysis that captures change in methods more easily than changes in identity. Nevertheless, through qualitative research, we can identify tension and symbiosis between collective identity and collective action methods.

An exchange on October 6, 2000, between two Northern Ireland politicians on *Talkback*, a popular radio talk show, illustrates tension between collective identity and persuasion. In the conversation, the late David Ervine (a prominent politician representing the Progressive Unionist Party, PUP, which has links to the loyalist paramilitary Ulster Volunteer Force and Red Hand Commando) expressed his shock at hearing Martin McGuinness (a Sinn Féin member of the Legislative Assembly [MLA], deputy first minister, and former IRA commander) declare at a Labour Party conference that the peace process is primarily about the partition of Northern Ireland from the Republic of Ireland, thus calling British sovereignty into question. At the time of the interview, McGuinness was serving as minister of education. Unionists, such as, Ervine, feel they have made exceedingly difficult compromises while many Republicans consider the peace process a stepping stone toward a united Ireland.

> McGuinness: Our position is spelled out, and our support for the Good Friday Agreement does spell out the fact that we are dealing with a status quo, but one that we believe that we can change. And then, we are about the business of persuading people about a united Ireland.

> [The moderator, David Dunseith, asks McGuinness if he is as open to being persuaded as he is to persuading others, which Dunseith calls "parity in the matter of persuasion."]

> McGuinness: We will present our political preference, and we will listen carefully to those who honestly have a different perspective. But, you know, I'm an Irish republican because I am already convinced that that is the logical and sensible outcome…and I think I can convince others who have a different perspective from me about the logic of my position.

> Dunseith: Fair enough, but then, you would say you are a democrat in these matters; you would have to accept the logic of others.

> McGuinness: I would have to take account of the logic of others, and I am stating to you, in answer to your question, that I am prepared to listen to those arguments. But, I think I have a very convincing case, and I really would welcome the opportunity to discuss my analysis with those of the unionist persuasion. I do think that the fact that there is such unanimity within broad nationalism tells you that people, even at the instinctive level, recognize the, if you like, the flow of history. And, I believe that when you look at the divisions within unionism that clearly those same forces are at work…but it is my conviction that will eventually result in constitutional change which should be by agreement.

When McGuinness was pushed on the issue of persuasion, he went to significant lengths to make it clear to others, and probably to himself, that politics and the use of persuasion did not require him to sacrifice his "conviction," the ideology and principles of his republicanism. Dunseith suggested that, logically, his position required that he also be open to persuasion, to which McGuinness agreed, but McGuinness also felt bound to declare, "I'm an Irish republican because I am already convinced that that is the logical and sensible outcome." Mr. McGuinness appears caught between a strategy that relies on political persuasion, but one which brings with it a logic that challenges the sanctity of republican ideology.

Similarly, Aretxaga (1997) describes the cultural work Bobby Sands undertook while he and other republican prisoners refined hunger strikes to strategic advantage while also preserving their Irish collective identity:

> Sands was simultaneously reinterpreting while enacting a myth model deeply rooted in Irish culture (i.e., redemptive Christian sacrifice) by fusing it with mythological images of Gaelic warriors and socialist ideals of national liberation. Simultaneously, Sands was fighting with rational instrumentality a concrete political battle that influenced, at least temporarily, the balance of power between Britain and the republican movement in Northern Ireland, a fight that led the latter to a political reconfiguration. (p. 81)

For Aretxaga, Sands had to ensure that the prisoners' actions were consonant with the warrior ethos of republican mythology and ideology while recognizing that the prisoners were without the usual tools of armed struggle, and they had begun to appreciate the effectiveness of political struggle (Shirlow and McGovern 1998). These tensions suggest a relationship between strategy and identity that I will pursue further through analysis of evidence gathered among committed unionists and loyalists in Northern Ireland who seek to participate in a new political and social dispensation in which militarism and exclusion offer increasingly few benefits but for which they must develop new ways of contending and relating.

■ PEACEBUILDING AND CONFLICT TRANSFORMATION WITHIN COMMUNITIES AND TRADITIONS

John D. Brewer (2003) has presented a comprehensive theoretical frame for conflict transformation by drawing on Mills's (1959) work on the "sociological imagination." Brewer interprets the monumental political changes in Northern Ireland and South Africa at the end of the twentieth century as products of a complex interaction between biography or individual experience, social structural factors, such as, demographic trends and economic changes, and political processes, all situated within the *longue durée* of history: "The lives of individuals cannot be adequately understood without reference to the institutions (political and social) and historical forces within which their biography is enacted, and societies are composed in part of the biographical experiences, historical and contemporary, of the people they comprise" (p. 34).

Living through the Troubles within this web of forces created a "tension between two forms of ontological insecurity that pulled in opposite directions" (p. 158). War weariness inclined people toward a desire for peace, but fear of the other and the uncertainties of peace mitigated against taking the risks involved with compromise. However, key leaders were able to consolidate sufficient interest in a new negotiated political arrangement because of changes in local and international circumstances, such as, a declining economy, and because of a reevaluation and reinterpretation of people's biographies.

Similarly, Ruane and Todd (1996) show how ethnopolitical division in Northern Ireland is a reflection of a "structure of dominance, dependence and inequality" that was forged and reproduced over the course of four hundred years of British and Irish economic and political history (pp. 11–12). The reproduction of the system is also, however, perpetuated across socially constructed dimensions of cultural and ideological difference that are themselves the product of structured social relations. Thus, like Brewer, they "present structural relations, ideas and meanings as interpenetrating in all areas of social life" (p. 5). Ruane and Todd work on understanding how such deep division has come to exist but with a critical eye to the potential for unwinding the mutually reinforcing structures, practices, and schemata that maintain "communal division." Ruane and Todd call their assessment of what is necessary for Northern Ireland to move toward a sustainable democratic future "an emancipatory approach to the conflict" (pp. 290–316), and I share their commitment to discerning what is necessary to escape the downward spiral of violence, fear, and retribution that characterizes intractable conflict.

In conflict situations, a transition from defensive or violent action to persuasion is rarely precipitous. Nonviolent empowerment and the adoption of effective organizing skills require changes in worldview and vice versa. New methods are considered, debated, experimented with, and tried, in some cases alongside violence. The internal politics of developing and adopting new nonviolent strategies takes places slowly and incrementally, behind closed doors and with careful consideration. Eventually, organizations and the communities in which they are embedded endorse or reject new innovations. Even after cease-fires are called, the task of maintaining support for new strategies or "making politics work" is central to avoiding a return to violence.

Similarly, the transformation of collective identities occurs incrementally, and it is most effective when it occurs from *within* communities. In order to shift from intractable ethnopolitical violence to less-violent or nonviolent democratic arrangements, there must be a sense that to do so does not violate sacred trusts. A new appreciation of the strategic advantages of engaging constructively and nonviolently in conflict can provide an important impetus for adopting new modes of operation, but some sense of continuity with long-held collective identities must also be maintained, especially when they have been forged over years of suspicion and trauma. Minimizing this kind of insecurity while mitigating support for coercion in favor of more constructive methods, such as, persuasive ones, constitutes the core tasks of conflict transformation work (Liechty and Clegg 2001; Brewer 2003; Ganiel and Dixon 2008).

I want to focus attention specifically on the construction and reframing of identity and difference in iconic and ritual moments (Schirch 2001). Studying the innovation and reinterpretation of the narratives, rituals, symbols, and modes of collective action that sustain and shape core identities provides an important window onto the transformation of polarized ethnopolitical relations in Northern Ireland.

Conflict Transformation

"Conflict transformation" has become a familiar term among academics, professionals, and government officials. It emerged in the late 1980s at a time when realist schools of international politics were struggling to address a proliferation of nonviolent people power movements, not the least of which led to the fall of the Soviet Bloc (Kriesberg, Northrup, and Thorson 1989; Väyrynen 1991a; Rupesinghe 1995a; Smithey and Kurtz 1999). Suddenly, the literatures on strategic nonviolent action, peacebuilding, globalization, and critical theory gained new relevance (Ryan 2007:1–14). The potential for significant changes in the geopolitical landscape and the apparent importance of popular movements demanded a reassessment of many conflicts and raised hope that such large-scale nonviolent change could be encouraged elsewhere. Conflict resolution and conflict management studies had much to offer, but they were not suited to the dynamism and complexity of many large-scale conflicts that were the products of a wide range of factors (Dunn 1995; Ruane and Todd 1996; Miall 2004; Reimann 2004). These include economic inequalities, colonial legacies and borders, segregation, class makeup and inequality, third-party interventions, and social movement mobilization. All interact to influence the trajectory of a conflict. Even when they might be said to end with the cessation of violence, the laws of unintended consequences tend to contribute to new conflicts over different issues and in new areas. Thus, conflict never ends but transforms in rolling waves of contention.

Conflict transformation shares the basic goals of conflict resolution and conflict management in ending violence through nonviolent negotiation and dialogue, but it envisions horizontal and vertical linking and long-term, multidimensional problem solving in pursuit of societal arrangements where former enemies can coexist and cooperate (Lederach 1997; Reimann 2004:10–13). Students of conflict transformation understand that conflict can be constructive but, soberly, they recognize that transformation must be as multidimensional as large-scale conflicts themselves. Change must take place across personal, communal, and institutional levels (Väyrynen 1991b; Lederach 1995; Lederach 1997; Brewer 2003; Miall 2004; Ryan 2007). The scope of the challenge has spurred a host of subfields of research in contact theory, coexistence, reconciliation, consociational politics, development diplomacy, alternative dispute resolution, and peace education, to name only a few. All the while, scholars and practitioners have struggled with the extent to which prescriptive programs can be effective when every conflict is unique and interpreted within the bounds of local culture.

One prominent strand of conflict transformation has recognized the importance of intersubjective meaning-making and issues of culture, education, socialization, and public narratives, all of which widen the scope of analysis beyond elites to include civil society (Deutsch 1991; Nordstrom 1995; Schirch 2001; Ryan 2007). Distinct periods of political negotiations are important but not sufficient to develop sustainable peace. Fundamental social psychological and structural changes at the grassroots are necessary to empower and undermine alienation and fears (Ryan 2007). According to Kumar Rupesinghe (1995b),

> Ultimately, transformation can be meaningful only if it is not merely a transfer of power, but if sustainable structural and attitudinal changes are also achieved within the society and new institutions emerge to address outstanding issues. Applied to conflict transformation, non-prescriptive methods of analyzing root causes and exploring mutually acceptable compromises involve empowerment of local people. (p. 77)

I would add that part of empowerment entails the discovery of nonviolent action and political participation as powerful and productive means of conducting conflict, but even then some parties may not have sufficiently developed the skills and ability to feel fully empowered. Transitions from one mode of conflict into another are often uneven and burdened with old ways of understanding conflict and opponents, besides the obvious challenges of negotiating the transition with opponents. One of the primary tasks of building peace is ensuring that a new nonviolent and political mode of conflict is effective for all communities and fully undermines the insecurity that fueled violent conflict.

I would like to make two orienting assertions in relation to conflict transformation. First, the empowerment to which Rupesinghe refers can be considered a continuation of conflict by increasingly nonviolent means. Peacebuilding aims not only to encourage prejudice reduction but to facilitate more constructive interaction between groups in conflict. We often think of important activities such as, relationship building, dialogue, or mediation. However, in ethnopolitical conflicts, the ways in which disputing parties publicly and symbolically represent themselves can constitute ongoing conflict, even while cease-fires hold and demilitarization is under way. Observers of Northern Ireland know only too well how public events, symbols, and slogans can project claims and threats. In much the same way that peacemakers seek to deescalate violence, negotiate cease-fires, and encourage opponents to engage in democratic politics, peacebuilders encourage activists at the grassroots level to reconsider how they represent themselves and how to adopt alternative means of pursuing group interests. As communities become empowered, they also become less defensive and less prone to resort to destructive or intimidating actions that break down trust and make cooperative politics impossible. As they become more confident in their ability to pursue their interests nonviolently, through effective grassroots organizing or democratic politics, they can begin to engage around interests that cut across racial and ethnic divides over which conflict was previously waged destructively.

Second, we should recognize the centrality of culture and identity to grassroots opinion about what kind of collective or representative action is acceptable and thus how conflict is conducted (Northrup 1989; Ross 1993:152–60; Kriesberg 2007; Ross 2007). The adoption of constructive tactics and strategies requires changes in worldviews since collective action agendas and collective identity are so closely related. Fundamental shifts in how groups perceive their identities and *modi operandi* will nearly always come slowly since to introduce new ideas or strategies too quickly risks dissent and fractures, a trend that seems especially prevalent in the Protestant population in Northern Ireland, where community esteem and confidence has often been placed outside of local communities in institutions such as, the state and its security services, both of which have undergone significant change over the course of the political peace process. The grassroots process of developing and negotiating new practices constitutes an important facet of conflict transformation. Without an integration of new schemata that prioritize and legitimize constructive and less exclusive practices, alienation and the seduction of violence threaten to undermine the progress toward peace that has been made in Northern Ireland.

These concerns underpin the British direct rule government's 2005 document *A Shared Future: Policy and Strategic Framework for Good Relations in Northern Ireland.* The framework calls for a "good relations" strategy based on the principle that the collective and subjective orientations of people to one another and the objective conditions in which they relate must be addressed in tandem (Northern Ireland Community Relations Council 2007). The document focuses on social psychological and cultural issues as then Secretary of State Paul Murphy states in his foreword: "The essence of reconciliation is about moving away from relationships that are built on mistrust and defence to relationships rooted in mutual recognition and trust" (p. 3). *A Shared Future* targets a "culture of intolerance" and refers to the 1978 Council of Europe for a standard of good relations: "A society's cultural life is rich if people in the society can communicate with each other, describe their reality and their experiences, voice their feelings, understand one another and thus in the end be in a position to respect one another" (p. 8). We might add, even as they continue to engage in the kind of constructive nonviolent conflict and collaboration that befits a fully democratic society.

In other words, a sustainable peace in Northern Ireland, requires that groups of people, distinguished from one another along familiar lines of ethnopolitical division, feel they have the wherewithal and opportunities for dialogue, collaboration, and constructive opposition. Conflict is thus transformed, not simply resolved. Whether polarized communities are prepared to engage effectively in transformed conflict remains an important question. One cannot expect that grievances, prejudices, and collective identities hardened over decades of violent conflict, especially among those who have borne the brunt of violent conflict, can be quickly pacified or dissolved. Furthermore, without the space and ability to organize effectively and nonviolently around collective interests, the temptation to retreat or employ defensive or intimidating tactics under conditions of uncertainty or perceived threat will remain. Thus, how groups with strong ideological or cultural commitments become prepared to engage in a shared nonviolent future warrants close examination.

Ultimately, the kind of cross-community contact, dialogue, and cooperation that has characterized community relations work in Northern Ireland is crucial. Whether Northern Ireland remains part of the United Kingdom (UK) or becomes part of a united Ireland or, like Scotland, devolves further toward the periphery of the union, the ongoing task of breaking down stereotypes and building relationships across the ethnopolitical divide will remain important. However, it is also important to understand those processes *within* the Catholic and Protestant populations. The changes in attitudes and sense of identity that must accompany cooperation will occur incrementally and in ways that are unique to each community in which it occurs.

A comprehensive transformation of conflict means that even those organizations that have been associated with maintaining the pillars of communal identity, often excluding, alienating, and even intimidating other communities in the process, must also find a way to become active participants in civil society. Some may decline or fade, but in other cases, ideologically oriented organizations can carry a credibility and capital with which to assist the change of attitudes and outlooks, or "'common sense' ideas," within their own communities (McAuley 1997:173; Brewer and Higgins 1998:175–76; Ganiel 2008a,b). Documenting the negotiation of changing political and symbolic strategies among unionists and loyalists in Northern Ireland constitutes the core task of this book, to which we will increasingly turn our attention.

Cultural Traditions and Multiculturalism

Cultural traditions work is a particular form of community relations work in Northern Ireland that recognizes the importance of addressing collective identities from the inside out. It operates from the premise that insecurity in the legitimacy or coherence of collective identities can lead to defensive attitudes and behavior. By encouraging groups to develop increasingly rich narratives and cultural expressions, cultural traditions work aims to undermine the ontological insecurity that has fueled ethnic division and direct energy into more communicative activities. Maurice Hayes (1990), the first chairperson of the Northern Ireland Community Relations Commission, described cultural traditions work in a lecture delivered in 1990 to the MSSc Irish Studies Forum at Queen's University in Belfast:

> In the same way as an individual needs to be secure in himself, and this indeed is one sign of maturity, so groups, especially minority groups in society, need to develop self-confidence. A self-confident group, secure in its own values, can deal with other groups much more constructively than a group which is insecure, lacking in self-confidence, or which sees itself as oppressed or undervalued by the wider society. Much of what presents as inter-group or ethnic conflict, is, I believe, determined by the self-perception of the groups concerned, their perception of others, and their preconceptions of others' view of them. Underlying most of these conflicts is a failure of communication, a lack of empathy and understanding which results in stereotyping and scapegoating, and a basic lack of trust without which no social, political or other contract is conceivable. (p. 5)

John, the director of an ecumenical religious organization, put the point more bluntly in an interview as he discussed the urgent need to make the Orange Order's Twelfth celebrations a much more welcoming event,

> I want to make it wonderful because I honestly believe, even though it is not the expression of who I personally am any more, I can identify enough with the Protestant community from which I come that, unless it recovers some sort of cultural pride and confidence, it will not be a fit partner to make peace and will actually be the seedbed for the next war.

Cultural traditions work aims to address psychocultural roots of the Troubles and invites partisans to become agents of peacebuilding within the context of their own cultural experience.

However, cultural traditions work has come in for criticism by those who fear that it encourages further development of the narrow and polarized sectarian identities that have legitimized division and violence (Rolston 1998; Ryan 2007:120–21). These critics feel it risks perpetuating the social psychological underpinnings of the conflict in a time when old ethnic identities should account for a diminishing share of a growing and diverse assortment of identifications. They argue that parity of culture relativizes and flattens our understanding of the colonial bases of conflict and replaces class analysis. Perhaps the most common critique of cultural traditions work deconstructs traditional "orange" and "green" identities as fundamentally abused and compromised by the political agendas to which they owe their origins. Both the romantic republican myth of an original Gaelic nation and the loyalist search for an equally unitary Protestant history with which to stake a legitimate claim in Ireland constitute historically impoverished and mutually alienating projects. Edna Longley (1987), who has been active in the Cultural Traditions Group, sees greater potential in developing rich cultural expressions that embrace the complexity of history and social experience in Ireland:

> The literature produced by Ulster people suggests that, instead of brooding on Celtic and Orange dawns, its inhabitants might accept this province-in-two-contexts as a cultural corridor. Unionists want to block the corridor at one end, republicans at the other. Culture, like common sense, insists it can't be done. Ulster Irishness and Ulster Britishness are bound to each other and to Britain and Ireland. And the Republic will have to come cleaner about its own de facto connections with Britain. Only by promoting circulation within and through Ulster will the place ever be part of a healthy system.

If one of the pillars of conflict since the late nineteenth century in Ireland has been the false supremacy of two broadly opposed identities, surely greater cultural diversity is a much-needed antidote. James Hawthorne, serving as chair in 1989, associated the Cultural Traditions Group with cultural diversity: "There is more than orange and green. We want to think of this spectrum as a very wide one with interesting colours everywhere in it" (1989:29).

The Cultural Traditions Group aims to reach a state of pluralism in which cultural identities become deconstructed or at least exposed to contradictions through the very process that aims to facilitate confidence among people who feel they are pursuing something innate within themselves.[7] However, one critic, Finlayson (1997), asks a provocative and useful question:

> CTG [Cultural Traditions Group] is concerned to foster cultural confidence and aware-ness of the respective traditions. How can it do both at the same time? How can it say "your cultural tradition is a contingent formation that can and should be changed. It has no essential validity," at the same time as saying "feel good about yourself, we respect your culture fully"? (p. 79)

Finlayson (1997) argues that identities are created by social and political discourse and are consequently best described as "identifications" with ideological positions (p. 83). He regards political hegemony as the primary social force behind the construction of collective identities. "Political activists open up spaces and offer them to a population. The victor is the one who convinces people of the over-riding validity of one category of belonging, and is able to keep on reaffirming it" (p. 83). Conflict among a growing variety of worldviews is desirable as it creates a more diverse and competitive market of identifications, increasing the chances of cross-fertilization and creating incentives for groups to modify their cultural offer-ings to capture greater market share. To this, he contrasts cultural traditions work which he claims entices ethnic groups into reconciliation while keeping them whole: "What we need is a process that seeks to problematise identities rather than resolve conflicts between them" (p. 85).

My aim is not to belabor Finlayson's critique but to offer a different way of thinking about collective identities and cultural traditions work. Finlayson is right to promote competition as a healthy feature of any successful liberal democracy (p. 84). However, it may be premature to discount the contributions of cultural traditions enthusiasts toward a maturing democratic landscape. When Finlayson questions whether cultural traditions can be both encouraged and changed, he seems to imply that this is an either-or proposition, but ethnic heritage is a social construction and is subject to experimentation and redefinition.

People are not mere consumers of political discourse, who absorb a cocktail of identifications. They play an active role in the construction of belonging, though clearly the discursive environment is an important factor shaping identity. Collective identities are not so rigid and static that they cannot change, even if adherents feel that they are essential or transcendent. They can be credibly trans-formed from within, using some pillars of tradition from which to modify or retire others (Liechty and Clegg 2001). Cultural enthusiasts and local leaders can intro-duce new elements of symbolic ritual or interpretations of familiar narratives that are less antagonistic toward other groups and thus make space for the kind of dia-logue, relationship-building, and reconciliation that has been the aim of community relations work as well as the kind of diverse democratic discourse that Finlayson envisions (Ascherson 2004).

Leadership and Cultural Entrepreneurship

Influential meaning makers or "agents of cultural reproduction" (intellectuals, artists, writers, poets, political and civic leaders) articulate group identity and represent communities to themselves through media, such as, publications, speeches, and symbolic actions (Ryan 2007:140). In the process of disseminating messages within the community, they can incrementally influence communal tastes and preferences through what McCauley (2002) calls "feet-first persuasion." He describes a "power of small steps to motivate larger steps in the same direction." One might consider it a slippery-slope model. The central mechanism lies in the setting of precedents within communities, instances of innovation, and moments in which groups redefine themselves and conduct conflict with opposing parties in less destructive ways. Even experimentation can set precedents for further development. McCauley roots feet-first persuasion in dissonance theory: "When we act in a way that is inconsistent with our attitudes and values, we are likely to change our beliefs to rationalize the new behaviors. The motivation for the change is to avoid looking stupid or sleazy to ourselves or others." Consequently, values, narratives, and ideologies that serve as referents underlying collective identities may be modified to align with novel actions.

The depth of this kind of social psychological work suggests that new strategies and less polarizing worldviews are best developed as closely as possible to sources of communal legitimacy. Joseph Liechty and Cecelia Clegg (2001) have aptly stressed the importance of internal transformation in their work on religious sectarianism and reconciliation: "What is far more constructive is for a community to learn to hear its own ancestral voices anew, with or without the aid of outside voices.... When destructive ancestral voices are countered from within the tradition, they are weakened and silenced as effectively as they ever can be" (p. 178). Despite somewhat primordial language, Liechty and Clegg make a strong argument for the articulation of constructive alternative visions from *within* communal traditions (cf. Miall 2004:4).

According to the 2005 Young Life and Times Survey (YLTS) of sixteen-year-olds in Northern Ireland, 45 percent of respondents identified their family as the most important influence on their views about the other religious community. Nineteen percent identified friends as most influential, suggesting that out-group attitudes are largely sustained within communities and families (Schubotz and Robinson 2006:2). Contact theory asserts that projects carefully designed to diminish prejudices by bringing opposed groups into contact with one another, when executed with the initiative or approval of local community leaders, allow greater freedom for participants to experiment with new orientations toward outgroups (Amir 1969; Pettigrew 1998). When local community leaders and authority figures propose to alter familiar expressions of communal identity, they do so with a credibility and legitimacy that is often not part of programmatic or state-sponsored community relations initiatives (Boulding 2000; Ryan 2007:149–51).

Brewer (2003) notes that key individuals have had significant influence on peace processes in Northern Ireland and South Africa. Figures such as, F. W. DeKlerk, David Trimble, Gerry Adams, and Martin McGuinness have, from (sometimes tenuous) positions of authority within their own communities, moved their constituencies toward important compromises. "It was precisely because their individual backgrounds and biographical experiences were unimpeachable in right-wing terms that they were able to take doubters along. And both were successful in presenting the peace process to many confused, bewildered and powerless people in a way that it made sense for them to support change" (Brewer 2003:96).

Leaders' abilities to shape collective identity and cultural expressions operate within limits, however, because authority is a communal product. Authority is not something that political leaders possess; authority is a resource that resides within their constituencies, which they can access through familiar symbol and ritual (Kertzer 1988:42–45). Leaders command cultural capital that allows them to speak in such a way that their language is recognized as legitimate (Bourdieu 1991:170). They tap into wells of meaning that make up collective identity and represent the group to itself in innovative ways, but leaders who go too far in jettisoning the cultural trappings of their community often find themselves with diminished influence (Lederach 1997:40). And yet, political representatives must maintain some measure of freedom to innovate in order to be effective negotiators when peacemaking opportunities arise. Politicians in Northern Ireland are no strangers to the dilemma. Since the early 1980s, Sinn Féin's political leadership has worked tirelessly to hone the party's ability to utilize the deep well of republican myth and the cachet of the armed struggle while cultivating politics as an equally powerful strategy within the republican movement.

Leaders involved in any sort of negotiation must deliver their constituencies, so they must pay careful attention and present themselves as representatives of core beliefs and commitments. However, to be effective negotiators, they must also stretch their constituents to embrace new ideas and jettison some former commitments. Cathy Gormley-Heenan and Gillian Robinson (2003) refer to this careful dance as "elastic band leadership" (p. 268). The process of introducing new ideas and opening the community to new possibilities is often a slow one. Collective identities must have ontological continuity; they must have authenticity and be recognized as having the imprimatur of the community. Moving too quickly can endanger ontological security and create a backlash and a retreat to insularity (Brewer 2010:35–36).

Nevertheless, local leaders in communities can innovate and contribute to reframing their communal identities and the way in which conflict is conducted. John Brewer (2003) asserts, "In some cases local spaces are opening up in which, for example, grassroots peacemaking and reconciliation are possible, and in which new identities can be experimented with and perceived as possible or in which existing identities come to be seen as more flexible and inclusive than previously imagined" (p. 150). In these cases, collective identities and their cultural expressions can be subtly altered in ways that are ontologically consonant but that open the group's orientation to hear adversaries in a new constructive way or at least minimize the alienating effect of a particular cultural expression. Liechty and Clegg (2001) refer to this process as "mitigation"; practices that threaten outgroups can be modified so that they are less likely to cause offense and feed destructive relations (pp. 226–29).

■ CONFLICT TRANSFORMATION IN NORTHERN IRELAND

Intractable ethnopolitical conflict consists of a set of intertwined conditions that usually include economic, political, and social inequalities; the construction of social psychological boundaries and their expression through cultural practices; and the quality of interaction, from the structuration of daily life in a divided society to revolutionary struggle and state security policy (Dunn 1995; Ruane and Todd 1996). To fully grasp the transformation of complicated intractable conflicts requires a range of theoretical and methodological approaches. Historical and political analyses abound, but the cultural and social dimensions of conflict and division also deserve thorough treatment. Sociological and anthropological work in Northern Ireland has shown how cultural practices have contributed to division in Northern Ireland (Rolston 1991; Bryson and McCartney 1994; Loftus 1994; Jarman and Bryan 1996; Jarman 1997; Buckley 1998; Bryan 2000; Jarman 2005), but we also need research that examines the unraveling of division, particularly in those corners where the most polarized worldviews have prevailed.

One of the critical dynamics operating in both the deepening and alleviation of sectarian division in Northern Ireland lies in the relationship between the collective actions that groups and communities undertake and the mutually polarized identities they maintain. Elaborate rituals and cultural displays mark boundaries of group identity as well as physical territory. They reference narratives that provide meaning in traumatic circumstances and cultivate in-group solidarity and ontological security. Once violence and coercion become prominent in repertoires of contention, and victims and martyrs become symbols within the powerful narratives of victimization that Volkan (1997) calls "chosen traumas," less coercive methods can often be considered weak and even traitorous.

However, new and more constructive methods can be introduced. Why and how strategic innovations are adopted and what forms they take are crucial questions for understanding conflict transformation, especially when ethnic group identities are so closely related to the ways in which opposing communities deal with one another. In the chapters that follow, we examine several cases in which Protestant unionist and loyalist organizations, such as, the Orange Order, cultural organizations, bands, and community development groups, have begun to modify or abandon traditional practices. Loyalist paramilitary organizations have begun to decommission weapons,[8] but they have encouraged their members to direct their energies into community work. The Orange Order and the Apprentice Boys of Derry have agreed to engage in dialogue with protesting nationalist residents' organizations. Increasingly, the Orange Order and loyalist bands have sought to remove unruly and offensive behavior among parade participants and supporters and incorporate historical themes and a more festive atmosphere.

In each case, new initiatives have been undertaken in attempts to build political and social capital. The defensive and coercive modes of operation that have characterized unionism and loyalism are being traded for more persuasive and diplomatic ones. Overall, we find a transitional process under way in which many of the beliefs and practices that have been antipathetic to Catholic nationalists remain but in less staunch forms. The trend is remarkable, but it is not simple. Progress has been slow. Credible rationales have to be developed that are consonant with familiar narratives and principles, but embracing persuasion and negotiation introduces new rules for public discourse with nationalists, new opportunities for cross-community dialogue, and new grounds for reflecting on fundamental premises of unionism and loyalism.

■ Notes

1. Liechty and Clegg (2001) illustrate the levels of exclusion attached to a variety of sectarian statements in their "scale of sectarian danger." A similar analysis of rituals and cultural expressions, such as, parades, murals, flags, and music, could be undertaken to assess the extent to which they are likely to exclude and intimidate others.

2. For contributions by social psychologists to the study of persuasion and attitude change, see Chaiken, Gruenfeld, and Judd (2000).

3. Strategies have often been counterposed as negative or positive sanctions, and other scholars have used similar tripartite models, such as, Morton Deutsch's (1973) *influence, threats* and *promises*, William A. Gamson's (1968) *persuasion, inducements* and *constraints*, or Kenneth Boulding's (1989) *threat, exchange,* and *love.*

4. Deutsch (1998) takes a similar position characterizing strategies with a concern for oneself, and not the other, as competitive and destructive while strategies based on a concern for oneself *and* the other are cooperative and constructive.

5. Deutsch's crude law of social relations holds that "the characteristic processes and effects elicited by a given type of social relationship (for example, cooperative or competitive) also tend to elicit that type of social relationship" (Deutsch 1991:31).

6. Persuasion and conversion, especially as conceptualized by Sharp (1973), are related but not exactly the same. Persuasion may or may not involve a broader conversion of an opponent; conversion is a consequence of persuasion, but also goes beyond it. Sharp also acknowledges the constructive potential of conversion and accommodation to diminish "the likelihood of bitterness, hatred and desire for revenge," factors that stand in the way of coexistence (p. 768).

7. Finlayson notes the use of the Irish Gaelic word *Dúchas* in the Cultural Traditions Group logo, which refers to "something deep inside people which makes them distinctive. It is an innate quality which resonates to the various elements of their cultural heritage" (Cultural Traditions Group 4 quoted in Finlayson 1997).

8. The Ulster Volunteer Force and Red Hand Commando undertook a decommissioning process in June 2009. At the time of writing, the Ulster Defense Association remained in discussions with the Independent International Commission on Decommissioning while trying to negotiate fissures in the organization in north and southeast Antrim.

3 Protestant Unionists and Loyalists

Some readers will almost certainly ask, "Why write a book on *Protestant unionists and loyalists* and conflict transformation?" Why not address conflict transformation across Northern Ireland including Catholic nationalists and republicans as well? After all, I have asserted that conflict and conflict transformation are imminently relational phenomena. The implementation of new, less coercive conflict methods and new cultural schemata for interpreting the conflict must take place in all quarters, and as some groups implement new policies and begin to adopt new definitions of the situation, their moves influence others, challenging each others' definitions of the situation and removing justifications for mistrust. A truly comprehensive account of conflict transformation would indeed require a wide lens. However, as is always the case, breadth usually means less depth, and convinced that much of the action of developing, testing, and approving new ideas often originates and ultimately must prevail at the grassroots, I focus my attention and resources on the work of constructing and enacting collective identities in one segment of Northern Irish society.

In many ways, looking at how republicans have transformed their struggle from an armed to a political and cultural one might have been more straightforward and no less important. However, I was compelled to determine whether a similar process could be identified among unionists and loyalists, who have long been in the position of defending the status quo and have long characterized themselves as perpetually unwanted and "under siege." I anticipated that innovations would stand out more starkly against the backdrop of Protestants' conservative predispositions. Conducting research on parading disputes among both Protestants and Catholics in two rural towns in County Down in 1999, I discovered an emerging pragmatism. Local Orange lodges were beginning to compromise on long-held positions and practices, even if for strategic leveraging of media coverage (Smithey 2002; Smithey and Kurtz 2003:356). The evidence suggested critical processes of grassroots change to be uncovered.

■ HISTORICAL BACKGROUND

Understanding changes in attitudes within any ethnic group requires historical background to appreciate how the collective experience of ethnic conflict informs contemporary attitudes. Ireland's history is one of successive invasions, and the "infiltration" of Celtic culture from as early as 1000 B.C. marked the beginning of a complicated multiculturalism. Consecutive invasions of Ireland extend well back into the ninth century with Viking raids, and the northern region of the island, now known as Ulster,[1] was given its name, *Ulaidh*, during the Norman invasion in the latter half of the twelfth century. In 1154, Ireland was granted to King Henry II by Pope Adrian IV based on Constantinian precedence that any island belonged to the Roman Catholic Church (Bardon 1992:32). Four hundred years later, in 1541, Henry VIII laid the first English monarchical claim to the whole of Ireland.

The reign of King James I brought the official plantation of colonists in Ireland at the beginning of the seventeenth century, laying the groundwork for religious, ethnic, and class divisions that evolved over time, aligning into two uneasy populations. Sectarian conflict in the middle of the seventeenth century included the 1641 massacre of Protestants, which has become incorporated into contemporary collective memory for many Protestants as an illustration of what they consider the Catholic threat.[2] Oliver Cromwell arrived in August 1649 to brutally put down the uprising. Catholics experienced some reprieve under the rule of Charles II, and in 1685, King James II, a Catholic, ascended the throne, but his reign was short. The Dutch Protestant King William III (of Orange) seized the throne and defeated James II on Irish soil at the Battle of the Boyne in 1690, a victory the Protestant Orange Order celebrates to this day. Nearly a century later, feuding between the Protestant Peep O' Day Boys and the Catholic Defenders resulted in the Battle of the Diamond and the formation of the Orange Order on September 21, 1795.

Meanwhile, the nationalist movement was taking its first revolutionary leap forward. Inspired by the French Revolution and the successes of American colonists, Wolfe Tone, a Dublin lawyer, mobilized the United Irishmen, culminating in the uprising of 1798. However, the movement failed, and shortly after the Act of Union of 1800 constitutionally joined Ireland to Britain. The remainder of the nineteenth century saw various unfruitful attempts at secession by the Fenian Brotherhood, Charles Stewart Parnell, William Ewart Gladstone, and other nationalists (Kee 1972; Hoppen 1989). The latter decades of the century were especially crucial as nationalism gained a unified voice during the Land War of 1879 to 1882 (Kane 2000), and Walker (1996) argues that the run-up to the 1885–1886 elections was central to the construction of polarized religio-political ideologies that have fueled modern conflict in Ireland. According to Aughey (1989), "It was only when Catholicism and nationalism became indissolubly linked together in the nineteenth century that divisions within Protestantism became secondary to the combined political and religious threat of Home Rule.[3] Denominational differences were subordinated to the political defence of the common heritage of civil and religious liberty" (p. 8). Prior to this period, religious and political distinctions were not always aligned. Like Catholics, Presbyterians endured penal laws, and Protestants could be found among republican ranks, such as, those who led the United Irishmen Rebellion in 1798.

Political and ethnic distinctions were well aligned by the Easter Rising of 1916 during which British forces put down a republican rebellion, martyring the insurgents and thus catalyzing popular support for physical-force republicanism. By

1920, guerrilla warfare had spread across Ireland, and partition was established under the Government of Ireland Act 1920, creating a clear Protestant majority in the new bounded Ulster. This in turn led to the establishment of Northern Ireland in 1921, the Irish Free State in 1922, and eventually the Republic of Ireland in 1937. Republican violence erupted sporadically, notably in 1954, up until the civil rights marches of 1968–1969.

The Northern Ireland Civil Rights Association (NICRA), consisting of community, labor, and political organizations, protested systematic discrimination against Catholics in housing and employment. Encouraged by the successes of the civil rights movement in the United States, activists used nonviolent direct action and won substantial reforms from the O'Neill government. However, after some reforms had been granted, students involved in the movement under the auspices of People's Democracy insisted on continued public protest via a march from Belfast to Derry/Londonderry. Loyalists, and in some cases off-duty police officers, repeatedly attacked the marchers, whom the Royal Ulster Constabulary (RUC) did little to protect. Eventually, the movement declined into violent riots, the regional government at Stormont was prorogued, and the British Army was deployed in 1972. The Provisional IRA splintered from the Official IRA in 1970 becoming the primary organization of republican armed struggle (Rose 1971; Bardon 1992).

At the start of the Troubles, governance in Northern Ireland was dominated by unionist parties that administered a state tainted with unjust voting laws and gerrymandering, though debate has ensued over the extent of discrimination. Some authors have declared that discrimination against Catholics after partition was "systematic and pervasive" (O'Hearn 1983: quoted in Whyte 1990:165), though after a review of the literature, Whyte (1983, 1990:164–69) has determined that there is little consensus. In characterizing the situation, McKittrick and McVea (2002) argue, "This was not Nazi Germany or anything like it. But it was institutionalized partiality, and there was no means of redress for Catholic grievances, no avenue of appeal against either real or imagined discrimination" (p. 17). Besides the obvious problem of injustice, however extensive, discrimination may have been most problematic in laying the groundwork for even deeper and self-replicating division in Northern Ireland (Ruane and Todd 1996:171). Soon, the divide deepened as violence swept away any short-term hope of focusing on social and political issues and developing a working political system that could address the larger issues of jurisdiction and sovereignty.

■ PROTESTANTS, UNIONISTS, AND LOYALISTS

The "damnable question" over sovereignty lies at the root of conflict in Ireland (Dangerfield 1976). However, the conflict has long since become institutionalized and embedded in collective memory and cultural routines. Northern Ireland is fragmented over a range of issues, identities, agendas, and loyalties that for decades defied political progress (FitzGerald 1988; Whyte 1990; Byrne and Carter 1996).

Despite the complexity of the field of ethnic and political identities, it is hard to deny the reality of two readily discernible blocs, "Protestants and Catholics." Due largely to the historical realities set in motion by plantation and British policy in Ireland and the reaction of Catholic nationalism in the nineteenth century, fundamental political and ethnic categories have aligned.

Consequently, PUL (Protestants/unionists/loyalists) is an acronym that is some-times used among grassroots organizations and appears in community relations and community development reports. To lump all three terms together oversim-plifies the political and cultural landscape, but one could also argue that its use is an attempt to at least acknowledge different currents of political thought that are related to one another and held by people who identify themselves as Protestants. I try to move accurately among the three terms, reserving "Protestant" for those points that refer specifically to a religious context or when referring to the population of people who identify themselves ethnically as Protestants. I tend to rely more heavily on the terms "unionism" and "loyalism" because the content of my inter-views with individuals did not revolve around religious doctrine or organizations.

In her seminal article, "Two Traditions in Unionist Political Culture," Jennifer Todd (1987) established a basic set of ideological distinctions between unionism and loyalism that has guided most attempts to describe the terrain of Protestant politics (Todd 1987; Aughey 1989; Whyte 1990; Bruce 1994b; McGarry and O'Leary 1995; Aughey 1997; McAuley 1997; Cochrane 2001; Farrington 2008; McAuley 2008). Todd defines Ulster loyalists as those who prioritize identification with fellow Ulster Protestants over British identity, and for whom evangelical Protestantism and anti-Catholicism often frame political struggle and conflict as a spiritual zero-sum battle of good against evil. She identifies the Orange Order, the Democratic Unionist Party (DUP), and working-class loyalists as archetypes of this mode of unionism (Todd 1987:3; see also Ruane and Todd 1996:60–61). Bruce (1994b) takes a similar approach by describing Ulster Loyalism as the "evangelicals and the gunmen" embodied in Paisley, the DUP, and loyalist paramilitaries, who coexist uneasily but maintain a conditional loyalty to British governments and share similar understandings of Northern Ireland as a uniquely Protestant province under threat (Miller 1978). Rose (1971) refers to this category as "ultras"; McGarry and O'Leary (1995:92) describe them as "ethnic"; Porter (1996:72–126) discusses "cultural unionism"; and Tonge (2005:65, 74–81) calls them "Orange skeptics."

The Ulster British, Todd's second category of ideological unionism, subsume a regional Ulster identity of identification with Great Britain. If Ulster loyalism encompasses working-class Protestants, the Ulster British are more likely to be middle- or upper-class unionists, who embrace British values of progress, industry, civilization, and democracy (Ruane and Todd 1996:60–61). Academics alternate between using political and cultural criteria in characterizing unionism, but descriptions of "traditional," "conventional," or "constitutional" unionism generally align with Todd's Ulster British category and refer to the political fundamentals of unionism, without the evangelical Protestantism and ethnic nationalism that characterize Ulster loyalism (Buckley 1989:189–90; Cochrane 2001:36–40). Despite the enduring utility of Todd's scheme, scholars have continued to struggle with the optimal way to describe what Cochrane (2001) calls "a multi-layered phenomenon which almost defies categorization" (p. 39). There seems to be a perpetual degree of slippage and overlap in the use of terminology throughout the literature, especially as important distinctions *within* unionism and loyalism emerge.

Unionism

Unionism has often been characterized along two general lines: old, traditional, or conventional unionism and new, liberal, or civic unionism (Todd 1987, 1988; Aughey 1989; Bruce 1994b; McGarry and O'Leary 1995:119–21; Porter 1996; Aughey 1997; McAuley 1997; Cochrane 2001:37–38). Conventional unionism focuses on the constitutional relationship linking Northern Ireland and Great Britain alongside a deep appreciation for British identity and the historical empire's military and industrial strength. Northern Ireland is considered a beacon of British values and democratic political structures against which the Republic of Ireland is contrasted as parochial and backward (Todd 1988; Porter 1996:133). Conventional unionists' intense focus on the United Kingdom and Britishness has made it difficult for them to acknowledge and engage nationalists (Todd 1988:16; Whyte 1990:162; McGarry and O'Leary 1995:105–6; Porter 1996; Farrington 2006:3).

"New unionism" refers to attempts to shake conventional unionism from its fixation on Northern Ireland's constitutional status and provide rationales that allow for greater political maneuverability. Arthur Aughey's (1989) work epitomizes "liberal unionism," a branch of new unionism. He emphasizes a philosophical commitment to the state and procedural democratic principles and deemphasizes ethnic and regional identity in favor of secular citizenship. Liberal unionism has come in for criticism, however, with McGarry and O'Leary (1995) declaring it revisionist because it glosses over British colonial history in Ireland, and it overestimates the United Kingdom's commitment to a perfectly liberal and enlightened citizenship. Similarly, Porter (1996) says it seeks to escape the faults of cultural unionism by idealizing the British state and its ability to realize liberal principles of equality and justice. It thus prioritizes union with the British state over and above the liberal principles that the state is believed to protect. Cultural unionism is no better as an alternative because it relies too heavily on exclusive ethnic and religious identifications, preserves the already hard political ground, and distances unionists from their fellow British citizens. Instead, Porter proposes a "civic unionism" that acknowledges the importance of collective identity in unionist life in Northern Ireland. He draws on a civic republican model that prioritizes quality of social and economic life and the importance of developing a strong civil society. To the extent that the state facilitates space for the development of strong civic participation, a primary political goal of unionism has been achieved.

Loyalism

Within loyalism, distinctions have also been made between strands of political thought and action, particularly between Ulster loyalism and new loyalism. Loyalism has often been defined simply as physical force unionism that was primarily situated in working-class areas. These are Bruce's (1994b) "gunmen," whom he connects, albeit tentatively, with "evangelicals" (pp. 2–18, 31–36).[4] More inclusive definitions of Ulster loyalism have included loyalist paramilitaries, the loyal orders, and evangelical Protestants (Bruce 1994b:1–2; Mitchell 2008a:150–51).

New loyalism refers to the emergence of politicians and political organizations connected to loyalist paramilitaries, in particular the Progressive Unionist Party (PUP), which has drawn leadership from the Ulster Volunteer Force, notably David Ervine and Billy Hutchinson. The New Ulster Political Research Group (NUPRG, founded in 1978) and later the Ulster Political Research Group (UPRG; launched after the demise of the Ulster Democratic Party, UDP, in 2001) were formed to provide political analysis for the Ulster Defence Association (UDA), and they have developed some of the most innovative proposals for a negotiated political agreement (Elliott and Flackes 1999:477–78; McAuley 2008:17–18). NUPRG's 1978 *Beyond the Religious Divide* called for a negotiated independent Northern Ireland and the UDA's 1987 document, *Common Sense*, called for the kind of proportional representation (including the D'Hondt mechanism) and power sharing that appeared over ten years later in Strand One of the Belfast/Good Friday Agreement (Bruce 1994b:102–5). More broadly, new loyalism refers to the development of working-class loyalist agendas that distinguish them from traditional unionism by advocating community politics and conflict transformation programs, in many cases with the assistance of local community organizations, community relations workers, and socially minded churches (Bloomer 2008; Farrington 2008; McAuley 2008; Mitchell 2008a).

Other fault lines in unionism and loyalism have been identified, such as, the integration versus devolution debate within unionism, support or opposition to the Belfast/Good Friday Agreement, and radicalism versus pragmatism (Cochrane 2001:40, 99–113; Farrington 2006:61). These distinctions are analytically helpful, but they do not always hold up well empirically. For example, the PUP, an unambiguously loyalist political party, has often focused on its role in unionist electoral politics and policy (Bloomer 2008). Conversely, the DUP is often referred to as part of an "Ulster loyalism" that extends beyond loyalist paramilitarism. Ian Paisley, an evangelical long considered the most staunch anti-agreement figure in Northern Ireland, became First Minister in 2007. Loyalist politicians and political thinkers connected to paramilitary organizations have not always been the most reactionary but have instead articulated "discourses of transformation," advocated power sharing long before the main unionist parties, and developed socially progressive platforms (McAuley 2002).

It is helpful to have the kinds of typologies that Todd and others have developed, and while there is no doubt that distinctions can be made between schools of unionist and loyalist thought, they can be difficult to disentangle on the ground, where individuals often draw from more than one strand and collaborations cross categorical boundaries. Thus, I frequently use "unionism" and "loyalism" together. Among interviewees, it was often difficult to describe them as only one or the other. I encountered middle-class community workers who identified themselves as Protestant but indicated no enthusiasm for unionist politics (McGarry and O'Leary 1995). Others, such as, staunch unionists working with loyalist organizations, were openly critical of loyalist paramilitaries. Conversely, working-class loyalists, sometimes sympathetic with paramilitary organizations, could be quite bitter about what they considered the failure of traditional unionist political parties to advocate for their communities' interest. Yet, many of these same people often vote DUP, now the largest unionist party.

If the organizations encountered in this research project were to be plotted within the field of classificatory schemes that already exist, many would fall within Todd's general category of Ulster loyalism, which includes the Orange Order, and secular working-class loyalism. The research is attuned to working-class or middle-class individuals, communities, and organizations that, in many cases, could be identified as part of cultural unionism and new loyalism. Upper- and middle-class Ulster British or liberal unionists are not represented as thoroughly.

Religion

"Protestant" and "Catholic" are often used to describe the broadest divide in Northern Ireland, even though, for many, the content of those identities does not always focus on religious concerns. Some scholars have relegated religion to secondary status, arguing that it serves as a boundary marker that merely contributes to an essentially nationalist conflict bound up in political and economic inequalities. They view religion through an institutional lens that focuses on church policy (especially regarding education and intermarriage) rather than through a cultural or social psychological lens. Others, however, have demonstrated how religious worldviews contribute significantly to division that is also reproduced politically, economically, and socially (Porter 1996; McVeigh 1997; Brewer and Higgins 1998; Jordan 2001; Liechty and Clegg 2001; Mitchell 2006; Ganiel 2008a). Bruce's (1994b, 2007) work on Ulster Loyalism and Paisleyism notes that even though most supporters of the DUP (now the largest unionist party) are not evangelicals, they identify at some level with Paisley's evangelicalism and the way in which it helps them to interpret their circumstances in Ireland (1994b:22–26).

Liechty and Clegg (2001) describe the social construction of difference that takes place in myriad and mundane ways. In many cases, the process is subtle or passive, such as, when one group repeatedly overlooks the concerns of other groups.

> Most of what is required for the system to continue to flourish is for the majority of ordinary, decent citizens to keep colluding in low level sectarianism and subtly re-inforcing the divisions between groups. The silence and inaction of the majority can be, and has been, taken as a mandate by the tiny minority who espouse violence. (p. 109)

Belittling, demonizing, and dehumanizing others can take many forms, often drawing on religious ideas that have been incorporated into institutions, traditions, and habits.

Faith systems and churches have played a mixed role in the polarization of Catholics and Protestants. Sectarianism can reside in religious organizations and inject a powerful emotional dimension to out-group categorization (Liechty 1993; Brewer and Higgins 1998; Higgins 2000; Liechty and Clegg 2001). Religiously segregated schools and the stigma that accompanies mixed marriages only serve to reinforce the consistency of divisions along religious lines in other institutions, such as, political parties and law enforcement. Churches are "markers of identity" and "carry many of the cultural memories of Northern Ireland," but they have also often served as voices of reconciliation, even if their role in promoting social and political change has been underdeveloped (Morrow, Birrell, Greer, and O'Keeffe 1994:258; Ganiel 2008a; Ganiel and Dixon 2008; Mitchell 2008a; Brewer 2010:56–67).

In the debate over the relevance of religion, which ranges from dismissal to according it status as one particularly significant component of division in a sophisticated cocktail, the latter position emerges as the more compelling one (cf. Whyte 1990:103–11). Though many in Northern Ireland who identify themselves as Protestant do not attend church or think of themselves as particularly religious, rates of religious participation in Northern Ireland rank among the highest in the industrialized world. It is important to understand that Protestantism is not a purely secular ethnicity, and yet, religion's contributions can be more subtle and difficult to disentangle than political ideologies. Religion is perhaps all the more important as a result.

Protestant Politics

Arthur Aughey (1989) begins his book, *Under Siege: Ulster Unionism and the Anglo-Irish Agreement,* with "Unionists think of themselves as a much-misunderstood people" (p. 1). Faced with their own fears that the British government may abandon them and the political and cultural successes of nationalists, unionists, and loyalists have struggled to adapt (Miller 1978; Dunn and Morgan 1994; Cochrane 2001:68). Their position since the Home Rule movement has been primarily defensive and conservative. Unity among Protestants, whatever their religious denomination or political party preference, has revolved around the preservation of the union. Nationalist movements that swept Europe in the nineteenth century clarified the divide between Irish Catholics, who increasingly

emphasized their Gaelic origins, and British Protestants who embraced an ideal-
ized vision of British civilization and modernity. Prior to the nineteenth century,
the divide was less clear, with many Old English settlers adopting the Gaelic culture
of their fellow Catholics in the seventeenth century and Presbyterians playing
prominent roles in nationalist uprisings in the eighteenth century (Ruane and
Todd 1996:24). By the turn of the twentieth century, however, nationalistic trends
had begun to crystallize into two mutually opposing political camps.

> Nationalism described an Ireland economically laid waste by centuries of British rule,
> whose rightful owners had been dispossessed, their religion persecuted, their culture all
> but destroyed – but which once free would use its talents and resources to rebuild itself.
> Unionism described a backward Ireland to which Britain had brought political order,
> cultural advance and religious liberty, and whose resources Irish Protestants of British
> stock had developed using their talent, education and enterprise; outside of the British
> context Ireland and Irish Protestants would undergo irreversible decline. (Ruane and
> Todd 1996:29)

Staving off that decline has become the sine qua non of Protestant unionism.

The partition of Northern Ireland in 1921 and the establishment of government
at Stormont was, in the minds of most Protestants, to be the end of the "Irish
problem." Protestants in Cavan, Monaghan, and Donegal were sacrificed to the
Irish Free State, but a region had been secured, within which a Protestant unionist
majority could maintain British culture and citizenship. Ulster was to be a beacon
of British democracy in Ireland, but the civil rights movements of the 1960s called
that vision into question. To Protestant unionists, Northern Ireland was perched
on the edge of a chasm into which it could potentially slip. Vigilance was necessary,
and unionists interpreted the civil rights movement as a security threat from
within, or at the least, they were unsure about how to respond to it (Ruane and
Todd 1996:127).

As the civil rights movement was replaced by the violent campaign of the
Provisional IRA, unionists felt increasingly threatened. A long-standing insecurity
that Britain regarded Northern Ireland with less loyalty than unionists reserved
for Britain was compounded by fears that they would fare poorly in a united
Ireland with a strong Catholic ethos, often pointing to the declining numbers of
Protestants in the Republic after partition (FitzGerald 1988; Dunn and Morgan
1994; Hennessey 1997).[5] Though fundamental tenets of unionism are widely
shared, such as, a claim to a distinctive heritage and an insistence on union within
the United Kingdom, long-standing disagreements about the best way to preserve
the union and attempts to establish a workable government in Northern Ireland
have provoked internal disputes among unionists and loyalists. They disagree, for
example, on whether devolution of authority to Stormont or integration into the
United Kingdom is the most effective form of union (Whyte 1990:146; McGarry
and O'Leary 1995:92–97; Cochrane 2001:99–105; Farrington 2006:61–74). Though
unionism is technically the position that defends the union of Great Britain and

Northern Ireland, relations between unionists and British governments have been tense, as many unionists, unsure of British support, argue that limits on security policies and reforms instituted under Direct Rule signal weakness and encourage republican paramilitaries to continue their struggles.

The imposition of Direct Rule in 1972 was perceived as a betrayal by the British government. Subsequent attempts at negotiated political arrangements were opposed by unionists and raised further suspicions about Britain's commitment to maintain the union. The first power sharing experiment to include constitutional nationalists in 1973 was received by some unionists as a sufficiently benign change in the status quo, but others were deeply uncomfortable with plans to include "an Irish dimension" in the governance of Northern Ireland. Unionist and loyalist groups, such as, the Reverend Ian Paisley's Democratic Unionist Party, the Vanguard Party, and the Orange Order, formed the United Ulster Unionist Council in protest, and the fledgling power sharing government was essentially toppled by the loyalist Ulster Worker's Council strike of 1974.

Protestant fears were heightened with the 1985 signing of the Anglo-Irish Agreement by Prime Minister Margaret Thatcher and Garret Fitzgerald, the Irish Taoiseach.[6] The agreement formally acknowledged a role for the republic's government in the affairs of Northern Ireland. Unionists were appalled, fearing the agreement introduced a slippery slope leading to a united Ireland. Most unionists saw Margaret Thatcher as a staunch ally and were thus shocked when she signed the agreement without fully consulting the unionist parties. Thatcher was trying to secure greater cross-border cooperation on security issues, but unionists abhorred the idea of the Irish government having an official albeit consultative role in the affairs of Northern Ireland, even if Dublin officially recognized Northern Ireland and accepted the principle of consent (Cochrane 2001). An anti-agreement campaign ensued, with massive protests and some rioting. While unionist outrage was widely shared, coordination of the resistance campaign faltered amid divisions in the unionist leadership and disagreement over the advisable limits of civil resistance (Cochrane 2001:165–80). In any case, the agreement had attracted international support and was ratified by the House of Commons.

Despite ongoing violence and political polarization, the seeds of the peace process were being planted during the 1980s. As unionists were reeling from the betrayal of the Anglo-Irish Agreement, republicans discovered the power of popular political support during the hunger strikes and began debating the strategy of armed struggle, which was increasingly being understood as a hurting stalemate with British security forces. The Hume-Adams talks between constitutional nationalists and physical force republicans got under way in January 1988 and further persuaded republicans of the prospects of a political strategy. The peace process could be largely characterized in terms of this shift.

During the 1990s, unionist politicians recognized that they were failing to defend their political positions. They were unable to persuade their own fellow citizens in the UK, never mind nationalists, the Irish government, or influential

Irish Americans. Attempts to articulate a "new unionism" sparked debate among academics and within unionist political circles over the core tenets of unionist ideology and identity (Aughey 1989; Porter 1996; Farrington 2006:28–34). Public relations initiatives were launched to present their case more proactively, but most unionists had internalized what McAuley (2002) calls a "discourse of perpetuity" by which all developments are assumed to contain a threat to Protestant interests, even if not immediately apparent (pp. 113–18). For example, unionists had not been consulted on the development of the Anglo-Irish Agreement, which introduced a nationalist logic via the prominent new role of the Irish government, and thus any new political initiative to develop a political process was suspected by unionists to lay the foundations for further erosion of the union (Cochrane 2001:272; Farrington 2006:39).

Nevertheless, by 1992, having spent five years debating with the loyalist UDA/ UPRG and each other over a political way forward, the main unionist parties, the Ulster Unionist Party (UUP) and DUP, were engaged in multi-strand exploratory talks, but they were intent on limiting the influence of the Irish government in northern affairs. The Brooke-Mayhew talks and secret separate dialogues between the British and Irish governments and republicans in the early 1990s helped produce the 1993 Downing Street Declaration and the 1995 Framework Documents in which the principle of consent championed by Hume and Adams was further reiterated by the two governments. The Irish government promised to amend its constitutional claim on Northern Ireland in the context of an agreed settlement, but unionists remained skeptical, and the DUP and UUP continued to spar with one another over the mantle of defenders of the union (Cochrane 2001). They were predictably irritated at the 1993 joint statement between John Hume and Gerry Adams, which they interpreted as the forging of a pan-nationalist front. However, they were pressed by the first temporary IRA and loyalist cease-fires in 1994 amid growing international support for the Framework "twin-track" approach of decommissioning weapons and negotiations. When the more public phases of the peace process began in 1995, unionists were still unwilling to negotiate directly with republicans, but by 1997, UUP politicians had begun to meet with Sinn Féin politicians. Remarkably, the process survived an escalation of loyalist violence in reaction to the Hume-Adams dialogue, the Drumcree parading crisis, which flared up in 1995, and the IRA's Canary Wharf bombing in London in February 1996 (Cochrane 2001:305–6).

Following a renewed cessation of violent activity by the IRA in 1997, difficult all-party talks, chaired by U.S. Senator George Mitchell, brought the Ulster Unionist Party fully into the process. Both unionist parties remained deeply suspicious of republicans' sincerity on decommissioning, and they were concerned about the details of power sharing and cross-border institutions. The loyalist UDP and PUP parties were significantly more supportive of the process (Cochrane 2001:356).

Despite the massive and traumatic bombing of Omagh by the Real IRA on August 15, 1998, and continuing loyalist violence, the Belfast or Good Friday

Agreement was presented on April 10. The deal was finally endorsed in dual (north and south) referenda on May 22. Seventy-one percent of voters in Northern Ireland supported the multi-strand agreement, though unionists were evenly split in their support for the agreement. Prisoner releases proved a bitter pill for many unionists. Policing reform and decommissioning continued to plague the process, but a significant change had taken place within unionism.

> Pro-Agreement unionists had actually achieved the return of devolved powers to a Stormont Assembly, brought the reviled Anglo-Irish Agreement to an end and secured much sought-after reforms to Articles 2 and 3 of the Irish constitution. This altered the structure of intra-unionist politics quite significantly. Unionist parties were not simply providing alternative critiques of British government policy to their constituencies. After the Agreement, the UUP were able to point to a tangible set of achievements and articulate a positive vision of the future as a result of such achievements. (Cochrane 2001)

Unionism was split over the wisdom of compromising cherished values and institutions in order to share power with republicans who still held arms, but the result of the referendum nevertheless marked a major change in unionist and loyalist political strategy.

With further shepherding by Senator Mitchell, the Northern Ireland Executive that administers the governmental ministries was established in December 1999. The Northern Ireland Assembly was subsequently suspended three times as unionists' fears over the extent of IRA decommissioning and republican demands for significant policing reform dogged the process. The DUP, which at the time remained staunchly anti-agreement, benefited, emerging with Sinn Féin from the 2003 Assembly elections as the two parties with the greatest support, a result they repeated in the 2007 Assembly elections. After over three years of suspension, the Northern Ireland Assembly reconvened on May 15, 2006, and an executive was formed after Ian Paisley and Gerry Adams announced their parties' intentions to share power, returning local governance to Northern Ireland. Paisley and Martin McGuinness, icons of Ulster loyalism and republicanism, were sworn in as First and Deputy First Ministers, respectively, on May 8, 2007. Paisley was later replaced by Peter Robinson when he stepped down from the position of First Minister in 2008.

Peace and "The Empty Chalice"

Unionists' concerns over political arrangements and the security of Northern Ireland's constitutional status should be interpreted in the context of changes across a range of important domains that include demography, ecology, economics, politics, ideology, and the military (Ruane and Todd 1996:141). In each dimension, Northern Ireland's Protestants' advantage has diminished. For nearly ninety years, they held the larger share of institutional political influence. Between 1970 and 2005, unionists prevailed in every election, which one would expect to confer a considerable level of confidence, but they have also seen their political share decline steadily. The 1974 Westminster election saw unionist parties gain 64.2 percent of the vote, but by 2005, their lead had diminished to 51.8 percent. The same trend holds true for local government and European elections (Melaugh 2010).

Protestants have also been unequally represented in other institutions of the state. The Northern Ireland civil service, judiciary, and security forces have historically been dominated by Protestants, who feel an emotional attachment to the Royal Ulster Constabulary (RUC), which they considered their primary defense against Republican paramilitaries. However, the Patten policing reforms adopted in 2001 mandate 50–50 representation of Protestants and Catholics to redress the overrepresentation of Protestants in the police force. In 2001, 58.5 percent of Protestant participants in the Northern Ireland Life and Times Survey felt policing reforms had gone too far; 27 percent said they were about right. By contrast, 43.6 percent of Catholics felt the reforms had not gone far enough, and 38.3 percent thought they were about right. The figures held steady when the question was asked in 2003, two years after the Police Service of Northern Ireland (PSNI) replaced the RUC (ARK 2001, 2003). Policing has undergone significant reforms, and in 2007, Sinn Féin took up their seats on the Policing Board, further eroding any exclusive association between Protestants and policing. Like the RUC, the Ulster Defence Regiment (UDR), a local mainly part-time Army regiment evokes deep sentiments among Protestants; it was merged with the Royal Irish Rangers in 1992 (Ruane and Todd 1996:140). The completion of decommissioning by the Provisional IRA was accompanied by the demolition of army bases and the downsizing of military forces, but a military presence remains.

Economic advantage has favored Protestants since plantation in the seventeenth century, when British policy transferred ownership of prime lands from Catholics. Protestants remain the demographic majority in Northern Ireland according to the 2001 census (53.1 percent),[7] though Catholic numbers have been catching up (Northern Ireland Statistics and Research Agency 2001: Table KS07c: STATED CURRENT RELIGION). Protestants continue to dominate the more prosperous eastern half of Northern Ireland, but their numbers have declined elsewhere; they represented only 3.8 percent of the population of the Republic of Ireland in 2006 (Central Statistics Office Ireland 2007). Protestants later came to control major industries, especially the linen trade and shipyards (Ruane and Todd 1996:151). However, from World War II, the Northern Ireland economy became increasingly dependent on British subvention. As British governments gained increasing influence over Northern Ireland affairs, especially during the period of Direct Rule, they were able to introduce reforms to practices, such as, hiring, that had privileged Protestants. At the same time, unemployment rose and the traditional industries, such as, shipbuilding, declined and required increasing support from British taxpayers.

On the cultural front, when unionists controlled government in Northern Ireland, Protestants could draw a measure of confidence from the association of recognizable symbols and narratives with the state (Bryan and McIntosh 2005).

> A distinctive Northern Irish Protestant culture emerged, a blend of Protestant and pro-vincial British values. It stressed respectability, uprightness, honesty, order, respect for authority, work ethic, cleanliness and tidiness, modesty and informality in social rela-tions, social and political conformity. There was an unquestioned belief in the superiority of this culture to the one emerging simultaneously in the South. It became an integral part of Protestant identity, functioning as "cultural capital" in relations with the state and in the search for employment or electoral office. (Ruane and Todd 1996:182)

However, as unionists lost control of the levers of the state, they also lost control of public space. Disputes over parading on public roads, the flying of flags on public buildings, and the building of bonfires on public lands have all become increas-ingly contentious.

Unionists and loyalists have tended to frame their experience of change in Northern Ireland in terms of loss or the perpetual potential for loss. Only in the context of the union could they prosper and maintain institutions that would express and protect Protestant values and aspirations. Consequently, unionists' political attention has been focused on British governments (Cochrane 2001:395). Compared with nationalists, unionists have failed to develop the robust political frames that nationalists have used to garner support in Britain, Europe, the United States, and farther afield. The decline of industries, the greater parity of cross-border economic prosperity, the waning political influence that unionist members of parliament (MPs) could wield in that body, republican decommissioning, and international pressure undercut the rhetorical and procedural strategies on which unionists and loyalists have traditionally relied. Those strategies were rarely designed to generate political solutions or recruit new allies but rather assumed that the unionist position had been settled under the terms of the Government of Ireland Act 1920. Besides, Northern Ireland's political and economic systems were considered superior in contrast with their Irish counterparts. The economic suc-cesses of the region and the political superiority of majoritarianism were consid-ered sufficient rationales to maintain the union.

Yet, a shifting political environment marked by paramilitary cease-fires, decom-missioning, and the repeal of Articles Two and Three of the Irish constitution has challenged unionists and loyalists to reframe their political arguments. The pro-cess of transitioning into political engagement with nationalists on an increasingly international stage has strained unionist solidarity.[8] The DUP and UUP adopted distinct and contradictory positions with David Trimble cajoling the latter (with considerable difficulty) into power sharing before full decommissioning in order to pressure republicans into conformity with the principle of consent. The DUP remained anti-agreement, though it participated in the Assembly and eventually, having become the largest unionist party, acquiesced with Sinn Féin in accepting the proposals on policing and power sharing put forward by the British and Irish governments at St. Andrews, after which Paisley became First Minister in May 2007. Following the Belfast/Good Friday Agreement, Protestants were almost evenly split over the wisdom of sharing power with republicans, and by 2001, only one-third supported the agreement (English 2002:95; Tonge 2005:59), a number that remained essentially constant through 2005, according to the Northern Ireland Life and Times Survey (ARK 2000–2005).

Since then, however, Protestant attitudes have warmed to the agreement. By 2007, 57.5 percent of Protestant participants in the Northern Ireland Life and Times Survey reported they felt "the Good Friday/Belfast Agreement was a good thing for Northern Ireland" (ARK 2007).[9] The results signal greater Protestant investment in power sharing and a willingness to rely less heavily on external British support. This seems to be a time of transition, even if the general experience of unionists and loyalists has been one of alienation and division, as Richard English (2002) comments:

> Put bluntly, if one wants a community traditionally accustomed to advantage to yield some of that advantage lastingly, smoothly and peacefully, then the worst context in which to do it is one where that community is fractured, internally embittered, and substantially lacking in confidence in itself, its government, and its neighbours. That is the situation we have faced, and continue to face. (p. 103)

Perceptions among Protestants that they are politically and socially fragmented are commonplace. The Belfast playwright Martin Lynch expressed concern about Protestants' failure to take up work and meet needs through the voluntary sector when he was interviewed with Norman Hamilton, a minister from North Belfast (now Presbyterian Moderator) on the British Broadcasting Corporation's (BBC) *Sunday Sequence* on February 3, 2008.

> Where the Catholic community is bursting with energy, creativity, ideas, all the rest of it, the Protestant community is almost the opposite. If you look at major voluntary and community sector organizations like NICVA [Northern Ireland Council for Voluntary Action], they struggle to get a decent cross-representation on their executive and so on, which they obviously strive to do. In a community that still has a Protestant majority, they have an imbalance of Catholic membership.

Hamilton readily agreed. At one point in the interview, the host, William Crawley, interjected, suggesting that Catholic youth were more likely to stay and help build their community. Crawley's comment was derived from a common view that the Protestant population in Northern Ireland suffers from "brain drain" by which Protestant youth who undertake higher education tend not to return to their local communities, either moving into more affluent suburbs or never returning to Northern Ireland (*Orange Standard*, February 1990, August 2007). The Ulster Unionist Party has frequently expressed alarm over Department for Employment and Learning (DELNI) statistics showing that Protestant students (53 percent) are more likely than Catholic students (34 percent) to pursue higher education in Great Britain. Furthermore, of those who study in Great Britain, most (56 percent) remained after graduation (Schubotz 2008).[10] Unionist concerns over Protestant "brain drain" illustrate one way in which many Protestants feel that besides the ever-present risk of nationalist irredentism and the republican threat, they are also at risk of disintegrating from within. As the external threats diminish, the internal ones remain.

Despite the UUP's and DUP's leadership in the Assembly, there is a persistent feeling among Protestants that the Belfast/Good Friday Agreement has not benefited them as much as Catholics (Hughes and Donnelly 2003:654–55). Among respondents to the Northern Ireland Life and Times Survey in 2008, 50.7 percent felt that Protestants and Catholics had benefited equally from political changes since 1998. Thirty-four percent felt Catholics benefited either a little or a lot more, and only 4 percent felt that Protestants benefited either a little or a lot more. Catholics (63.9 percent) felt more frequently than Protestants (39.4 percent) that Protestants and Catholics benefited equally while 50.2 percent of Protestants felt Catholics benefited either a little or a lot more than Protestants. Very few Protestants (1.7 percent) or Catholics (7.8 percent) felt that Protestants had benefited more than Catholics (ARK 2008a).[11] Over time, a majority of Protestants and a significant minority of Catholics are increasingly likely to report that nationalists benefited either a little or a lot more than unionists. The trend is especially stark for Protestant respondents (see figure 3.1).

Research by Blackbourn and Rekawek (2007) further documents perceptions of inequality. They report that across several measures, including education and employment, Protestants are more likely than Catholics to feel relatively

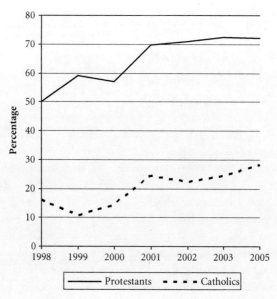

Figure 3.1 Nationalists Benefited from the Good Friday Agreement Either a Little or a Lot More than Unionists.

disadvantaged (Blackbourn and Rekawek 2007:38–39).[12] The fear of being over-whelmed by a growing Catholic and nationalist population persists, with more than 50 percent of Protestants believing that Northern Ireland is becoming more Catholic, nationalist, or republican in character when in fact increasing numbers of people are identifying themselves as Northern Irish and neither nationalist or unionist (Blackbourn and Rekawek 2007:56). Recent studies into "social exclusion" and community development have raised persistent concerns over the marginal-ization of Protestants and poor community development capacity, dynamics that undermine confidence in the peace process (Sandy Row Project Team 2004; Shirlow, Robinson et al., 2005b; Shirlow, Graham, McMullan et al., 2006). Adam, one of my working-class loyalist interviewees, referred to the peace process as "an empty chalice" because he felt loyalists have failed to reap the tangible benefits that should have accompanied the new political dispensation:

> Certainly for my section of the community, but I think it's true for about 60–70 percent of the unionist community, definitely the lower down the social scale you go, the more it's true, but the Stormont Assembly and all its structures is an empty chalice at the moment for my people. There's a number of reasons why that has happened. One, because of money, socioeconomic issues, all the social ills that are being suffered in my communities. My communities come from the top 10 percent of the most socioeconom-ically deprived people in the whole of Northern Ireland. And the ability, the capability, the resources, the education levels, the lack of social cohesion, no depth of skills, low skills, in social development terms. Especially, [a lack of] social development has left us unable to take opportunities arising from peace, and because we've been unable to take opportunities arising from peace, we haven't been able to apply it fully or understand the importance of the ballot box voting, of participating, of developing arguments through nonviolence, in fact, learning how to win your argument through nonviolence. We have missed out on all that. And that's just our own fault.

Interestingly, his interpretation of the problem was directed inward as a critique of loyalists' democratic capacities. Unlike conventional unionist discourses that have focused on external threats, this man spoke as if the challenge was the loyalists' ability—or inability— to participate fully in political and civil society, not the legit-imacy of the new political arrangements. His comments, while negative, identify areas for empowerment and "social development" that have not been at the center of unionist and loyalist agendas.

Cultural and Civic Unionism

As I noted earlier, unionism and loyalism appear less monolithic and inflexible than commonly believed. English (2002) identifies "new unionism" and "the trans-formation of unionist politics" as an interest among unionists to negotiate new political arrangements with nationalists and reframe fundamental principles. Tonge (2005) describes an incomplete "realignment of unionism" that increasingly foregrounds a "rational civic" or pro-Belfast/Good Friday Agreement agenda that is based on political engagement. The DUP's leadership in the Assembly signals that the realignment continues to develop. Even Tonge's "Orange skeptics" are becoming less skeptical as Feargal Cochrane (2001) says of unionists generally,

> They are no longer outside the loop of influence. They are no longer constantly saying "No." They are no longer without friends or influence in government or further afield within the United States. The Good Friday Agreement has provided a focus of achieve-ment for unionism that has given it renewed intellectual coherence. (p. 396; also see Mitchell 2003)

McAuley (2002, 2004b) identifies "Unionist discourses of transformation," or "new loyalism," which he attributes to progressive loyalists, primarily of the Progressive Unionist Party, such as, Dawn Purvis, who have appreciated the pace of change on political, social, and economic fronts; have introduced class and gendered analyses; and have undertaken "serious investigations of their identity and politics" (2004b:86).

Most of these commentaries focus on party politics, but Porter (1996) begins to expand politics beyond parties to voluntary associations in the public sphere where creative dialogue and deliberation become shared values, and space is opened for the kind of creativity that has rarely existed in Northern Irish politics. McAuley (2002) characterizes the new loyalism embodied in the PUP in ways that echo Porter's "civic unionism." The PUP is arguably more oriented toward com-munity-level politics than other unionist parties. The party is embedded in working-class communities and incorporates "pluralist and liberal" discourses in its speeches and manifestos (p. 121).

Porter's (1996) civic unionism cherishes many of the same values as liberal unionism, but he adopts a civic republican model that prioritizes the ownership and working out of those principles in civil society. The chapters that follow seek to extend McAuley's and Porter's analyses beyond political parties into unionist and loyalist grassroots organizations where new agendas and discourses are being developed. These are often organizations involved in historical and cultural iden-tity work, and I am revealing a route via these activities from cultural unionism to civic unionism. Porter argues that cultural unionism is fundamentally problematic because it distinguishes Northern Ireland's unionists from other British citizens, it is not always historically sound, and it disposes its adherents to exclusive identities that are deaf to nonunionists (p. 126). Yet, the Northern Ireland to which Porter sees civic unionism contributing is one in which cultural unionists must partici-pate. Porter himself advocates a cultural flexibility: "difference through openness" must be cultivated (pp. 172–175). "Northern Ireland is different by virtue of being the site where British and Irish influences peculiarly converge and conflict and in the process get reworked in distinctive ways – ways that may yield senses of Britishness and Irishness unrecognizable in other parts of Britain and Ireland" (p. 172). But how do cultural unionists get there from here?

For Porter, politics should focus on building institutions that provide effective social services and protect speech, civil dialogue, and individual and group rights. Porter calls for the state to create space for citizen action, and citizens are encouraged to extend "due recognition" to one another's cultural identities and practices (pp. 190–195). Or, as Porter puts it,

> if efforts were concentrated on creating, protecting and sustaining such a way of life or vision new possibilities would open up and old hostilities would be put under severe pressure. Common ground would be discovered by citizens devoted to making Northern Ireland work; new forms of citizen attachment and identity might appear alongside traditional ones. New divisions would also undoubtedly surface, but at least they would not necessarily cut along predictable sectarian lines. (p. 180)

If public space for civic republicanism is created, the citizenry will be inexorably drawn into it. But surely this approach fails to address the extent to which collective identities are constructed within groups, how amenable they are to change, and how change is negotiated internally. In short, how is it possible for cultural unionists who strongly identify with Britishness or Ulster Protestantism and fear cultural and political nationalism to make the transition to multicultural democracy?

In 1987, Jennifer Todd argued that only abrupt and radical change imposed externally could shock Ulster loyalists into restructuring the pillars of their beliefs and ideologies.

> No new evidence or argument can prove that humiliation won't follow from loyalists' letting down their guard. It follows that there can be no gradual change in loyalism towards a more moderate or tolerant stance. There will be no slow "modernisation" of Ulster loyalist ideology. Change in Ulster loyalist ideology can only be radical change in the basic structuring binaries of thought. But there is little within Ulster loyalist ideology that could internally generate such a change. It appears that radical change can only be externally produced, when Ulster loyalists face what they have perceived as defeat and humiliation and if they find the experience different from what they anticipated. (pp. 20–21)

What constitutes "radical change" resulting in "defeat and humiliation" is not clear. If the persistent sense of accelerating economic and political decline among loyalists counts, then Todd may have foreseen the development of the new loyalism identified by English and McAuley. If by radical change Todd means the end of the union, then questions arise about where new loyalism and transitional discourses come from. Obviously, much has changed since Todd wrote her seminal article in 1987 on unionist political culture, and to her credit, she was well attuned to the importance of identity change for the prospects of peace in the region (McAuley 2007). Elsewhere in this book, I have drawn on her more recent writings on incremental identity change.

Following Todd's more recent lead, I intend to delve more deeply into the processes of discourse and identity change that McAuley (2002) has described:

Sections of working-class loyalism in particular have begun to critically examine their historical and cultural identity in a meaningful way. This experience needs to be understood in the changing context of dramatic economic decline, political disarticulation and ideological disintegration within unionism. The period of the peace-process has opened up much deliberation within loyalist working-class communities, one possible reading of which suggests a marginalization of sectarianism as a fundamental organizing principle. (p. 118)

Where is this deliberation taking place, and what does it look like? Is it hermetically isolated from the kinds of activities, such as, parading and commemoration, that have been so closely associated with what Todd (1987) describes as "dominance legitimated and garbed in imaginatively rich and coherent ideas," or can those activities and organizations constitute spaces in which new discourses can be developed (p. 11)? The research I undertook in Northern Ireland from 2005 to 2007 was designed to cast light on these questions.

■ GRASSROOTS UNIONISM AND LOYALISM

In order to gauge the prospects of grassroots conflict transformation, it is helpful to look at those conservative segments of the Protestant unionist and loyalist population for whom ethnic identity is considered most important and expressed most prominently. I follow Shirlow and Murtagh's lead (2006) when they call for further research into the most isolated communities:

The types of lifestyles and identities located within segregated communities have generally been ignored within academic deliberation. Such groups are generally regarded as reactionary and overtly violent. Ultimately, there is a rejection of them and their ideology and representation. In a sense they do not display the "rationality" that academics require to provide corroboration to them or to espouse their cause. (p. 173)

Data collection was not limited to organizations in urban loyalist areas, where segregation is usually high, but they figure prominently in the research. Loyal institutions, bands, Ulster-Scots enthusiasts, historical and cultural enthusiasts, and loyalist paramilitaries constitute nodes of self-conscious expression of ethnopolitical identity within the PUL population. Along with churches and other voluntary or community development associations, this *constellation* of organizations reflects a *grassroots unionism and loyalism* that is by no means unitary, but the organizations share general unionist political and cultural preferences and are occupied by many of the same interests in maintaining and expressing an ethnic Protestant identity. The term "grassroots unionism" is an analytical convention, as it would not be widely recognized among Protestant unionists and loyalists. Few such labels generate much consensus. The meaning and use of the terms "Protestant," "unionist," and "loyal" or "loyalist" overlap with one another, and yet, each carries its own connotations which, in isolation, are often unacceptable to any given individual or organization. One working group formed by a range of Protestant community workers who perceived a need for greater coalition building among Protestant organizations adopted the terminology "Protestant/unionist/loyalist" (PUL) when they found it difficult to come to an agreement about a name that used only one or two of the terms (2000).

The descriptor "constellation" expresses a loose but discernible clustering of interest groups among which there is often little or poor communication, and in some cases, tension. Any close examination reveals a complicated landscape of attitudes and orientations that often overlap but also constitute rifts within the Protestant population. The range of perceived distinctions and levels of polarization across class, rural-urban, religious, political, strategic, and ethnic-national dimensions makes generalization challenging, even when similarities and trends exist.

Loyalist Paramilitaries

Journalists and political observers pay considerable attention to loyalist paramilitaries and the difficulties of forging a path to decommissioning and "standing down" organizations, and recent research addresses transitional projects undertaken by these organizations (Gribbin, Kelly, and Mitchell 2005; Shirlow, Graham, McEvoy et al. 2005a; Gallaher 2007; Mitchell 2008b). Loyalist paramilitaries have adopted the term "conflict transformation" to describe initiatives they have developed to move their organizations from active status to more benign forms that include veterans' associations, skill-building organizations, and community development. Whatever one thinks about the speed at which this transformation is progressing or the ethical or moral implications of allowing paramilitaries space to redefine themselves, their programs reflect principles of conflict transformation. These are attempts to shift from destructive violent conflict to nonviolent conflict (politics and civic involvement) by groups of people who come to see such shifts as compatible with their collective identities, and thus the ideological and narrative schemata that justified violence in the past must also be redefined. The project is contested and incomplete, as evidenced by the withdrawal in 2007 of funds earmarked for loyalist communities under an initiative agreed between Minister for Social Development Margaret Ritchie and the Ulster Political Research Group (UPRG), which provides political analysis for the UDA. For that matter, the process of developing consensus *within* paramilitary organizations is also contested, illustrated in recent years by conflict between the southeast Antrim faction of the UDA and the rest of the organization (Hall 2006).

Grassroots Organizations

To focus only on paramilitaries, however, bypasses the range of grassroots organizations where one finds a persistent perception that loyalist communities are misunderstood, "behind," and in need of empowerment (Hall 1994b). These include community development organizations, local churches, Orange lodges, bands, historical and cultural societies, and youth clubs. Outside the memberships of loyalist paramilitaries, the stakes may be less sensational, but among grassroots unionists, an ability to maintain a sufficient level of ontological security and continuity with the past while adapting to new political and economic circumstances is crucial to the overall trajectory of community relations and the prospects for sustainable peace in Northern Ireland.

■ METHODOLOGY

Sixty semistructured interviews were conducted between June 2005 and December 2007, involving sixty-seven interviewees, with fifty-one of them coming from within grassroots unionist organizations or communities, either through residence, membership, employment, or participation in specific projects or initiatives (see Table 3.1). Fieldnotes detail participant observation at cultural events and organizational meetings. Documentary data include governmental and nongovernmental reports, mainstream news media, organizations' annual reports, and minutes of meetings. Each interview has been transcribed, and fieldnotes, along with the majority of documentary data, have been coded or categorized along predetermined and emergent themes. Hundreds of photographs and video clips of rituals and symbolic artifacts, such as, parades, commemorations, murals, memorials, bonfires, and flags, also inform the analysis.

Three-quarters of the interviews were conducted with interviewees who work or reside in the greater Belfast area, especially in working-class loyalist East Belfast

TABLE 3.1 *Profile of Interviewees*

Profile of interviewees*	
Men	52
Women	15
Community workers	20
Paramilitaries or ex-combatants	12
Loyal Orders	12
Cultural workers or enthusiasts	11
Politicians	10
Ulster-Scots	7
Clergy	6
Muralist	4
Band members	3
Civil servants	3
Nationalists	3
TOTAL INTERVIEWEES	67

* The sum of profile characteristics does not equal the total number of interviewees as some individuals could be represented in two or more rows in the table.

and the Shankill Road areas. Other interviews draw in rural and middle-class per-spectives, but the data are skewed toward urban experience. The relative weight given to working-class loyalism is partly methodologically driven. A decision was taken to use the available time and resources to cover a range of organizations and cultural expressions that are influential in loyalist and unionist communities while also delving as deeply as possible into local networks. This approach was facilitated by focusing on densely populated urban areas. Rural Protestant populations will share many of the same attitudes and experiences with urban Protestants but will also be faced with their own conditions that shape decision making about cultural expressions. Interest in Ulster-Scots heritage, for example, seems to have particu-larly strong support in rural and border communities where cohesion is higher, and cultural expression, such as, dancing and music, provide opportunities for Protestants, who are spread out geographically, to interact socially. By contrast, murals are more common, and paramilitary organizations figure more promi-nently among working-class urban Protestants.

This is largely a book about men, even though they make up less than half of Northern Ireland's population. Surely conflict transformation, as a process that includes broad-based cultural change, must involve both men and women. Yet, when it comes to the narrow but high profile set of symbolic practices that are widely identified as unique expressions of Protestant ethnopolitical identity, they are usually planned, debated, and executed by men and organizations with male membership (Cochrane 2001:47–52).

Women's views were sought out to ensure that they are incorporated in the research, but adult men are nevertheless overrepresented as they are often con-sidered the keepers of public cultural expressions in Northern Ireland. With the exception of dancing, nearly all other "traditional" PUL activities are carried out primarily by men (bands, parades, murals, historical pursuits, reenact-ments, etc.), which suggests that the very notion of what constitutes traditional cultural expressions deserves reconsideration within PUL communities. Until then, we are overlooking an important segment of the population, and the loss of women's contributions and memories leaves the public consciousness impoverished and may mean that they also miss out on opportunities for empowerment. Thankfully, important research has been undertaken to docu-ment women's political, economic, and cultural contributions to the pursuit of a sustainable peace in Northern Ireland (Morgan 1995, 2004; Ward 2006; Potter 2008; Brewer 2010).

■ CONCLUSION

Unionists and loyalists have been significantly slower than nationalists in devel-oping a collective sense of alignment with the "new Northern Ireland" that is emerging both politically and economically. They are sometimes referred to as "at sea," and yet, they appear increasingly aware of a need to engage in public discourse in order to advocate effectively for their interests. A felt need to build confidence and communal esteem prevails in a time when—despite the cease-fires, the inclusion of the principle of consent in the Belfast/Good Friday Agreement, and the support of republicans for policing—a sense of uncertainty remains during these early days of power sharing. The challenges of reorienting collective identities present themselves starkly in working-class communities that have borne the brunt of the Troubles. Protestants there feel that the dividends of the political peace process have not reached them, and they are skeptical that their political representatives will advocate for them effectively in a quickly changing political and economic landscape. Power sharing with republicans and what Protestants perceive as preferential treatment in the development of nationalist communities abrade fundamental assumptions of their collective identity as loyal British citizens in Northern Ireland. Yet, one finds an interest in local civic empowerment. A range of often disparate community organizations has undertaken initiatives to modify traditional cultural expressions and experiment with various historical rationales for a positive shared heritage. Simultaneously, one finds a prevailing frustration at their capacity to engage more effectively with the media, statutory bodies, and in some cases, nationalist neighbors.

■ Notes

1. "Ulster" is a term often used to refer to the province of Northern Ireland. Actually, partition by the Government of Ireland Act in 1920 excluded three of the nine counties that historically comprised Ulster.

2. The validity of Protestant claims regarding the massacres has been questioned by historians, but the massacres have remained a part of unionist political history in Ireland (Bardon 1992:137–39).

3. Home Rule campaigns called for the transfer of political power from Westminster to Dublin.

4. Mitchell (2008a) also notes the paradoxically close relationships between many conservative churches and the loyalist communities where they are located, but these relations are tempered by pre-millennial other-worldly theologies (pp. 154–55).

5. Whyte (1990) references work by Walsh (1970), who finds that Protestant decline since 1946 was instead due to a high death rate and a low birth rate (p. 153).

6. The Taoiseach is the proper title of the prime minister of the Republic of Ireland.

7. Those reporting "No religion" in the 2001 census were asked what religion they were brought up in. Adding those numbers to those who declared themselves Protestant or Catholic produces the following results: Catholic 43.8 percent, Protestant 53.1 percent (Northern Ireland Statistics and Research Agency 2001: Table KS07c: Stated Current Religion).

8. Claims of increasing unionist division are overwrought, according to Farrington (2006), who notes that diversity and cross-party coalitions have been a common feature of unionist politics (pp. 183–85).

9. Nearly 11 percent felt it was a bad thing, 27.6 percent felt it did not make any difference, and 4 percent reported they did not know (ARK 2007).

10. The perception of brain drain constitutes the relevant point here, but note that using data from the Northern Ireland Young Life and Times Survey, Schubotz (2008) found that

Protestant sixteen-year-olds are more likely than their Catholic counterparts to *intend* to stay in Northern Ireland and more likely to plan to return if they do leave (p. 16).

11. The results of a similar question collected between 1998 and 2005, about how *unionists or nationalists* have benefited, reveal similar results, though respondents reported that Protestants and Catholics were more likely to benefit equally than unionists and nationalists.

12. Blackbourn and Rekawek (2007) document differential perceptions among Protestants and Catholics regarding which population benefited more from the Belfast Agreement, but they question whether those perceptions reflect real differences in social and economic benefits and call for further research.

4 Mitigating Murals and Loyalist Cultural Innovation

Murals and other means of publicly expressing loyalist identity provide windows onto a critical process in conflict transformation: changing perceptions of the conflict and softening out-group boundaries by incrementally redefining collective identities in ways that maintain continuity and yet, are less polarizing. If murals and other forms of public expression of collective identity serve a double function of both expressing and shaping collective identity, they can constitute a mechanism for reshaping attitudes about ethnicity. Murals, parades, and other cultural expressions have, of course, been used to encourage insular and parochial attitudes, but as a vehicle for framing collective identities, they may help redefine collective identities in less polarizing ways.

Walking the streets of loyalist working-class East Belfast or the Shankill Road, one encounters political and cultural expressions ranging from hastily daubed slogans and acronyms of paramilitary organizations to flags, banners, and elaborate wall murals. The murals celebrate historic victories and crises in loyalist mythology, commemorate fallen comrades and neighbors, and valorize paramilitary organizations and local bands. They have become striking and sometimes shocking hallmarks of Northern Ireland's Troubles, and in recent years have become the objects of a growing conflict tourism industry. However, a new trend of cultural exploration and innovation appears to be developing among a range of loyalist organizations. Initiatives have been emerging that reform cultural practices, such as, paramilitary murals, Orange Order parades, and bonfires, to make them more rich, sophisticated, and less offensive.

One now encounters murals in East Belfast featuring local historical and cultural topics, such as, the building of the passenger liner *Titanic* and C. S. Lewis's book *The Lion, the Witch, and the Wardrobe*. The redesign of paramilitary murals and modification of other traditional forms of cultural expression reflect shifts in political and cultural perspectives and modulate the tone of loyalism, even if only relative to the ubiquity of martial themes that have reinforced siege mentalities among Protestants and alienated Catholic nationalist communities.[1]

■ MURALS AND A SHIFTING SYMBOLIC LANDSCAPE

Historically, murals have primarily been found in unionist and loyalist neighborhoods, where they have been permitted, if not approved, by the state (Rolston 1987). Their origins can be traced to the era of the Home Rule debates and the availability of mass-produced commercial paint at the turn of the twentieth century. They became increasingly common as partition was established in 1920 and Northern Ireland remained part of the United Kingdom (Jarman 1992; Loftus 1994). The Northern Irish state that followed ensured unionist ascendancy, and murals became a widely accepted means for Protestant communities to signal their support for unionist politics, and such expressions of British loyalty were approved if not officially sanctioned by the unionist-controlled Stormont government.

Early loyalist murals featured reproductions and adaptations of Benjamin West's 1780 painting of King William of Orange crossing the Boyne River atop his steed during the Battle of the Boyne in 1690, during which the forces of the Protestant "King Billy" defeated the deposed Catholic King James II and his Jacobite army. Loftus (1994:31) identifies John McClean's 1908 mural in the Beersbridge Road in East Belfast as the first such mural. Some murals have been connected to annual July Twelfth commemorations of the battle, when new murals were often unveiled, or older ones were retouched to supplement other traditional activities, such as, the erection of arches, bunting, and flags; the painting of curbstones; and parades by the loyal institutions (Rolston 1991; Jarman 1992:151; Sluka 1992:193–95; Jarman 1997; Bryan 2000).

Between World Wars I and II, mural painting peaked, with varied subjects including the *Titanic*, the Battle of the Somme, and the coronation of King George VI (Sluka 1992:194). As Rolston (1991, 1992) reports, the comfortable relationship between Protestants and British governments became strained with the onset of the Troubles in the late 1960s, and as the local Stormont government was superseded by direct rule from Westminster in 1972. Loyalist murals declined amid unionist and loyalist confusion over their status as British citizens who were, nonetheless, increasingly dissatisfied with British policy in Northern Ireland. The murals that did appear largely abandoned traditional themes of Britishness and Protestant ascendancy and turned to iconic references to Ulster, such as, the flag of Northern Ireland, which features the Red Hand of Ulster (a reference to Irish mythology) and St. George's cross (the prominent red cross found in the flag of England). After 1984, and into the 1990s, largely in reaction to the Anglo-Irish Agreement, republican hunger strikes, the seventy-fifth anniversary of the Ulster Volunteer Force (UVF) in 1987, and growing numbers of republican murals, loyalist murals proliferated and became militant, featuring loyalist paramilitary organizations, such as, the UVF, the Ulster Defense Association/Ulster Freedom Fighters (UDA/UFF), and the Red Hand Commando. Traditional images, such as, those of King William of Orange, did not disappear, but young politicized painters increasingly produced less sophisticated images of balaclava-clad paramilitary members wielding automatic weapons surrounded by flags, slogans, and emblems (Rolston 1987; Sluka 1992:210; Loftus 1994; Jarman 1997:209, 15, 26). Intimidating murals in both loyalist and republican neighborhoods remain common and have served to mark territory and project threat to outsiders while discouraging dissent within communities. In loyalist areas, paramilitary murals have also been used to distinguish territories controlled by rival paramilitary organizations.

Like other forms of collective cultural expression, murals represent communities to themselves. They help define collective identity by shaping collective memory, commemorating lost comrades and community members, declaring that the community is under pressure or attack, or memorializing a long history of sacrifice. Rolston (1992) describes the expressive character of murals:

> Through their murals both loyalists and republicans parade their ideologies publicly. The murals act, therefore, as a sort of barometer of political ideology. Not only do they articulate what republicanism or loyalism stands for in general, but, manifestly or otherwise, they reveal the current status of each of these political beliefs. (p. 27)

Murals exhibit political ideology, and in the case of Northern Ireland's loyalists, the decline and resurgence of mural painting as well as its content have reflected the broad outlines of the unionist and loyalist psyche. This, incidentally, is not to assert that all residents of loyalist neighborhoods appreciate or condone paramilitary activity or the murals that valorize it. In fact, murals are often placed without the consent of local residents under an unspoken threat of intimidation, ensuring that paramilitary organizations can claim territory through the placement of murals. Though loyalist murals constantly refer to defense from outside attack, they can also constitute means of internal control as paramilitary organizations assert their influence. Nevertheless, Neil Jarman (2005) argues that murals have promoted solidarity in both loyalist and republican neighborhoods. From the beginning, "Murals helped to transform 'areas where Protestants lived' into 'Protestant areas,'" and "All murals create a new type of space, they redefine mundane public space as a politicized place and can thereby help to reclaim it for the community" (pp. 176, 179). However, it is important to understand that murals' functions are not merely conservative.

Murals are not static; their contents evolve, stretching old ideas and testing new ones. Murals, in particular, have exhibited a kind of fluid impermanence and malleability, often changing over time. "They can be added to and changed as required. In this sense, a mural need never be regarded as complete or finished," according to Jarman (1997:211–12). They are often replaced or may take years to complete (Jarman 2004; Kelly 2004). Jarman (2005) claims that collective expressions, such as, murals, can be appropriated in innovative ways for new agendas, and thus, I would argue, have the potential to *shape* collective identity. The resurgence of loyalist murals, for example, has been used to challenge traditional Britishness and Orange unionist leadership, as working-class loyalists have grown increasingly skeptical of elite unionism. While loyalists originally appropriated the mantle of unionism by employing symbols, such as, the crown, "God save the Queen," and the Union Jack, some (especially in areas affiliated with the UDA) have turned inward, seeking new sources of identification and displaying Independent Ulster flags and appropriating Irish mythology, in the form of Cúchulainn whom some loyalists regard as an archetypal defender of Ulster (Jarman 1997:219–20, 26, 28).

Two points bear special note. First, murals are not confined to a perfectly rigid and unchanging symbolic formula, though they no doubt conform to certain rules within their own genre. The second point, which follows from the first, is that murals reflect loyalists' attitudes and beliefs, but they also mediate the development of new ideas and agendas, as their component parts can be introduced alongside and sometimes under the cover of familiar and legitimated ones. This process is covered more fully in chapter 5, but for the moment, we are primarily interested in the potential for murals, flags, bonfires, and other traditional cultural expressions to be altered and yet, retain their basic functions of performing identity and maintaining ontological security.

If it is not uncommon for traditional cultural expressions to change, we can ask whether they can be modified in ways that less clearly legitimize violence and suggest nonviolent strategies, even if they often continue to express grievances and convey a highly ideological narrative of conflict in Ireland. Presumably, less-violent murals can help improve community relations by lowering the levels of intimidation felt by neighbors at interfaces and among viewers of media coverage, though Jarman (1997) asserts that nationalist and loyalist murals are primarily designed for internal consumption:

> The two bodies of mural works have developed in parallel over the past decade or so, and depict many similar themes and images; but the two communities are not engaged in a debate with each other via the murals – rather it is the shared socio-political environment that has helped to generate the similarities. The murals remain a part of two largely separate internal discourses. (p. 209)

This is a point on which Sluka (1992:191) disagrees. The truth probably lies somewhere between Sluka's and Jarman's positions; there is not a tight correspondence between the messages embedded in most loyalist and nationalist murals. They are, nonetheless, part of discursive exchanges, and they communicate beyond their immediate locales, interacting within a larger political and social environment.

Murals, especially nationalist ones, may provide symbolic commentary on current events. Sluka (1992) argues that in the 1980s, nationalist murals often responded to events, such as, the hunger strikes and the running struggle between the IRA and security forces, and he cites instances in which loyalists have used graffiti to react to events. He asserts that the proliferation of loyalist murals in the late 1980s was a reaction to the growth of republican murals after the hunger strikes, though I would argue that there may be other equally relevant explanations, such as, the affront and disorientation unionists felt at the signing of the Anglo-Irish Agreement in 1985 (p. 212).

Sluka also notes the intentional way in which murals became a propaganda tool in the hands of Sinn Féin operatives who appreciated their appeal to international journalists and ensured that they were in their best condition when journalists were most likely to take pictures of them and thereby broadcast arguments about British imperialism, discrimination, and injustice. Loyalists have not used murals in nearly such politically calibrated ways, though the recent shift in the content of loyalist murals has received considerable media attention, and several of my contacts talked about having been interviewed by local and international journalists and appreciate the opportunity to project a new image of their organizations and neighborhoods.

Murals communicate internally as well. By interrupting the frequency of violent, martial, and sectarian images, murals and other symbolic displays can dial down the atmosphere of mistrust and fear that has prevailed during the Troubles and improve quality of life, enhancing the chances of cross-community work and political peacemaking. The placement of more benign murals as part of regeneration efforts is not new. Bill Rolston (1991) describes a community arts scheme sponsored by the Belfast City Council that operated between 1977 and 1981 and recruited students from the Arts College in Belfast to create more than forty nonpolitical and nonsectarian murals in underdeveloped areas of Belfast (Sluka 1992:197). Direct rule ministers worked from the premise that beautification and economic progress were related and would help create an environment for political progress, a perspective that still underpins regeneration efforts today. The project was generally well received, though in some cases the artwork did not sufficiently reflect the experience of local residents and met with disapproval. Rolston reports that consultation was a necessary but not sufficient factor within a complex range of factors that determined the acceptability of each mural within the community. In those cases where the murals were appreciated, the community members felt they provided a welcome distraction from the Troubles and enhanced their otherwise bleak urban surroundings. Themes included jungle and pastoral scenes, mythical fairytales, and local street scenes; murals that represented local community members were especially appreciated.

While the community arts program murals most likely influenced local communities by instilling a modicum of pride in their neighborhood, the murals studiously avoided the conflict, one of the most prominent features of daily life at the time. It is also worth noting that the community arts program was administered by the Belfast City Council through its Community Services Department and was thus imported *into* the neighborhoods. In many cases, the residents were consulted and were involved in the design and construction of murals, but there does not seem to have been direct involvement of hard-line and conservative organizations, such as, the paramilitaries or the Orange Order. As such, the community arts murals project was disconnected from the predominant mural tradition and did not fully engage ethnopolitical identity.

By contrast, loyalist murals since approximately 2003 have played an increasingly notable role within *local* community development initiatives. These initiatives have adopted some of the aspirations of the earlier community arts program but also use symbols and narratives that reflect loyalist memory, aspirations, and grievances. Where the community arts program avoided politics at all costs, loyalist activists are themselves deeply immersed in loyalist political perspectives, which many commentators and observers would assume to be particular and revanchist. Yet, for a variety of reasons, as I discovered, they have tried to reframe loyalism on the walls in ways that are less intimidating and offensive.

Redesigning, Replacing, and Removing Murals

"Cultural murals," as they are often called, highlight community history and achievements and thus sustain community identity while simultaneously "tweaking" it by replacing overtly sectarian themes with others that define "us" without direct reference to "them." Many return to subjects featured in murals painted between the world wars, such as, the construction of the Titanic and the Battle of the Somme (Sluka 1992:194; Loftus 1994). Even murals that make political arguments about grievances in the Protestant community, such as, the conditions placed on parades or the disbanding of the Royal Ulster Constabulary (which Protestants have seen as a defense against Republican violence), signal an engagement in political discourse that is more nuanced and constructive than murals that emphasize the paramilitary defense of loyalist neighborhoods, tit-for-tat retribution between loyalist and republican paramilitaries, and factional infighting among loyalist paramilitaries.

Newsnight, a BBC news television program, cleverly borrowed one of their video segment titles, "The Writing on the Wall?" from a mural redesign initiative in East Belfast titled, "The Writing's Not on the Wall" (Sillito 2003). These titles refer to a growing recognition among loyalists that a return to majoritarian governance is impossible, but a desire to influence their own future remains. They feel that they suffer from poor public relations and have failed to develop the necessary political skills to effectively engage nationalists and act as advocates for their communities. Many have come to believe that cultural activities provide an important vehicle for the development of their public image and political confidence.

When I arrived in Northern Ireland in 2005 to begin research for this particular project, local mural redesign was still in its relatively early days and had only begun to receive media attention. The most extensive of the mural schemes in East Belfast, where I resided with my family, had been developed by a coalition of local clergy, community development organizations, representatives from local paramilitaries, and statutory bodies, such as, the Northern Ireland Housing Executive, and Police Service of Northern Ireland (PSNI), a collaboration that is notable on its own in terms of cooperation between a range of state and nonstate organizations. As early as 2003, the forum was involved in the creation of nine new community-themed and cross-community murals. In all, at least nine murals were placed or redesigned featuring local historical themes that included the building of the *Titanic* in the East Belfast shipyards, the famous footballer George Best, Protestant reformers, a local primary school, Belfast native C. S. Lewis's novel *The Lion, the Witch, and the Wardrobe,* and Northern Ireland's football team (see figures 4.1 and 4.2).

Figure 4.1 Harland and Wolff—*Titanic* mural in East Belfast. Dee Street at the Lower Newtownards Road. September 6, 2007.

Each of the new murals represented a deliberate move to shed the trappings of paramilitarism and to foreground alternative symbols and narratives. The scheme was not arrived at lightly. The coalition engaged in six months of protracted discussions over whether mural redesigns could be undertaken. Some of those in favor of the program emphasized economic concerns, arguing that paramilitary trappings scare away inward investment. Others expressed concern over paramilitary murals' impact on children. At the same time, paramilitary representatives within the coalition harbored concerns over their credibility within their organizations, especially in relation to younger more radical members. Could they be seen as loyal while taking down images that, in some cases, commemorated fallen comrades? In the end, they were convinced to support the project, in part because advocates pointed out that republicans had reaped political benefits from similar activities that foregrounded distinctive ethnic activities, such as, music, language, and literature, through events, such as, the West Belfast Festival. At least one paramilitary organization subsequently took their own initiative to redesign a few additional murals and became more involved in community development issues.

Figure 4.2 C. S. Lewis Mural in East Belfast, Island Street. September 14, 2007.

Later, another organization, the East Belfast Historical and Cultural Society (EBHCS), completed a series of murals in Thorndyke Street that follows a progression of events the society considered crucial in Protestant, loyalist, and local history. Many of the panels that span the long wall depict Protestants under siege or heraldic declarations of loyalty to Britain. References to paramilitary organizations are notably absent save for a panel that depicts "Defending the community" against IRA attacks in the early 1970s (a period during which the UDA was formed from local community associations) and subtle allusions to paramilitary emblems and slogans among the insignia of local bands (East Belfast Historical and Cultural Society 2006). EBHCS has overseen the production of additional murals that remain politically edgy but have abandoned the normal fare of flags, emblems, and armaments that have predominated since the 1980s in favor of political argument, commemoration, and historical narrative.

Similar initiatives have been taken up in other areas of Belfast. A pilot program of the Northern Ireland Housing Executive's Community Cohesion Unit led to the redesign of murals beginning in 2006. The program called for the removal of tattered flags and emblems, painted curbstones, and graffiti, and facilitated discussion of local bonfire issues as well as workshops to examine alternative expressions of culture. The West Belfast Athletic and Cultural Society (WBACS) has sponsored new mural designs, and in June 2009, the Lower Shankill unveiled ten newly redesigned murals under the sponsorship of Belfast City Council's Re-imaging Communities program (*Newsletter*, June 17, 2009).

These are only a few of the redesign projects that have spread across Belfast and are captured in an analysis of photographs I took or collected between 2005 and 2007. This analysis is restricted to 212 loyalist murals in Belfast. The photographs constitute a convenience sample covering five geographical areas for which I will provide descriptive statistics. The ideal approach would involve either a full photographic survey of all murals or, alternatively, random sampling of a series of areas with repetition of the process from one year to the next. Doing so would provide a better foundation from which to draw generalizations about the prevalence of themes in murals at any given period of time or over time and geographic location. That approach was not feasible given other data collection demands, and so the results should be interpreted with caution. Even so, there is no immediately obvious basis from which to anticipate patterned bias in the results. I did not, for example, formalize the coding scheme I use here until well after the pictures were taken. Murals were photographed without regard for their content or aesthetic quality. It is, of course, possible that I unconsciously expected to see certain themes in some areas or years and so noticed more murals that reflected those themes, though this seems unlikely, since at least all first encounters, and often subsequent encounters, with murals of any content resulted in a photograph being taken. It also bears emphasizing that the themes presented here reflect the growing interest in mural schemes that has been identified in the interviews and other sources of information presented in this chapter.

All the photographs were taken in five areas of Belfast: Belfast (central and south Belfast), East Belfast, North Belfast, Sandy Row, and Shankill. By far, the most pictures were taken in East Belfast (121) because the area is much larger, it contains a greater concentration of loyalist neighborhoods, and I resided there with my family for six months in 2007. The Shankill Road area, a deeply loyalist enclave and paramilitary stronghold, which is geographically much smaller and surrounded by nationalist neighborhoods in West Belfast, produced the next greatest number of murals (50).

A review of the photographs suggests that they can be usefully categorized along the following prominent themes, some of which appeared concurrently (see table 4.1).[2] Paramilitary themes dominate the collection, followed closely by historical themes, which often co-occur with paramilitary themes, usually in the form of commemorations of World War I veterans (see figure 4.3).

To compare the prevalence of murals that might be considered contentious, antagonistic, or intimidating and those that feature less controversial themes, two indices were created using the themes in table 4.1. The first index (MCONT) consists of arguably contentious thematic content including paramilitaries, security forces, and the loyal institutions (which incorporates Orange Order and Battle of the Boyne themes). The loyal institutions theme is less overtly inimical than the former

TABLE 4.1 *Frequency of Mural Themes*

Theme[1]	Count	%	Theme	Count	%
Bands	18	8.5	Peace	1	0.5
British	8	3.8	Politics	6	2.8
Entertainment	1	0.5	Religious	7	3.3
Historical	73	34.4	Security Forces	5	2.4
Industry	7	3.3	Social	2	0.9
Local	35	16.5	Sports	11	5.2
Loyal Institutions	8	3.8	Ulster-Scots	5	2.4
Memorial	27	12.7	United States	4	1.9
Mythology	4	1.9	Victims	9	4.2
Paramilitary	86	40.6	Youth	13	6.1
			TOTAL	N = 212	100

[1]Please see Appendix 4.1 for descriptions of the themes.

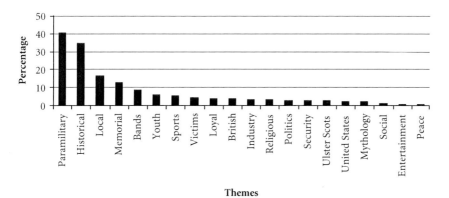

Figure 4.3 Percentage Frequency of Mural Themes.

ones, but was included because of the perceptions of the loyal institutions by many nationalists as conspiratorial, discriminatory, and triumphalist organizations. One hundred fifteen instances (54.2 percent) of mitigated (less or noncontentious) themes were identified, leaving 97 instances (45.8 percent) of contentious themes remaining. The nearly equal proportions of contentious and less-contentious exhibits may surprise some readers who tend to associate murals with paramilitary organizations (see figure 4.4). Among the less-contentious content, historical, memorial, bands, local, sports, and youth themes emerged as most common. Historical and memorial themes can often be found with both contentious and less-contentious themes, though historical themes are far more likely to accompany less-contentious themes, which are becoming increasingly common (see figure 4.5).

If we look at the Shankill Road and East Belfast areas, where the largest number of pictures (171) were collected, we find that, overall, mitigated themes appear slightly more frequently (52 percent) than contentious ones (48 percent). Murals with historical and mythological themes can still prove intimidating when they

Figure 4.4 UDA/UFF mural in Tullycarnet estate. January 6, 2008.

depict vintage weapons such as, swords or lances, simply because they suggest violence, though they are arguably less intimidating than those depicting contemporary paramilitaries and automatic weapons. Consequently, I calculated a more conservative estimate (MCONTW) of the potential antagonism associated with murals by counting murals displaying weapons, soldiers, military units, or their emblems, and adding them to the former index of contentious themes. Taking into account the presence of weapons adds thirty-two murals to the original collection of murals with contentious themes, and now, under the new classification (MCONTW), the percentage of contentious murals (60.8 percent) surpasses mitigated ones (39.2 percent), suggesting that even as fewer murals focus on loyalist paramilitaries, they often maintain martial elements (see figure 4.6).

Since murals were photographed at different rates, and often in different locations from year to year, and given that a consistent sample was not replicated in each of the three years, the variation in frequency of themes in murals for which I can verify the dates from 2005 to 2007 is not particularly meaningful.[3] However, given that murals were photographed regardless of their content, the *percentages* of mural themes across years becomes interesting (see table 4.1 and figure 4.3; all

Figure 4.5 One of a series of panels on Donegal Road bridge commemorating the German Luftwaffe's attacks on Belfast during World War II. September 18, 2007.

percentages reflect a proportion of the 212 murals represented in the collection.) Table 4.2 reports the results for mural themes without consideration for the presence of weapons.

The overall and longitudinal results, in light of the ethnographic data presented in this chapter, suggest that the complexion of loyalist murals may well be changing, becoming less contentious, abandoning paramilitary, military, and Orange themes (see figure 4.7).[4] The frequency by percentage of contentious murals decreased from 2005 to 2007 while all others necessarily increased. The overall magnitude of percentage change in themes—increase and decrease—across these years is 18 percent for murals regardless of the presence of weapons (MCONT). Among the most common themes (paramilitary, historical, memorial, and local), we find in figure 4.8 a clear decline in the percentage of paramilitary murals accompanying equally prominent increases in the percentage of murals with historical themes and a wide selection of less-contentious themes (those besides historical, memorial, and local themes). The percentage frequency of memorial and local themes remained fairly constant between 2005 and 2007, with a slight uptick in local themes between 2006 and 2007.

Paramilitary themes are being replaced by a range of less-contentious themes (see figure 4.8). Given these trends, one might guess that the steady proportion of murals with memorial themes would increasingly commemorate individuals

Figure 4.6 Obsolete weapons, such as, muskets, often appear in historical murals. Thorndyke St. murals, East Belfast. July 1, 2005.

TABLE 4.2 *Contentious and Mitigated Mural Themes over Time (MCONT)*

		2005	2006	2007
Contains contentious themes	Count (%)	25 (56.8)	34 (48.6)	38 (38.8)
Without contentious themes	Count (%)	19 (43.2)	36 (51.4)	60 (61.2)
	TOTAL %	100	100	100
				N = 212

without associations with paramilitaries. However, instead, the percentages of coincidences of paramilitary and memorial themes rise by more than 10 percent. Thus, one feature of the changing complexion of murals is that even for the proportions of paramilitary murals that persist over time, they are turning attention to legitimating the past and constructing memory as opposed to valorizing a contemporary struggle (see figure 4.9). Meanwhile, fewer murals without paramilitary themes are memorializing individuals. The incidences of non-paramilitary and historical themes seem to be on the rise, though the results are not clear and the net increase is not large.

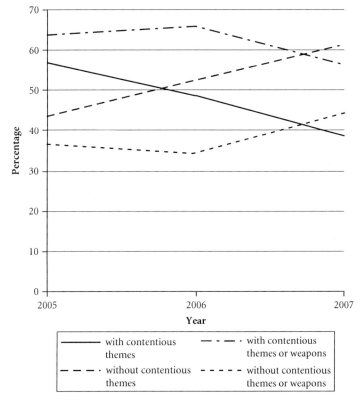

Figure 4.7 Percentage Frequency of Contentious and Mitigated Mural Themes over Time (MCONT).

By the even more conservative estimate that includes all instances of weapons (MCONTW), the general direction of change toward less contentious murals remains, though to a lesser degree. The comparative difference in percentage frequency between contentious themes with weapons and less-contentious themes differed by a more modest net change of 7.5 percent between 2005 and 2007, and mitigating themes only surpassed contentious ones in 2007 after the latter continued to predominate in 2006. We can surmise that many historical and memorial themes still coincide with representations of weapons from the seventeenth century, World War I, and World War II.

In comparison with characterizations of loyalist murals since the 1980s as militant and simplistic, photographs collected between 2005 and 2007 suggest a shift away from paramilitary and other contentious themes that nevertheless reinscribe Protestant or loyalist identity. However, until data collected under more rigorous sampling are available, we should be cautious about assigning too much importance to the findings presented here.

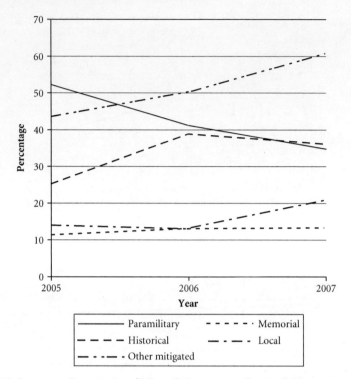

Figure 4.8 Percentage Frequencies of Selected Themes over Time.

Loyalist murals have not become politically or ethnically neutral, even as they have not taken up the kind of political themes that often appear in nationalist murals. They have not ceased to employ exclusive historical narratives. The prominent display of British and Northern Ireland flags in many murals will not resonate with most Catholics. Historical and mythological themes often incorporate weapons or references to British military units as they depict World War I battle scenes and commemorate veterans. The ubiquitous embrace of the British military may alienate many nationalists, though there has been a growing willingness among nationalists to acknowledge the service of Catholics in the British military during World Wars I and II, which may go some way toward normalizing historical murals.

Even celebrations of industry can remind Catholics of their exclusion from employment in factories and shipyards. Murals with political themes can portray nationalist agendas as anathema. Sports murals can reinscribe social division by laying claim to certain teams that are supported by loyalists. Victims murals make direct reference to the violence of the Troubles and could reopen old wounds, frustrating those who would prefer to "draw a line under history" (Brewer 2010:166) Nonetheless, noticeable shifts in the character of murals away from paramilitary and other contentious themes suggest a process in which cultural schemata are in flux.

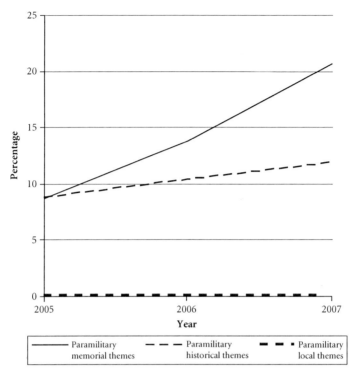

Figure 4.9 Percentage Frequencies of Themes Coinciding with Paramilitary Themes over Time.

Downsizing Bonfires

Murals are not the only cultural activity that has been undergoing modifications in loyalist neighborhoods. Annual bonfires have been noted for their displays of sectarianism and antagonism. Each year, on the night before the Twelfth parades, unionists and loyalists across Northern Ireland gather around enormous bonfires, usually constructed on waste ground out of a mélange of wooden pallets, industrial spools, scrap lumber, old furniture, and tires. The Northern Ireland Housing Executive (NIHE) reported 1,203 bonfires on property under their jurisdiction in 2003 (Interagency Working Group on Bonfires 2006:21). Children begin collecting material for the bonfires weeks in advance, and the piles grow steadily until July 11. The largest bonfires can reach heights of twenty to thirty feet, and heavy machinery is sometimes used to lift materials onto the stack. Collecting materials is a rite of childhood and adolescence in loyalist communities as youths compete against others in nearby neighborhoods to gather the most materials, often camping out at the bonfire sites to make sure the completed bonfires are not lit prematurely by saboteurs.

On July 11 or shortly before, the bonfires are constructed as adults become involved. Hundreds of residents (depending on the location) gather around the bonfire as midnight draws near, usually after many have patronized local pubs. Even around the bonfires, open bottles or pint glasses of beer are common, and one usually finds adolescents and adults who are clearly under the influence of alcohol. Local vendors hawk the usual red, white, and blue souvenirs, such as, flags, hats, scarves, and audiotapes; the ever-present hamburger and chip vans keep the crowds plied with food. Dance music, band tunes, or paramilitary tributes blare from loudspeakers mounted on lorry flatbeds that serve as stages. Often, small bonfires are lit for the entertainment of children. Neighbors catch up with one another while young kids soak up the excitement of the crowds and the joys of cotton candy and fluorescing toys.

Finally, at midnight, the bonfires are lit, and from an elevated vantage point, fires and smoke can be seen rising across the Belfast skyline. By the time they are alight, any number of nationalist or republican symbols may have been placed on the stacks (see figure 4.10). I have seen SDLP and Sinn Féin campaign posters,

Figure 4.10 Bonfire with tricolour and republican starry plough flags. Lower Newtownards Road. July 11, 2007.

tricolours, pictures of the pope, various republican flags, effigies, and hastily scrawled names of republican hunger strikers consumed to the cheers of the crowd. In staunchly loyalist areas, local paramilitary units used to take advantage of the rare opportunity to address the assembled community and performed "shows of strength" by uniformed and masked men, usually involving the reading of a pre-pared statement and a volley of automatic weapons fire. Anti-social behavior asso-ciated with bonfires, such as, littering, loud music, under-age drinking, attacks on fire and security services, and alcohol and drug abuse, do little to improve the image of events that are already seen as aggressive and sectarian by nationalists and many middle-class Protestants.

According to popular history, bonfires were lit to commemorate important events, such as, King William's landing at Carrickfergus and his victory at the Battle of the Boyne (Jarman 1992:151). Today, older generations recall bonfires fondly as opportunities for renewing or building relationships in local communities (Byrne and Wilson 2007:44). However, like many communal activities over the course of the Troubles, bonfires have served contentious purposes. Sectarian music, para-military demonstrations of strength, the desecration of nationalist and Catholic symbols, and the gathering of large crowds have all contributed to intercommunal mistrust and fear.

Besides their incendiary ethnic dimensions, bonfires present a number of envi-ronmental and social challenges as well. The collection of bonfire materials in public spaces can begin as early as mid-February, creating eyesores for much of the year (Interagency Working Group on Bonfires 2006:7). Tires have been a popular material to throw on bonfires, but the toxic fumes they release can damage health and the environment. The Interagency Working Group on Bonfires (2006) esti-mates that 30 percent of bonfire materials consists of tires, and opponents, such as, the SDLP's deputy leader, Dr. Alasdair McDonnell, have campaigned against them on environmental and health grounds (*Observer*, June 29, 2008). Wooden pallets constitute 31 percent, and trade wastes make up 70 percent of bonfire materials that can smolder for days or weeks (pp. 8, 21).

The immense heat generated by bonfires can damage streets and nearby prop-erties. Belfast City Council estimates that cleanup costs per bonfire can reach £5,000 (*Times*, July 11, 2009), and in 2004 district councils spent approximately £173,224 on cleanup and repairs (Interagency Working Group on Bonfires 2006:10; *Times*, July 11, 2009). The fire service received emergency calls as frequently as every eighty-five seconds on the Eleventh Night in 2007 (down 40 percent from the previous year), and costs across Northern Ireland reach £200,000–250,000 each year. Costs are also incurred by the Northern Ireland Housing Executive for cleanup of sites and nearby properties (£119,013 in 2003). The Police Service of Northern Ireland often must respond in support of the fire brigades and attend to public disturbances, activities that cost £206,623 in July 2002 alone. Overall, con-servative estimates of costs to taxpayers reach £1 million (Interagency Working Group on Bonfires 2006:3–5, 21).

In recent years, initiatives have been undertaken to organize bonfire events in ways that redress many common criticisms. Instead of building bonfires on empty, dilapidated lots, dedicated multipurpose sites have been proposed on which other activities can take place during the rest of the year. Some have suggested that organizers downsize bonfires to "beacons," maintaining their symbolic value but diminishing their environmental impact. The village of Stoneyford lit an elevated beacon and shot fireworks instead of a bonfire in 2007 (see figure 4.11). The Pitt Park bonfire in East Belfast featured a large fireworks display as well. In 2009, the Woodvale neighborhood on the western end of the Shankill Road erected, for its second year, an environmentally friendly beacon constructed of a large metal cage filled with carbon-renewable willow chips placed on top of sand. In an attempt to promote multiculturalism, organizers invited a Dublin historian to speak, and a

Figure 4.11 Beacon in Stoneyford Village. July 11, 2007. (Photo credit: missfitzphotos. Reproduced under the terms of a Creative Commons License 2.0).

Northern Ireland football team played a match with a team made up of international players. Five other neighborhoods in Belfast also lit similar beacons in 2009 (*Irish News,* July 8, 2009; *BBC News,* July 10, 2009; *Times,* July 11, 2009).

Some attempts have also been made to restrict the burning of nationalist symbols and ensure that bonfires are not used to propagate sectarian threats. Local community organizations are beginning to work more closely with local authorities in the fire and police services to plan and marshal parades, and activities leading up to bonfires have been developed to set a festive tone. Local community organizations hold block parties with music, historical reenactments, Ulster-Scots performances, food, and activities for children, such as, games, large inflatable recreations, and mini-parades. Local organizations train stewards to help police antisocial behavior, and curfews are established.

Unfortunately, these kinds of initiatives are not universal, and in Belfast, they represent only a small fraction of the eighty-six bonfires that were lit in the city in 2009 (*Irish News,* July 11, 2009; *Times,* July 11, 2009). Nationalist and Catholic symbols are still burned on many bonfires, and in one shocking case in 2007, the names of two recently deceased Catholics were placed on a bonfire in Coleraine alongside the question, "Who's next?" (*Belfast Telegraph,* July 12, 2007).

Regulating Flags and Emblems

One of the most prominent and controversial displays of unionist identity involves the erection of flags on public buildings and the hanging of flags and bunting, especially during the summer months, through towns, villages, and neighborhoods across Northern Ireland. The national flags of both the Republic of Ireland (the Irish Tricolour) and the United Kingdom (the Union Jack), as well as those of paramilitary and other organizations constitute clear and highly mobile symbols of political allegiances. Flags and emblems have been commonly used to mark territory and signal the legitimacy of activities (parades, policing, commemoration) and locations (public buildings, Orange halls, churches). Between partition and the institution of Direct Rule in 1972, the Union Jack was flown regularly on public buildings and not only on designated United Kingdom flag days but on popular Protestant holidays, such as, July 12. The 1922 Civil Authorities (Special Powers) Act and the 1954 Flags and Emblems (Display) Act ensured unionist control of symbols in public space, and in the latter case, it legislated a special exemption from restriction for the Union Jack (Bryan and Stevenson 2009:70–71).

The hanging of flags and emblems has accelerated since the cease-fires of the mid-1990s, especially in loyalist areas, as conflict moved from the martial to the symbolic realms. Loyalist paramilitary feuds also made flags an important means of marking out territory between the warring organizations (Bryan and McIntosh 2005; Bryan and Stevenson 2009:75–76). However, since the signing of the Belfast/Good Friday Agreement in 1998 and the establishment in 2005 of the *A Shared*

Future community relations policy, public agencies have gone to considerable lengths to address the contentious display of ethnic and national symbols, including flags. The PSNI has developed a protocol for monitoring and removing flags, which does not rely primarily on enforcement but on community-level consultations and efforts to persuade local organizations, especially paramilitary organizations, to abandon all paramilitary flags and ensure that flag flying is restricted to shorter periods of time around major celebrations (Bryan and Gillespie 2006:44–45; Bryan and Stevenson 2009:79).

Field surveys conducted between 2006 and 2008 by Dominic Bryan, Gordon Gillespie, Clifford Stevenson, and their researchers show that unionists and loyalists put up the majority of public displays of flags and emblems (compare 4,571 unionist displays in the lead-up to the Twelfth celebrations in 2008 versus 1,192 nationalist displays by the end of the summer following republican commemoration of the Hunger Strikes; Bryan and Gillespie 2005; Bryan and Stevenson 2006; Bryan, Stevenson, and Gillespie 2008:27, 2009). Over the course of 2006–2008, these researchers counted between four and fourteen times as many unionist displays as nationalist ones. The raw numbers of symbols on display has remained essentially unchanged, but they note some improvement in the removal of symbols between the first and second rounds of their surveys (53.7 percent removed by September in 2006; 65.8 percent in 2007, and 58.8 percent in 2008). However, this means that a significant number of flags remain on display, deteriorating in the weather (Bryan, Stevenson, and Gillespie 2007:70; Jarman 2007; Bryan, Stevenson, and Gillespie 2009:31).

The display of flags and emblems remains problematic in light of public opinion. Eighty-four percent of respondents to the 2008 Life and Times Survey (NILTS) reported that they do not support the flying of flags on lampposts in their own neighborhoods, and Bryan, Stevenson, and Gillespie's work demonstrates that although there seems to have been progress in the removal of flags, many remain (ARK 2008a). At the same time, however, the timely removal of flags has become one activity by which some loyalist organizations have endeavored to improve their public image. The results have proven limited so far, according to field surveys, but the adoption of flag policies constitutes an intentional attempt to modify a traditional display, similar to new mural designs and the downsizing of bonfires.

Both Loyalism in Transition and the Beyond Conflict Initiative, associated with the mainstream UDA and the Southeast Antrim brigade of the UDA, respectively, welcome a reduction in the number of flags, which they acknowledge has been perceived as a threat by some residents and businesses. According to its Web site, the Beyond Conflict plan proposes to consult with residents in estates to determine what flags might be acceptable and where they should be flown and notes some initiatives that have already been taken, such as, limiting flags to the entrance of estates or replacing flags with weather resistant vinyl bannerettes sponsored by local businesses. A similar protocol was adopted by the East Antrim Athletic and

Cultural Society to monitor flags and negotiate the development of "fixed sites" for flags and a code of conduct for bands' color parties.

Vinyl bannerettes featuring the Queen, William of Orange, the Northern Ireland flag, and the ninetieth anniversary of the Somme were first adopted in 2003 by the East Belfast Historical and Cultural Society with the intention of replacing flags with a display that could be supported by local businesses, would not become tattered, and could be reused in subsequent summers. On their Web site, the society says they chose "symbol(s) that no one can complain about," which probably refers to avoiding paramilitary symbols but also reminds us of the importance of context for the interpretation of symbols. Symbols that do not seem contentious among loyalists could still be considered contentious or even antagonistic by nationalists, even if they are arguably less contentious or intimidating than paramilitary symbols. Plus, if flags are being hung alongside vinyl bannerettes and if, in some areas (not necessarily East Belfast), bannerettes have been designed to incorporate paramilitary symbols, as Bryan, Stevenson, and Gillespie (2007) report, the overall effect is to undermine the mitigating programs that have been adopted (p. 69). Nonetheless, the adoption of banners was a genuine move during which EBHCS claims to have "spent many hours debating" how to institute the new practice.

Similarly, the Broadisland Gathering in Ballycarry developed a "Townland Banners" component to their annual Ulster-Scots festival, which the organizers hoped would reflect an Orange tradition of carrying banners but would also avoid provoking the contention that some neighbors might associate with Orange parades. One of the event's organizers associated their decision to create townland banners with other decisions to diminish perceptions of sectarianism:

> We wanted something to add to the pageantry, and banners have always been a part of our common community identity if you like. I mean, ever since I was a young boy, I remember the Orange Lodge and the Black Lodge and so on with the banners. So, we thought, "Well, we'll design a different type of banner, an entirely new banner," and so the townland banner idea was born. I mean, it's the only place in Ireland that we have townland banners, so it's very, very unique. But we consciously, you know, we didn't want to make it just an Orange event, and we've always been very careful of the components of the parade and so on. At one stage, you know, the local flute band wanted to take part in the parade, and we said, "Yes, that's OK, but you know you're going to have to play hymn tunes."

In both the East Belfast and Broadisland examples, modifying flags or banners to take on new forms was considered feasible by organizers (though not necessarily easy) and was intended to be innovative and less exclusive. These initiatives do not constitute root-and-branch reform, but they indicate reflection on the process of displaying ethnic and political identity and a capacity to reinvent traditional practices.

■ MITIGATION AND MURALS, BONFIRES, AND FLAGS

In Northern Ireland, absolutist phrases, such as, "not an inch" or "not one bullet" and Ian Paisley's famous refrain, "Never, never, never",[5] are familiar sound bites. One of the defining characteristics of intractable conflict is a widespread fear that loss by one side constitutes a gain by others, making compromises difficult to reach. Anything of value militarily, economically, culturally, or otherwise is carefully guarded, and in a climate of fear, a loss on any one front raises the value of resources on other fronts, causing them to be even more closely protected. If certain resources are difficult to relinquish, because it is feared that such compromises inevitably create a disadvantage, we might alternatively ask whether, instead of being abandoned, they can be modified to diminish the kind of intimidation that raises suspicion and breaks down trust across ethnic divides.

Liechty and Clegg (2001) refer to this process as "mitigation." They argue that beliefs and practices that threaten and intimidate out-groups can be modified so they are less likely to cause offense and feed destructive relations: "By mitigation we mean the capacity to lessen or eliminate possible negative outcomes of a belief, commitment, or action. What cannot be negotiated can sometimes be mitigated" (pp. 228–29). The authors focus on religious beliefs and the kinds of claims-making by which Protestants and Catholics have alienated and even dehumanized one another. In some cases, polarizing truth claims can be renegotiated if they are not central to a belief system.

According to Liechty and Clegg, Catholic doctrines sustained by documents such as, *Dominus Iesus* (1998), which asserts that the Catholic Church is the only fully Christian Church, and *One Bread One Body* (2000), which denies Protestants participation in the Eucharist, are so fundamental to many Catholics that they defy significant change. Similarly, anti-Catholic tenets among fundamentalist Protestants that view the Catholic Church in error (or worse) lie at the heart of Protestants' identification with the Reformation. The authors point to *The Qualifications of an Orangeman* and its call for Orangemen to "strenuously oppose the fatal errors of the Church of Rome, and . . . by all lawful means resist the ascendancy of that church, its encroachments and the extension of its power" to illustrate a fundamental component of anti-Catholicism at the core of one of the island's largest Protestant organizations (pp. 232–37).

Dogmatic separation from Catholics might, however, be mitigated by shifting attention to other biblical tenets, such as, the call to "love your enemies and pray for those who persecute you," which remains alienating but tempers the dogmatism and aggression of *The Qualifications*. Liechty and Clegg also offer a useful "Scale of Sectarian Danger" on which to gauge the negativity of any given truth claim, ranging from simple difference (we are different, we believe differently) to dehumanization and beyond (you are evil and demonic; p. 245). Conflict transformation requires that the distribution of exclusive components in opponents' worldviews moves toward the former end of the scale. One of the questions that dominates this book is whether the same principles of change apply to both physical and ritual expressions of identity and to the kind of discursive formations that occupy Liechty and Clegg's attention.

The folklorist, Jack Santino (2001), writes of the principle of "folk assemblage" by which symbols do not communicate in isolation but in interaction with one another. They supplement and provide context to one another. The locations on which bon-fires are built have a particular quality because they are marked out by graffiti and flags during the rest of the year. Orange parades past the site of an IRA bombing take on special significance among those participating and amplify the righteous-ness of their cause. Thus, the assembly of public displays (flags, curbstones, murals, graffiti, and parades) contributes to an overall effect for those "experiencing the culturescape of a place" (pp. 50, 57). Mitigation of public displays alters the cultur-escape. A decline in the density of flags, murals that reference local sports heroes instead of feuding paramilitaries, or a lack of Orange arches all interact with one another in altering the experience of the locale for both locals and visitors.

As with all symbolic and social processes, the interpretation of statements and actions through the lens of identity is crucial, and changes in identities constitute one of the pillars of conflict transformation. In the production and consumption of symbols, however, cultural schemata become modified. As contentious sym-bols proliferated during the violence of the Troubles, so the adoption of less-con-tentious symbols should accompany the ending of violence. Greater fluidity in public representations of ethnic and political identification indicates shifting per-ceptions and strategies among loyalists that can contribute to a process of conflict transformation.

The development of new mural themes that gravitate away from the negative end of the scale of sectarian danger represents the potential for movement away from dogmatic and defensive cultural expressions and the collective identities to which they are closely associated. This process of mitigating "public displays," as Santino calls them, changes expressions (textual or otherwise) in small but significant ways by substituting some meaningful components within the genre or tradition with others that impart new meaning. As Liechty and Clegg assert, "A consistent, if not quite constant, feature of mitigation is that it seeks to lessen destructive consequences arising from within a tradition by appealing to resources from that same tradition. The tradition works to heal the tradition" (p. 229). Thus, familiar expressions cue legitimacy and credibility in the minds of those who iden-tify with them, and like a Trojan horse that never leaves Greece, new ideas can be smuggled into group consciousness.

Murals are familiar to many loyalists and help maintain a sense of continuity and ontological security, as one community arts worker, Mary, explained:

> There's this drive to replace like with like, you know, so it's all the things that people have in them, all the understanding they have of culture and how they would connect that to

their own cultural activity and how their cultural identity is connected to cultural practice, you know? They haven't linked that yet, because they see it all as: "If you take down a mural, you put up a mural." And a mural's easy to do with young people, and it also reinforces that sense of being part of what went before when you're replacing a mural with a mural.

The familiarity of murals can be frustrating for some artists and arts workers who would like to introduce novel media, such as, sculpture and mosaics (e.g., Wheeler 2007), and it may only be a matter of time until those become incorporated, but to sustain community support, painted murals have remained the most common outdoor medium.

At the same time, however, in a process of mitigation, as Liechty and Clegg put it, "the tradition works to heal the tradition," and thus narratives with ontological credibility can support the modification of other practices and ideas that have otherwise taken on an almost sacred significance and are often seen as inviolable. Paul at the Ulster-Scots Agency illustrated this process when he argued that programs to downsize bonfires are more accurate reflections of historical tradition than the large intimidating bonfires that have become common.

> Children in Belfast and throughout Northern Ireland, they love to build a massive, massive, massive, massive big bonfire, but they don't really know why they are building it, or the significance of why they are building it. Now, if we can change the mind-set to get them to understand what is the significance of bonfire—now, bonfire is not an Ulster thing, it's a British thing. Simon Schama, a professor of history at Oxford University, done the history of the British peoples for the new millennium there for the BBC. If you go on the Web site on the Internet, you can chase it up. They done, I think it was twelve programs, but program seven was called "Burning Ambition,"[6] and in it, he said, at the time of the [Spanish] Armada, the British warned each other with bonfire and a beacon and when the Armada was defeated, they celebrated with bonfire and beacon. Again, at the time of the threat of Nelson, they celebrated Trafalgar with bonfire and beacon, and the victory of Waterloo, bonfire and beacon. Outside of the First World War, [they] celebrated with bonfire and beacon, the same for the Second World War. For the British, bonfire became the vocabulary of democracy and freedom. Now, those were his words, and it's the same thing in the time of William and the Glorious Revolution, celebrated by bonfire, and Guy Fawkes, celebrated by bonfire. Now, it's a very British thing, and to me this is a nonsense of what they are doing with these massive high bonfires. We need to get their children and that's why, in East Belfast, we had hoped to introduce into this festival little plays or lectures which can educate children from the age of five to eleven. This is what it's about. It's not about building a mountain; it's not about putting [up] another country's flag on something, it's about having a small thing just to remind you of the significance of what is really important that you should be remembering here.

From this perspective, bonfires are not abandoned, but in the process of transforming them into beacons, they are reconnected to loyalist identity while jettisoning the desecration of nationalist symbols. One North Belfast community worker interviewed in the *Irish News* described Tiger Bay's new 2009 beacon and alcohol-free celebration, "This is not about stripping away our loyalist culture. It's about embracing it and celebrating but in an inclusive, family-orientated way" (*Irish News*, May 23, 2009).

Similarly, Tim, a muralist from East Belfast, who has collaborated with nationalist muralists, told me that the introduction of new themes reflects a greater sense of possibility among loyalists that has accompanied the ending of violence, but, he claims, it does not signal an abandonment of loyalism.

> Yes, there will be a balance to be had, and that balance is now and only now achievable because of peace, because we are a post-conflict society, even though its only a relatively new post-conflict society, but now we can go about creating that balance [of older paramilitary themes and new themes], whereas before, when you were living in conflict, the opportunity wasn't there, nor was the want to go down that road by the larger part of the community where now we are sort of treading different waters, and that's all changing. I believe that, yes, there will be a balance had. I believe that, yes, we will still have gunmen, but possibly only on the murals that are commemorating the dead; I don't know that we will need them the way they are now, [where] pretty much every street corner needs a gunman. I think we are moving, and we have been moving, even before the formation of a government, we have been moving away from those types of murals into more cultural, more educational murals that are still political but maybe not just as political as the gunmen murals were. They have a more subtle nature, but they are still promoting loyalism; they are promoting unity with Britain. They are still doing the same thing, but as the old saying goes: there is more than one way to skin a cat.

As Tim describes it, the more "subtle" expression of loyalism in new murals is possible after the end of violence, but it is not likely to suddenly replace the insecurity, bravado, and intimidation that have characterized loyalist murals over the course of the Troubles. Instead, "cultural" murals continue to sustain a particular worldview but in ways that are based less on division and intimidation.

Public Opinion

Mitigating murals, bonfires, and flags has become increasingly common in loyalist communities and organizations, but how have these initiatives been received? To what extent do such changes in public expressions improve the environment for cross-community engagement from the perspective of those inside and outside of loyalism? Can the modification of cultural expressions shape opinion and facilitate the lowering of defenses by diminishing perceptions of hostility and danger, improving the social-psychological landscape across which relationships can be built?

The Northern Ireland Life and Times Survey (NILTS) offers some insight into public attitudes about loyalist public displays (ARK 2000–2008). This publicly available dataset includes two questions that have often been incorporated into the survey since 2000. The first question asks, "And has there been any time in the last year when you personally have felt annoyed by Loyalist murals, kerb paintings, or flags?" (variable LOYMUR2 available 2004–2008), and the second asks, "And has there been any time in the last year when you personally have felt intimidated by loyalist murals, kerb paintings, or flags?" (variable LOYMURAL available 2000, 2002–2008). These questions allow us to examine how attitudes have changed among Protestants, unionists, Catholics, and nationalists over recent years during which mitigating schemes have been undertaken.

Between 2004 and 2008, 32 percent of NILTS respondents who responded to the question have found loyalist murals, curbstones, and flags annoying. Twenty-one percent surveyed between 2000 and 2008 (with the exception of 2001, when the question was not asked) report feeling intimidated. Those identifying themselves as nationalists express slightly more frequent annoyance (35.5 percent) than unionists (31.3 percent; chi square test value 7.30, $p < .007$) though there is no difference between Catholics' and Protestants' feelings of annoyance. Catholics (24.5 percent) have felt somewhat more intimidated than Protestants (18.1 percent; chi square test value 63.73, $p < .01$) and nationalists (26.3 percent) report intimidation one and a half times as often as unionists (17.4 percent; chi square test value 83.67, $p < .01$). Incorporating questions from the survey that measure strength of political identity shows that the stronger one's nationalist identity, the more annoyed and intimidated one becomes; 67.3 percent of "fairly strong" or "very strong" nationalists report intimidation (chi square test value 9.27, $p < .01$) and 87.6 percent report annoyance (chi square test value 10.96, $p < .01$). Strength of unionists' identities introduces little additional information, with roughly one-third of all unionists expressing annoyance and approximately 20 percent expressing intimidation, perhaps because unionists are less likely than committed nationalists to feel targeted by loyalist paramilitary themes.

Interestingly, if we look at NILTS survey results over the years for which each question is available, we find that respondents identifying themselves as Protestants and Catholics and those identifying themselves as unionists and nationalists report similar patterns of attitudinal change.[7] With but a few exceptions, intimidation connected with loyalist murals, curbstones, and flags grew slowly but steadily between 2002 and 2005, a trend that parallels measures of annoyance between 2004 and 2005. Around 2005 and 2006, however, reports of annoyance declined among all Protestants, Catholics, unionists, and nationalists (see figure 4.12). Protestants' and unionists' feelings of intimidation declined more than those of Catholics, but by 2006, nationalists' levels of intimidation had essentially returned to their 2002 levels after fluctuation that at least resembled the attitudes of Protestants, Catholics, and unionists (see figure 4.13).

Given the growing interest in redesigned murals and new mural designs that began appearing in 2005, or only shortly before, one wonders whether the declining number of loyalist paramilitary murals encouraged participants in the Northern

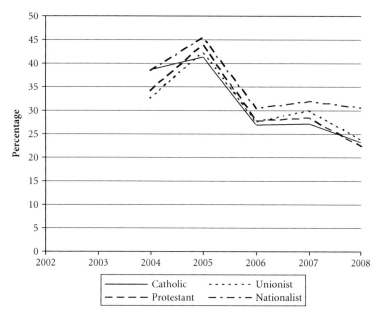

Figure 4.12 Reported Feelings of Annoyance by Loyalist Murals, Curb Painting, or Flags.

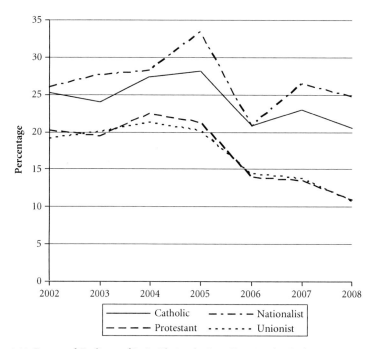

Figure 4.13 Reported Feelings of Intimidation by Loyalist Murals, Curb Painting, or Flags.

Ireland Life and Times Survey to report less annoyance and intimidation. Unionists report a similar decrease in annoyance and intimidation connected with republican murals, curb paintings, or flags. However, without a similar and corresponding analysis of republican murals, it is difficult to assess any associations with changing mural content in republican areas, and thus I will limit the scope of discussion here to attitudes regarding loyalist murals.

We should consider what else might account for declining annoyance and intimidation from 2006. Lower levels of intimidation by loyalist paramilitaries in general might encourage such responses, and 2006 saw considerably fewer political (or potentially political) deaths (four deaths) than 2005 (twelve deaths), and none of the 2006 deaths were conclusively linked to loyalist paramilitaries. However, deaths attributed to loyalist paramilitaries also declined in 2004 (to three from seven in 2003) without provoking declines in annoyance or intimidation among Catholics for that year (Melaugh 2009).[8] A more likely hypothesis holds that attitudes improved in the wake of multi-party talks at St. Andrews in October and the installment of a transitional assembly in November 2006 (while NILTS interviews were being conducted). However, the NILTS survey asked respondents about their experience of murals over the previous year, most of which passed *before* the talks. Plus, when respondents in the 2006 NILTS survey were asked how they would vote in a referendum on the St. Andrews Agreement, between 67 percent and 77 percent in each category (would vote yes; would vote no; wouldn't vote; don't know) said they were not annoyed by loyalist murals. Expecting to vote yes in such a referendum corresponded with a slightly *higher* rate of feeling annoyed by loyalist murals, curbstones, and flags. The results are similar regarding feelings of intimidation. Attitudes about the St. Andrews Agreement would not then seem to account for the post-2005 declines in intimidation and annoyance.

If we look at the distribution of annoyance and intimidation across class (measured by type of occupation),[9] we find that the higher respondents' occupational classifications the more intimidated and the more annoyed they feel. Those who have never worked and the long-term unemployed prove the exception, with slightly higher levels of annoyance and intimidation than those in routine and semi-routine occupations. We also find interesting longitudinal trends. All classes were equally annoyed over loyalist murals in 2005 (between 42 percent and 46 percent reporting annoyance), but after 2005, all classes (except for the higher professional classes, which follow suit one year later) become less annoyed and do so in such a way that the lower one's class, the more quickly one becomes less annoyed (see figure 4.14). Perhaps changes in mural content are recognized as more significant among lower-class respondents, who are more likely to reside in areas where murals exist. The same is true for intimidation, with the exception that the trend for higher professionals strangely does not last, and they report being as intimidated in 2007 as in 2003, despite expressing less annoyance.

Among nationalists, a trend of diminishing annoyance appears to be in effect, though attitudes across class fluctuate enough to diminish the predictive utility of

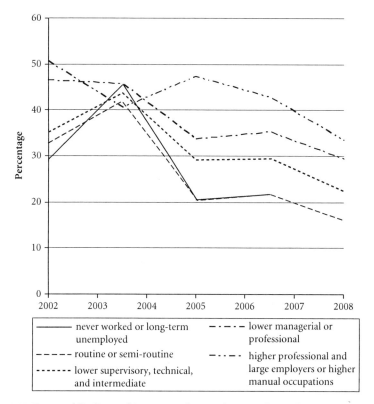

Figure 4.14 Reported Feelings of Annoyance by Loyalist Murals, Curb Painting, or Flags by Occupational Class.

class occupational background. While class has little impact on nationalists' attitudes about loyalist murals, for unionists, the lower one's class, the more steadily and deeply one's annoyance or intimidation over loyalist murals declines after 2005 (see figure 4.15). This is the case with one exception: rates of intimidation reported by higher professionals plummet in 2008 to match those of routine and lower supervisory respondents. Perhaps, by 2008, they had become more aware of changing themes in working-class areas, enough to catch up with the attitudes of the lower occupational classes.

The overall impact of class among unionists, in comparison with nationalists, may suggest that lower classes, who report declining feelings of intimidation, are more likely to live in areas where loyalist murals exist and were exposed to shifting mural content around 2005. The exact influence on attitudes of mural redesign and removal is difficult to disentangle given the wording of the relevant survey questions and lacking a comparative content analysis of republican murals, but the survey evidence reveals a compelling confluence of change in mural themes and changing public perceptions of murals.

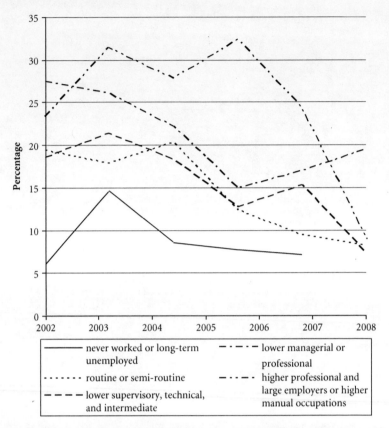

Figure 4.15 Reported Feelings of Intimidation by Loyalist Murals, Curb Painting or Flags among Unionists by Occupational Class.

Official Reimaging and Bonfires

While many of the initiatives presented in this chapter have been developed and executed by grassroots unionist and loyalist organizations, mitigation has been adopted by government officials who believe that improving the symbolic landscape can improve community relations. The *A Shared Future* (2005) community relations policy document includes a section titled "Tackle the Visible Manifestations of Sectarianism and Racism" (section 2.1, p. 19) and envisions a future without *any* flags, bunting, graffiti, or "paint" on public property, reserving the right to unilaterally remove such displays from roadways (section 2.2.3, p. 22). The document prioritizes community involvement alongside government agencies and thus implies room for negotiation and space for local organizations to develop their own plans for mitigating public displays. The policy recognizes that public displays represent attitudes and beliefs that are genuinely held by a significant number of people whose interpretations of their own communities are bound to a historical and political context (Santino 2001:17; Bryan and Gillespie 2005:35, 2006:43). Like the architects of *A Shared Future,* Santino (2001) appreciates the extent to which ethnic displays are embedded in sophisticated cultures:

> Some people suggest doing away with the bonfires legislatively, as if this would erase the sectarianism they are used to express. But as I have tried to demonstrate, the appeal of the large outdoor fires is as broad as it is deep. They are not only about sectarianism and political identity, though these dimensions are very much there. They are also about bonding with friends, about self-esteem, about family and neighborhood and even season. To legislate against the bonfires would cause deep resentment; to do away with them, even if possible, would be to do away with all of this. (p. 24)

The Interagency Working Group on Bonfires (2006) adopts a similar position, calling for close coordination between community representatives and statutory agencies (section 6.1, p. 24).

Developing relationships between community organizations and statutory agencies can prove challenging, however, as many unionists have feared that one side effect of the political dispensation would be the elimination of bonfires (Byrne and Wilson 2007:43). Nevertheless, a number of funding schemes and public works projects have been established to encourage and facilitate the mitigation of contentious public displays through partnerships with community organizations. Initiatives include the Police Service of Northern Ireland's flags protocol, which incorporates the Department of the Environment, Department for Regional Development, Department for Social Development, Office of the First Minister and Deputy First Minister, and the Northern Ireland Housing Executive (Bryan and Gillespie 2006:49). The Arts Council launched its £3.3m Re-imaging Communities program in 2006 to place "artists in the heart of communities to work with local people to tackle visible signs of sectarianism and racism to create a more welcoming environment for everyone." The council aimed to complete 60–80 projects and actually funded 109 (2005a). Similar work to "address the physical manifestation of contested space" through environmental improvements has been undertaken through the Creating Common Ground consortium, which includes the nonprofit organization Groundwork Northern Ireland and the Housing Executive (A Shared Future 2005b:34).

District councils have increasingly launched their own initiatives to mitigate ethnic and political displays. Coleraine District Council, inspired by the work of the Ballysally Community Association's management of their bonfire, undertook an Equality Impact Assessment beginning in 2001, and by 2003 had produced a Code of Practice based on "the rights of vulnerable people and people of other traditions and circumstances to feel safer at or near bonfires" (Coleraine Borough Council 2003: section 6.3, p. 12). By 2006, ten councils had produced codes or informative leaflets to advise the public on how to improve bonfires. Ballymena Borough Council established a "Best Bonfire Site Competition" and Down District

Council formed a Bonfire Liaison Committee in partnership with its Community Safety Partnership, a multi-agency coalition of community, voluntary, and statutory organizations (Interagency Working Group on Bonfires 2006:9,18; Byrne and Wilson 2007:39).

Belfast City Council initiated pilot schemes in 2005 at eight bonfire sites where organizers agreed to a set of principles (regarding collection, materials, sectarian displays, cultural awareness, and community involvement) and received £1,500 for event planning. Eleven unionist communities and one nationalist community participated in the program in 2006 (Byrne and Wilson 2007:40–42). The council launched its £90,000 Bonfire Management Program in 2007, collaborating with the Housing Executive, Community Relations Council, the Community Relations Unit of the Office of First Minister and Deputy First Minister, and the council's Community Safety Partnership (Belfast City Council Community and Recreation Committee minutes, October 18, 2005; *BBC News* July 12, 2006; Byrne 2008). By 2008, the council had sponsored improvements at fourteen bonfire sites, and in 2009 had placed beacons filled with willow wood-chips at six sites. An evaluation of the scheme conducted by the Institute for Conflict Research "concluded that it has significantly improved the environmental and cultural aspects of bonfires within the city." The group reported increases in "family and festival events that surrounded the bonfires" and significant declines in police- and fire-related incidents at the sites sponsored by the council. "Overall the Bonfire Management Programme is making a considerable difference to ways communities celebrate the Eleventh. They are becoming more empowered and confident in the processes, and are beginning to explore the cultural significance of bonfires within a more historical framework. No longer are they synonymous with paramilitary shows of strength, instead they are being transformed into festival events that are much more than just about the bonfire" (Byrne 2008:12).

■ CONCLUSION

The mitigation of intimidating or polarizing cultural expressions is a modest but important contribution to improved community relations. Changing the content of public displays alters the symbolic landscape and the character of one arena of public discourse. The changes are material but, more important, they are cultural and psychological. Gareth, the community worker in Portadown, highlighted the psychological impact of removing paramilitary displays:

> The area around interface management is one that I see as crucial. In terms of that interface, the interface isn't essentially that physical impediment. It's up here [taps his forehead]. Now, how we approach issues is about saying, "Right, there are issues here within our community." How do we do things that allow this community to live with this [situation] and work toward its removal as opposed to [saying,] "They're a pack of

Fenian this or whatever," and how we have been able to do that is by softening that whole interface. The removal of paramilitary displays significantly softens the area.

From this perspective, the process of mitigating intimidating public displays can contribute to the process of breaking down deep psychological barriers, both within loyalist communities and with regard to cross-community relations.

That said, we need not be naïve and trumpet mural replacement and redesign as the primary catalysts of change in loyalist paramilitaries or other loyalist organizations. Jim Wilson, a local loyalist community activist interviewed by the BBC in 2003, acknowledged, "There's only so far you can go in asking people to remove murals, you cannot wipe away history and you cannot wipe away what has happened in this country in the last thirty-five years just by taking murals down" ("Catholic Face," BBC 2003). Paramilitary murals are still commissioned, and paramilitary leaders are careful not to appear as if they are selling out their organizations, and they will be wary of removing murals without reciprocation among rival paramilitary organizations ("Old Masters Change Murals," BBC 2005). This is, not surprisingly, a contentious and conflicted process. Mitigating murals is part of a process of conflict transformation, not merely the development of "non contentious artwork" as Belfast City Council describes its Art for Arterial Routes program (Wheeler 2007:58).

A subtle and incremental softening of in-group and out-group boundaries is desirable, but in the long run, cosmetic change without cross-community engagement and new attitudes runs the risk of glossing over the division and trauma of decades of sectarian violence. For now, mural redesign initiatives do not often constitute cross-community work, though some muralists have developed collaborations across the communal divide (*Belfast Telegraph*, June 8, 2007). A recent replacement of a particularly offensive mural in the staunchly loyalist Tullycarnet estate commemorates the bravery of a Catholic man from the Falls Road, who was the only person from Northern Ireland to receive the Victoria Cross for bravery during World War II. According to a resident of Tullycarnet, whom I interviewed,

> We brought Catholics from Dublin and Donegal and all over, into Tullycarnet Estate, who had never been before. And they marched up the middle of the road with an Orange flute band, with a military band, and everybody just walked up the middle of the road around to the community center where we all had a knees-up after it, and it was fantastic. So there's an educational side, there's a capacity-building side, there's a confidence-building side, and there's a dealing-with-the-past side, and there's this thing: Do you learn anything from it not to make the same mistakes in the future?[10]

The development of a new inclusive narrative reveals at least a potential for community workers and former combatants in Northern Ireland to introduce symbols and narratives that subvert old psychological and emotional barriers and facilitate cross-community engagement. Note in this case, however, that Catholics who participated in the Tullycarnet event traveled from the Republic of Ireland

and would not necessarily have harbored the same suspicions as Catholics in Northern Ireland.

In order for mitigation of public displays to contribute to the transformation of conflict and improve the prospects of reconciliation, it must lower thresholds for contact, engagement, and dialogue among nationalists and unionists in Northern Ireland, even if it does not erase them. A council worker in Derry/Londonderry was enthusiastic about the Re-imaging Communities program, but she echoed concerns about ethnic divisions that have often dogged cultural traditions work.

> A conversation that we had earlier in the year [about reimaging projects] was this demarcation of space, and it's still territorial. It's just not as aggressive. You know, so it's still about keeping the separateness and the identity. And even within, say, Derry City Council's corporate plan, one of the development elements on it is that people can say that their culture has been protected rather than that their culture has been broadened. So, can you retain your culture while still broadening it?

This community worker felt that mitigation projects have been successful, and responses from the Northern Ireland Life and Times Survey suggest that they may have begun to impact levels of annoyance and intimidation that would otherwise diminish the prospects of cross-community engagement and cooperation. Mitigation's long-term value lies in the opportunity for in-groups to experience and internalize less reactionary and defensive orientations toward out-groups, to challenge stereotypes, and to remove rationales for maintaining division. However, the ratio of attention paid to protecting exclusive identities and to transforming them will have to be maintained at a level that opens opportunities for greater cross-community engagement.

For the moment, across the political divide, nationalists and unionists are skeptical of mitigation projects. SDLP politician Alban Maginness responded with incredulity to the Reimaging Communities Programme when it was announced by Minister David Hanson of the Northern Ireland Office (NIO) in July 2006, "It is clear that any paramilitary murals designed to intimidate or mark out territory should be removed. . . . Indeed their very existence is illegal. That is why today's announcement really beggars belief" (2006).

Maginnis was objecting to the injection of funds for removing loyalist paramilitary murals, which from his perspective, should simply be eradicated as a social ill. One can certainly understand his argument, and the SDLP, a nationalist party without links to paramilitaries, is in a strong position to offer such criticism. However, imposing policy with regard to symbolic displays risks alienating the very sectors of Northern Irish society most in need of transformation. Whether mural redesign projects serve as a convincing and effective tool of identity and attitude change in loyalist communities and further diminish intimidation and annoyance among nationalists remains to be seen, though there is evidence that progress is being made.

■ ACKNOWLEDGMENT

Parts of this chapter originally appeared in Smithey, Lee A. 2009. "Conflict Transformation, Cultural Innovation, and Loyalist Identity in Northern Ireland." In *Culture and Belonging in Divided Societies: Contestation and Symbolic Landscapes*, edited by M. Ross, pp. 85–106. Philadelphia: University of Pennsylvania Press, 2009.

Appendix 4.1
This appendix describes prominent loyalist mural themes that were identified during field research.

Bands: Bands murals display the crests, emblems, and mascots of local flute and blood-and-thunder bands, sometimes making overt connections with local paramilitary units, usually with the UVF. Some may allude to paramilitary connections through reference to the UVF and the 36th Ulster Division of World War I.

Battle of the Boyne: The Battle of the Boyne has historically been one of the most common themes for loyalist murals, usually featuring King William of Orange atop his horse. These murals have diminished since the 1970s (Rolston 1987:13; Loftus 1994).

British: Many murals display British flags, but the murals in this category celebrate Britishness by commemorating members of the royal family or by mythological references to the Roman goddess Britannia.

Local: Local themes refer to a local person, event, or organization.

Entertainment: Entertainment themes refer to popular forms of entertainment or entertainers, such as, the film adaptation of C. S. Lewis's *Chronicles of Narnia*, or the recording artist, Van Morrison.

Historical: Historical themes present events and individuals considered to have historical importance.

Industrial: Industrial themes celebrate local industry, such as, the East Belfast shipyards and aircraft factory, but they may reflect a Protestant identification with work and manufacturing.

Memorial: Memorial murals commemorate the lives of people who have died, often victims or members of paramilitary organizations.

Mythology: Mythology is much more likely to appear in nationalist murals, but some loyalist murals draw on Irish, Scottish, and Roman mythologies.

Loyal institutions: Loyal Institution murals referred to the organizations themselves, usually the Orange Order (not including the Battle of the Boyne).

Paramilitary: Paramilitary themes are the most common and, in these cases, make specific reference to contemporary paramilitary organizations. The line between many historical murals that refer to the UVF of the early twentieth century and contemporary paramilitary murals can be thin, but this category was reserved for present-day paramilitaries.

Peace: Peace themes include the word "peace," the symbol for peace, or peaceful images, such as, a view of the Earth from space.

Political: Political themes express political grievances or directly reference institutional politics, such as, Stormont, the peace process, or loyalist political parties (PUP or UDP).

Religious: Religious themes can be apolitical or evangelical, referring to Jesus or God, or they can appropriate scripture or historical events, such as, Martin Luther's initiation of the Protestant reformation.

Security Forces: Security Forces murals honor and commemorate the service of police and military personnel.

Social: Social themes usually address social problems and issues, including mental health, employment, housing, education, and alcohol and drug abuse.

Sports: Sports murals often celebrate the achievements of a local sports hero, such as, George Best. Others support particular football or rugby teams.

United States: Several loyalist murals depict U.S. history and often celebrate U.S. presidents with Scots-Irish ancestry.

Victims: Victims murals mourn the deaths of victims of Republican violence or in one case promoted victim-offender mediation. Victims murals with religious themes hold the Catholic Church responsible for seventeenth-century conflict during the British plantation of Ireland.

Youth: Murals with youth themes are prodigious and are usually apolitical, often located on the walls of community centers. They may use stylized graffiti and popular cartoon figures and feature favorite pastimes, such as, skateboarding and football.

■ Notes

1. Historical murals can also express sectarianism and militancy depending on their content. Images of vintage weapons and violence, such as, in the context of Cromwell's seventeenth-century campaign to pacify Ireland, can alienate and intimidate Irish Catholics.

2. Jarman (1997) focuses on several themes that also appear in this analysis: paramilitary, Orange/Billy, local identity, bands, honoring the dead/Somme/fallen comrades (p. 215). Sluka (1992) identifies two dominant themes: traditional (which includes King William, flags, the crown, and phrases such as, "No Surrender" and "Remember 1690") and paramilitary (p. 210). Bryan and Stevenson's (2006) Flags Monitoring Project also adopted similar overlapping themes: national, regional, paramilitary, sport, commemorative, Loyal Order, and political party/statement (p. 22). Photographs were coded for their most prominent themes.

3. Photographs taken in 2008 have been incorporated with those taken in 2007 as 95 percent of them were taken within the first week of 2008.

4. The results for a subsample of murals only in East Belfast and the Shankill Road, where the largest numbers of pictures were taken, reveal the same trend we find in the overall collection, suggesting that using the larger sample of photographs does not overly skew the results. It should be noted, however, that the net difference in percentage frequencies (2005–2007) between antagonizing and less-antagonizing themes in East Belfast and the Shankill was attenuated to one-third of the magnitude of the difference in the larger collection. This may reflect some sampling bias outside of these two neighborhoods or could be interpreted as evidence that easily accessible murals in areas outside of East Belfast and the Shankill are more likely to incorporate less-contentious themes.

5. At an "Ulster Says No" rally at Belfast's City Hall in November 1985, Paisley condemned the Republic of Ireland for allegedly harboring IRA operatives. He struck out at Margaret Thatcher and the Anglo- Irish Agreement for allowing Dublin greater input in the affairs of Northern Ireland, bellowing, "We say, never, never, never, never!"

6. Episode Six of *A History of Britain* was titled "Burning Convictions."

7. For example, nationalist feelings of annoyance, like unionists', grew in 2004 and 2005 and declined substantially afterward. However, reports of intimidation fluctuate enough between 2000 and 2008 to undermine their significance over time.

8. Melaugh warns that his figures (http://cain.ulst.ac.uk/issues/violence/deaths.htm) are intended to extend Sutton's Index of Deaths (1969–2001; http://cain.ulst.ac.uk/sutton/) and that they should be treated with caution as they may change as further information comes to light.

9. The Northern Ireland Life and Times Survey provides variables addressing class that are based on the Registrar General's Standard Classification of Occupations. Due to small cell sizes, some complementary and adjacent categories were merged when they contained similar reported attitudes on the issues in question. The resulting categories are as follows:

- never worked or long-term unemployed
- routine occupations or semi-routine occupations
- lower supervisory or technical occupations and small employers or own account workers and intermediate occupations
- lower managerial or professional occupations
- higher professional occupations and large employers or higher manual occupations

10. See also "Catholic Face," BBC, 2003.

5 The Orange Order: Mitigating Parades, Public Relations, and Identity Change

We focused in the last chapter on murals, static yet, rich representations of identity, but it is important to remember that redesign and reconceptualization are the practices through which individuals and groups experiment with new ideas and reconcile old cultural schemata with new ones. It is not surprising then that elaborate ritual practices also serve as vehicles for identity change. Parades in Northern Ireland offer the *rituel* par excellence among Protestant unionists and loyalists. Examining modification of parades by their most prominent practitioners, the Orange Order, the largest nonchurch voluntary organization in Northern Ireland,[1] provides an opportunity to follow further the potentially transformative relationship between collective identity and collective action. It also allows us to focus on one organization that has intentionally set about the contentious process of reframing itself in ways that are less defensive, more proactive, and more discursive. Parading has played a central role in the process. Toward the end of the chapter, we will broaden our scope and address identity change in more detail, expanding on some of the best work on the topic with a typology of modes of identity change as they relate to changes in practices.

■ ORANGE ORDER PARADES

The term "loyal institutions" refers to the collection of primarily male Protestant fraternal organizations in Ireland that have served to tie Protestantism to British nationality. They include the Orange Order, the Royal Black Institution, the Royal Arch Purple, the Apprentice Boys of Derry, and affiliated women's and youth organizations. The Orange Order is the most prominent, though it has ties with the Royal Black Preceptory and the Royal Arch Purple.

The Orange Order is perhaps best known for its parades, especially those held each year on July 12, which ritually celebrate the victory of the Protestant King William of Orange over the Catholic King James II at the Battle of the Boyne, symbolizing and reinscribing a Protestant myth of the salvation of Ireland. Parades link historic Reformation struggles and the emergence of modern European liberalism with the settlement of Ireland in a contemporary demonstration of Protestant unity. They have always been closely associated with Protestant political ascendancy. However, since the mid-1980s, and especially since 1995, they have become especially contentious, constituting a primary site at which nationalists and unionists have clashed, sometimes violently.

Loyal institution parades follow an annual cycle that includes, most prominently, the Orange Order's July Twelfth celebrations, the Royal Black Preceptory parades in August, and the August and December commemorations of the 1688–1689 Siege of Derry by the Apprentice Boys of Derry.[2] Over the weeks leading up to the Twelfth, arches, which display a range of biblical and other symbols holding special meaning in the rites of the Orange lodges, have traditionally been erected over main streets in Protestant areas, though they are less common today.[3] On the morning of July 12, lodges march in "feeder" parades through their own towns before boarding buses to attend much larger parades featuring the district lodges and their bands. Lodges rotate responsibility for hosting the main district event in their towns. The Belfast Twelfth, organized by the Belfast county lodge, differs in that lodge members walk from their prospective neighborhoods to Shaftesbury Square in the city center where they join up before proceeding to a field in Edenderry, or in recent years, to Barnett Demesne on the southern outskirts of the city (see figure 5.1).

Twelfth parades are colorful affairs, with Orangemen wearing shirts, coats, and ties, and Orange collarettes (sashes). Many don bowler hats and white gloves, and carry umbrellas. An elaborate banner carried between two staffs precedes each lodge. Banners often depict King William of Orange, deceased lodge members, popular unionist politicians, or biblical themes (Loftus 1994; Edwards 1999).

Figure 5.1 Orangemen on parade. July 12, 2009.

In rural areas, ornately decorated large "lambeg" drums that resemble enormous bass marching drums may be proudly played and displayed, though they are rarely carried in the parades. Lodges are often accompanied by their own affiliated and uniformed pipe, accordion, and fife bands playing traditional tunes or hymns. Families and friends line the sides of the street to catch a glimpse and a wave from their fathers, brothers, husbands, or friends. Vendors along the way hawk food and red, white, and blue Union Jack paraphernalia.

After all the bands have processed through the town, a rally is usually held in a nearby field. Vendors sell food, a stage is set up (usually a parked open lorry bed) from which speeches are made, and hymns are sung. Official resolutions on faith, loyalty, and the state are read, usually to a small crowd of Orangemen and supporters who gather at the stage while most rest, eat, and socialize. In a field in Dundrum, County Down, in 1992, I watched for my first time as the crowd was led in prayers, scripture reading, an address, and the singing of two hymns: "Onward! Christian Soldiers" and "O God, Our Help in Ages Past." Three resolutions affirmed the Orangemen's "devotion and loyalty to the Throne and Person of Her Most Gracious Majesty Queen Elizabeth II, Queen of the United Kingdom of Great Britain and Northern Ireland and Her other Realms, Defender of the Faith"; condemned false "teachers and preachers of a gospel which is not the gospel of Jesus Christ, the Church and the Bible"; and criticized the 1985 Anglo-Irish Agreement while condemning "the gunmen and their godfathers" and "encouraging" the police and security forces in their work. The format of the platform proceedings has changed little if at all over the course of the intervening eighteen years. After the platform exercises, the lodges and bands conduct "return" parades to their local Orange halls as they arrive back in their own towns, or neighborhoods in the case of Belfast.

Loyal institution parades are social events that give local Protestant communities an opportunity to come together to renew relationships and express a shared sense of identity. Most Twelfth celebrations are peaceful community affairs, especially in rural areas, and they exemplify a ritual practice that is filled with rich emotional meaning for many Protestants. David, a Methodist minister in East Belfast, described the way in which parades tap deeply into shared experience and emotion:

> I think the whole parades thing is so important to working class loyalism to a degree that most people don't understand…it's not just about marching. It's about family. There's a nostalgia that my father and my great-grandfather did this. It's hitting people at so many different levels. People just say, "Oh, it's a sectarian parade," but to many people actually it's not. There's a family link, there's an emotional [aspect], there's a physical [aspect], there's a spiritual [aspect], there's a mental [aspect]. It's hitting all those different buttons within people's lives. I guess unless you work in these areas [it is difficult to] understand it.

Even for those bystanders who do not participate directly, parades can still evoke feelings of shared identity, as a sense of natural continuity is cultivated.

Yet, the Orange Order has been undergoing considerable change in recent years. The organization has been under pressure from nationalists and the state regarding parades. Internally, the Order has suffered from declining numbers and rancorous debate over the core mission and principles of the institution. Much of the debate has centered on efforts to orient the Orange Order more fully toward a role as steward of Protestant cultural heritage. Currently, Grand Lodge leaders plan for the Orange Order to take up a prominent place in the civic unionism that Porter (1996) envisions (see chapter 3). Having lost its formal links with the Ulster Unionist Party in 2005, the Order is to become more community-oriented, trading on its long history and Protestant religious and ethnic identity.

Reforming its public activities has been at the top of the new agenda, though the Order's membership is divided over the necessity or wisdom of reframing the institution (Tonge, Evans, Jeffery, and McAuley forthcoming). Opening Orange halls for greater use, counteracting the image of parades as sectarian and sometimes dangerous affairs, engaging the media more effectively, and developing public, cultural, and historical events have all figured prominently. In the process, rituals long perceived as nonnegotiable have become open for modification, representing shifting priorities within the organization and testing new ideological ground.

■ PARADES, POLITICS, AND CONFLICT

For Orangemen, Twelfth parades have been one of their only public expressions of collective identity. For many Protestants, even those outside of the Orange Order, annual Twelfth parades serve an important unifying function as participants socialize, celebrate, and rehearse basic narratives of exceptionalism and ethnicity. Some nationalist residents find the parades benign, but others consider them annoying, triumphalist, and offensive. For many nationalists, the symbolism and frequency of loyal institution and band parades are disempowering reminders of inequality and discrimination under British and unionist rule (Irish Parades Emergency Committee & Brehon Law Society 2004–2008; Mulholland 1999). Orangemen feel equally strongly that parades constitute a civic right of public expression, which cannot be trammeled without violating fundamental principles of democracy and justice. Consequently, Orangemen have found it difficult to compromise on the scheduling, routing, and frequency of parades. As with most unionists, they believe that concessions merely portend an irreversible erosion of their position within the union.

Parades have thus become an important locus of antagonism, especially when organizations, such as, the Orange Order and the Royal Black Preceptory, parade through or near primarily nationalist neighborhoods.[4] With the beginning of the Troubles, loyal parades became contentious as violence tended to heighten ethnic territorial boundaries, which parade routes sometimes crossed (Bryan 2000:95). In some cases, the demographic growth of the Catholic population and the spread of Catholic districts has created mismatches between Orange parade routes and the political dispositions of residents (Kaufmann 2007:151). Increasingly, residents' committees have been established in towns and neighborhoods to contest the right of Protestant organizations, especially the Orange Order, to walk through nationalist areas (Edwards 1999:285–90; see figure 5.2). Under these circumstances, parades can operate as a microcosm of broader political struggles, symbolically recreating a history of division between Protestants and Catholics (Byrne 1995; Jarman 1997; Jarman and Bryan 1998).

Loyalist parades have predominated for both cultural and political reasons (Jarman and Bryan 1998). Functionally, they "perform memory" (Jarman 1997), but also, with Northern Ireland under local unionist control for most of the twentieth century, loyalists have been at greater liberty to exercise that function and to restrict nationalist parades. Yet, only a small minority of the parades that take place annually are considered a threat to civic order by the police service or the Parades Commission, which regulates parades and mediates parading disputes. According to police statistics, only 9 to 114 parades were rerouted each year between 1985 and 2007 while 1,731 to 2,694 parades took place (see figure 5.3). By 2007, according to statistics from the Parades Commission for Northern Ireland, 267 of 3,911 were considered contentious, and restrictions were placed on 58 percent of contentious parades (Parades Commission for Northern Ireland 2007:6).

Figure 5.2 PSNI Security at the Whiterock Parade. Belfast. June 24, 2006.

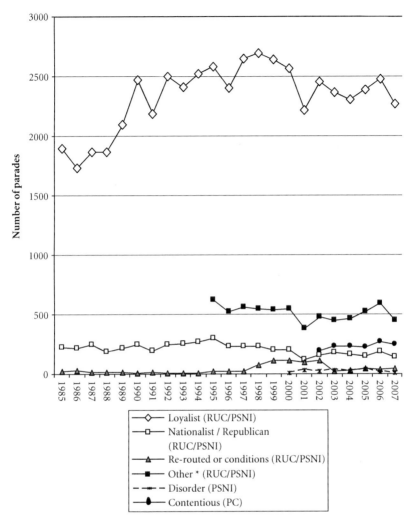

Figure 5.3 Frequency of Parades, 1985–2007.

Despite the small numbers of contested parades, a few loyalist parades that attract a great deal of attention have been prone to escalation and physical confrontation and thus have tended to define the struggle over parading issues. These hot spots include the Orange Order's annual parades and protest marches in Portadown, the Apprentice Boys' "Relief of Derry" parade in Derry/Londonderry, and loyalist parades on the Ormeau and Springfield Roads in Belfast as well as parades in towns such as, Bellaghy, Dunloy, Keady, Newry, and Pomeroy (Hughes 1998; Kaufmann 2007:152).

From one perspective, against the backdrop of the Troubles, parades have provided a *less* violent arena for ethnopolitical contention. Jarman and Bryan

(1996) describe the role that parades have played as part of a larger transformation away from martial violence and toward constitutional politics.

> In the past, parades have often served as a surrogate for low level warfare, and with the arrival of the cease-fires in 1994, the issue of parades became a prominent and highly visible means of displaying and mobilising behind traditional political demands in an alternative site of conflict. (p. 41)

While symbolically charged, parades are not often physically violent.

At the same time, although both loyalist and nationalist parading is in some sense technically nonviolent, it is also tied to coercion and intimidation. The symbols displayed in parades often recall coercive events that have been perpetrated by one community over another, such as, the Battle of the Boyne and Bloody Sunday. Orange parades in the late 1700s opposed the United Irishmen movement while nationalist parades around the turn of the twentieth century promoted Home Rule, devolution of power from Westminster in London. Parades are thus symbolic statements about the very issues that have motivated violence in Ireland.

Parades featured prominently from the start of the Troubles in connection with the growing tension around the civil rights movement of the late 1960s. Civil rights activists planned marches that raised questions of parity with loyal institution marches that had been routinely accepted by the state. However, they often ended in violent clashes with police and loyalists, and the Apprentice Boys' parade of August 12, 1969, which instigated the Battle of the Bogside between Catholic residents, security forces, and loyalists in Derry/Londonderry, is considered by many to mark the point of no return for the Troubles. In the years leading up to the Catholic civil rights movement and amid growing economic problems within Northern Ireland, relations between the British government and Northern Ireland's unionists and loyalists became increasingly strained, while fissures also developed within unionism (Bryan 2000:87; Fraser 2000). With the imposition of Direct Rule in 1972, Protestants no longer enjoyed the same relationship with the state that had prevailed under the Stormont regime. British ministers were far less familiar with the Orange Order and were primarily interested in security policy, and as parades were becoming sites of contention, restrictions were increasingly put in place by the RUC (Bryan 2000:82–96). As physical force republicanism, in the form of the Provisional IRA, came to replace the nonviolent civil rights movement within nationalist politics, a corresponding radicalization occurred within the Protestant community with the emergence of loyalist paramilitaries.

Parading reflected the trend as working-class loyalist parades took on a more aggressive tone in the form of "blood and thunder" or "kick the pope" bands that featured swaggering bass drums and sectarian tunes. Orange parades developed an increasingly rough character. They became known for public drunkenness, especially among the "blue-bag brigade," young people who support bands.[6] Loyalist Blood and Thunder flute bands playing loud sectarian tunes became more prominent, and connections with loyalist paramilitary organizations have consistently raised alarm among nationalists and moderate unionists (Bryan 2000:87, 96; Fraser 2000; Jarman 2000; Kennaway 2006:72–73).[7] Besides the ritual sermons, speeches, prayers, and resolutions, other activities in the "field" at the end of the outward parade can include public drunkenness, urination, and commerce in sectarian souvenirs, though news outlets have tended to sanitize many of these aspects (Bryan 2000:147–51, 63–68). Enormous amounts of litter are left behind the parade in Belfast, especially around Shaftesbury Square. In short, even though tens of thousands attend the Twelfth, Orange parades suffered in the court of public opinion as they became less respectable and more reactionary and coarse.

Parades have long operated within the context of political contention, often as a means of resistance. Excellent historical work has documented loyal parades and the ways they have been used to celebrate and show support for British rule while also celebrating and defending Ulster Protestantism apart from and often against British governmental policies in Ireland (Bryan, Fraser, and Dunn 1995; Jarman and Bryan 1996; Jarman 1997; Haddick-Flynn 1999; Bryan 2000; Fraser 2000; Ryder and Kearney 2001; Bryan 2004). For over two hundred years, Orangeism has often been both an "embarrassment" and a necessary ally for liberalizing British governments attempting to maintain some form of stable control in Ireland while under pressure from Irish nationalists (Loughlin 2000:27; Ryder and Kearney 2001:8–9).

Historically, parading has embodied a peculiar tension. Conflict over the best way to deal with the perceived Catholic threat and ensure British support for unionist policies has long existed *within* unionism, loyalism, and the Orange Order. Historically, Protestant elites used the latent threat of a large popular loyalist community, publicly manifested in Orange parades, to ensure due attention to the union by British governments. In return, the Orange elite were to keep the threat under control. Parades publicly manifested a growing fear of Catholic resistance and became a way to attach a level of "respectability" to a lower-class movement. This tension between raw populism and reputability constitutes a recurring theme in Anglo-Irish and Northern Irish politics. A similar tension has persisted in the Orange Order between its leadership and the grassroots, a schism that tends to fall along class lines but also reflects political (Ulster Unionist Party vs. Democratic Unionist Party), denominational (e.g., Presbyterian vs. Church of Ireland), and ethnic (Ulster-Scots vs. Anglo-Irish) distinctions (Kaufmann 2007:11–14).

Tension between conservative unionist Protestants and British governments were again placed under additional strain through the 1980s with the electoral rise of Sinn Féin, the establishment of cross-border institutions, and the British acknowledgment that the Republic of Ireland had a legitimate interest in the politics of Northern Ireland. Divisions within the unionist and loyalist communities were pressurized, and parades again became a site of resistance. Moderate unionist and Orange leaders sought to calm frustrated Orangemen and loyalists while hard-line leaders, such as, Orangeman Alan Wright, the UDA, and Ian Paisley, came to public prominence using parades as opportunities to mobilize working-class loyalists (Bryan 2000:159). From a unionist perspective, the Hume-Adams talks (between the nationalist Social Democratic and Labour Party [SDLP] and republican Sinn Féin leaderships), the Downing Street Declaration[8] by the British and Irish governments in 1993, and the 1995 Framework Documents constituted further erosion of the union with Great Britain. The 1994 cease-fires, while welcomed, also signaled a shifting political landscape that was increasingly open to republican involvement, foreshadowing power sharing and prisoner releases, both foreboding prospects for unionists (Bryan, Fraser, and Dunn 1995).

In this context, two developments marked the emergence of parades as an important venue for ethnopolitical conflict. First, nationalist residents' committees formed in some towns for the purpose of contesting loyalist parades through their neighborhoods. The committees have insisted on negotiations with parade organizers, but loyalists believe the residents' committees are republican fronts and are thus uncomfortable negotiating with them. In fact, majorities of both Protestants (84 percent) and Catholics (52 percent) in the Research and Evaluation Services (RES) report for the Independent Review of Parades and Marches stated they "thought that residents' groups were being manipulated for political purposes." It must also be said, however, that almost identical majorities agreed that "Loyal Orders were being used for political purposes" (Ward and McDade 1997). Second, an Independent Commission on Parades, established by the British government in March 1997, was authorized to review the parading situation and to ban, allow, and mediate parades.[9] Many Orangemen and loyalists disdain the commission and consider it an illegitimate body that violates their democratic right to parade. Some nationalists claim it is a biased instrument of the British government, though nationalists have been more open to working with the commission than loyalists.

Divisions within unionism had surfaced again at the outset of the peace process in January 1995 when Ulster Unionist Party (UUP) politicians agreed to negotiate with Sinn Féin while Ian Paisley's staunch Democratic Unionist Party (DUP) refused. During that summer, the bicentenary of the Orange Order, a high profile parading dispute developed in the primarily Protestant town of Portadown, where a nationalist community organization, the Garvaghy Road Residents Group, planned a counter demonstration against the highly symbolic annual "church" parade down the Garvaghy Road held by the local District Orange Lodge No. 1.[10] The Royal Ulster Constabulary (RUC) invoked legislation and banned the parade, but a standoff ensued, and the Orange Order established an encampment on the grounds of Drumcree Church (Church of Ireland). Each summer, from 1995 to 2000, security forces erected physical barriers including moats, barbed wire, and mobile steel barricades. The international media descended on the town to cover the standoff, and Drumcree and the Garvaghy Road became a locus of conflict in Northern Ireland, as central as paramilitary violence, policing, prisoner releases, and other points of contention.

At its height, the encampment maintained an almost festive atmosphere with flags flying and mobile food vendors selling chips and burgers. Hawkers sold

Drumcree paraphernalia, such as, commemorative lapel pins and refrigerator magnets, and during summer evenings, the church grounds became a place for working-class loyalists to congregate. It was generally only later in the evenings, as darkness fell and families dispersed, that young loyalists and paramilitary elements engaged the police across security barriers, dodging plastic baton rounds and throwing stones, petrol bombs, and in one deadly case in 1996, pipe bombs. The standoff today still features a brief parade-like display as Orangemen (often a delegation) proceed as far as a set of police barriers and present a statement of protest.

Today, parading continues to represent unionist and loyalist unease over the Belfast/Good Friday Agreement and British policy in Northern Ireland in addition to its usual functions of performing identity and appropriating a share of the symbolic landscape. Animosity toward the Parades Commission over the restriction and rerouting of parades has become one of the primary outlets for expressing opposition to any erosion of the union. However, while in the past parading signaled Protestant unity and an implicit threat (electoral or physical) through force of numbers, it is being reframed as an opportunity for engagement. Instead of projecting a defensive posture, the Grand Lodge leadership of the Orange Order is developing its outreach capacity on a number of fronts, including parading.

■ PARADES AND MITIGATION

As early as 1996, after Drumcree II, Orangemen who were annoyed by what they considered unfair treatment in the media began trying to influence media coverage (e.g., *Orange Standard* August 1996, p. 4; September 1996, p. 9; October 1996, p. 1; February 1997, p. 3; September 1997, p. 4). With the height of violence that was reached at the Drumcree standoff in Portadown in 1998, the leadership knew that parading had seriously eroded the institution's public image.[11] Grand Lodge has subsequently undertaken a range of initiatives to take charge of its image and its practices. Kaufmann (2007) addresses this trend in his thorough analysis of the Orange Order noting, "In the 1990s, the Order realized it was a cultural organization which could fit in well with the new liberal discourse of multiculturalism, cultural funding and group rights" (p. 303). Its Parades Strategy and Drumcree Winter Initiative 1998–1999 "embraced the 'soft' logic of secular human rights and public relations" as the institution increasingly set about recrafting its image (p. 301).

A raft of programs have been developed with these aims:

- To educate the public about Orange Order history and values
- To trim anti-social behavior, especially around parades
- To engage in dialogue with organizations and authorities that had previously been seen as out of bounds—such as, the Catholic hierarchy, representatives of the Republic of Ireland and nationalist residents committees protesting parades

- To widen community participation through cultural events that feature Orange and Ulster-Scots music, dancing, historical education
- Generally to present a softer, more progressive and inviting image than the stereotype of a staid, secretive, and defensive organization (Grand Orange Lodge of Ireland [GOLI] press release, November 9, 2007).

While we sat and talked over coffee and chocolate biscuits in the sitting room of his house in East Belfast, Robert, a prominent Orange clergyman, described the current moment of transition in which the Orange Order finds itself:

> We are coming to terms with a whole new society. And that's something people forget.... I think the Order is still looking where its role is. It was clear before the Troubles where its role is, but I don't think it's as clear now. We've gone through leadership changes. We've come out of thirty years of conflict in which three hundred eleven Orangemen were murdered in the Troubles, as were many other Protestants.... We then become the focus of all republican hatred through the parades thing. The parades dispute becomes the IRA campaign being fought at another level and without weapons. And we weren't ready for that. We didn't know how to deal with it. We made mistakes; we're probably still making mistakes; we're blundering our way through it, and I think we're coming out the other end. Not, I would have to say, because of any overt strategy, although we're strategizing more now, but because Sinn Féin has lost interest in the parades issue.... And I think we are changed, but I still think we're thrashing about where our role is in society.

This Orangeman articulated the way in which the Order feels thrust into new circumstances, a need to adapt, and a struggle to find how the Order can fit into civil society, "play its part," or "play a positive role in society." His comments reveal uncertainty, transition, and a new intentionality.

The Orange Order's initiatives to improve its image and to reach out to other sectors, domestic and international, have escalated in recent years and fall into at least six categories with considerable overlap.

1. Mitigation of traditional activities
2. Public relations and branding
3. Dialogue
4. Community outreach and education
5. Institutional outreach
6. International outreach and education

At the heart of these initiatives lies an attempt to rehabilitate the Orange Order's image, to build institutional credibility and social capital, and to secure the sustainability of the Order, both in terms of recruitment and its relevance within Northern Ireland's changing political and social landscape. Many of the institution's efforts have gone into modifying its parading practices.

Most Orange parades are not designated as contentious, and most participants on the Twelfth enjoy a festive social occasion. However, the loud and exclusive spectacle of Protestantism and unionism on the move can be intimidating for many Catholics, and the inclusion of paramilitary and sectarian elements over the past forty years has contributed to a negative image of the Orange Order. Many in the Order have become acutely aware of the problem and have taken deliberate steps to recast their parades by modifying some of the choreography and execution of these events to make them more festive and less intimidating. Much as mitigation efforts have been undertaken around bonfires and murals, the Orange Order has moved to make Twelfth parades a more welcoming event for families and tourists.

Orangefest and Flagship Twelfths

The Orange Order launched a wide range of celebratory events during the tercentenary of the Battle of the Boyne in 1990, but more sustained efforts have been undertaken since the turn of the century (*Orange Standard,* February 1990). Two projects, "Orangefest" and "Flagship Twelfths," are the most prominent examples of recent attempts to make over parades. Orangefest is an initiative of the Belfast County Lodge, and Flagship Twelfths are supervised by the Grand Orange Lodge, though Orangefest is often used to describe both. In 2007, the Belfast County Grand Lodge launched Orangefest to give the event greater historical and cultural depth and emphasize its pageantry and entertainment value (see figure 5.4). The project was originally conceived in the Grand Lodge's Committee for Educational Affairs, and as early as 2003, an application was submitted to Diversity Challenges, a funding organization (Grand Orange Lodge Ireland minutes June 23, 2003). Orangefest has focused on improving the traditional Twelfth activities in Belfast, a goal shared by the organizers of the Flagship Twelfth celebrations at selected District Lodge parades across Northern Ireland. The organizers have worked to ensure that basic amenities are available, such as, providing toilet facilities, training stewards, and cooperating with police.[12] They have tried to incorporate activities that are intended to convey an air of festivity or attach historical and cultural narratives to the formulaic rituals of feeder, district, and return parades intermitted by food and speeches in "the field."

The Reverend Martin Smyth, a former Grandmaster of the Grand Orange Lodge, encouraged lodges to construct historical floats in 1990 to transport older lodge members, who normally rode in cabs. In recent years, however, some parades have begun to incorporate floats and other mobile attractions that display Ulster-Scots music and culture and historical reenactment. A Grand Lodge press release from 2008 describes the use of floats in Omagh, which served as a Flagship Twelfth site.

> The Twelfth celebrations in Omagh will have an added element this year with the addition of carnival floats depicting scenes from the Battle of the Boyne. The idea is to create a more family orientated event and add a fun element to the parade. The

Figure 5.4 Reenactment in the field during the Orange Order's annual Twelfth parade. July 12, 2005.

centre float will be a rotating drum with eight different panels each showing different scenes of the story of the Boyne. Each panel will have a short verse which will be recited all along the parade route and will then be the nucleus of a performance piece which will take place at the assembly field as the crowd gather for the religious service. As soon as the verses are recited, a group of musicians and dancers will perform a pulsating set of tunes. The group will consist of bagpipes, electric bass, drums, keyboards, rhythm guitars and dances all leading to an exciting climax. (GOLI press release, June 19, 2008)

The floats in Omagh clearly drew on the historical references to the Battle of the Boyne that have always constituted the thematic focus of the Twelfth, but the press release emphasizes a focus on families that might have previously been taken for granted, and the incorporation of electric instruments and dance certainly signal a departure from the traditional rigid formula of the parade.

I joined the Belfast Orange lodges in the field in 2005 and 2006 and found that obvious effort had been put into providing entertainment and amusements for youth. In 2005, reenactors in period dress demonstrated the martial arts of medieval Scottish Border Reivers using lances and flintlock muskets (see figure 5.5). Willie Drennan and the Ulster-Scots Folk Orchestra and Ulster-Scots dancers performed on a mobile stage in 2006, funded at least in part by the Ulster-Scots Agency.

Figure 5.5 Reenactors and Ulster-Scots music in Belfast's Orangefest. July 12, 2007.

Flagship Twelfths and Cultural Tourism

"Flagship Twelfths," an initiative of the Grand Orange Lodge that is similar to the Orangefest project, aims to modify parading practices in an attempt to expand participation and challenge prevailing characterizations of Twelfth parades as sectarian and threatening. Orange leaders point out that more than 500,000 people attend the Twelfth each year and claim that hotels, restaurants, and other tourism-related businesses could benefit from "Belfast's largest visitor number event" (GOLI press release, March 8, 2009). The Northern Ireland Tourist Board began promoting the Twelfth in 2006, and announced in October 2007 that it would work to incorporate unionist culture in its promotional work. Tourism Ireland representatives began attending Twelfth parades in 2005. After representations to the tourist agencies, Orange Order officers arranged to select a limited number of venues, towns where lodges gather to parade on the Twelfth after having marched in their own local towns and village. Each of these parading events at the selected venues were organized to ensure that visitors would feel welcome and accommodated. Stewards were trained to police participants and welcome bystanders. Informative leaflets and basic amenities, such as, toilet facilities, were provided.

The first "Flagship" venues were Bangor and Enniskillen in 2006 and 2007, respectively. Tourist authorities provided "host training" beginning in 2007. Four towns, Belfast, Dromara, Tandragee, and Coleraine, were chosen in 2008 followed by Bangor, Banbridge, and Larne in 2009. In at least some cases, the Twelfth has been linked with other community cultural activities. In 2008, a Grand Orange Lodge press release described a series of events in towns hosting Flagship Twelfths that were to build interest leading up to the usual July 12 activities. These were to include a lambeg drumming exhibition, an event marking the end of World War I featuring the Ulster Military Vehicle Club, children's amusements, Schomberg Fife and Drums, Kirknara School of Dance, followed by a disco. A praise singing event in Ballymore Church was to be held to raise funds for Newry Hospice. A fancy dress parade was to include a dragon display by members of the local Chinese community and a fireworks display (GOLI press release, June 19, 2008; April 21, 2009).

Similarly, in Coleraine, plans were laid for events, such as, an exhibition of "culture and heritage" in the town hall with exhibitions of Ulster-Scots music, Irish and Scottish dancing, lambeg drumming, model helicopters, and fireworks. A "carnival pageant featuring the Ulster-Scots float, King Billy on horseback and Williamite foot-soldiers, Chinese lion dancers and an African samba band" were arranged to precede the Twelfth parade. Similar events were scheduled at the Lower Iveagh Ulster-Scots Festival in association with the flagship July 12 demonstration in Dromara as well as in other towns, which the Grand Lodge was careful to detail in its press release (GOLI press release, June 19, 2008).

A discernible pragmatism lies behind the reinvention of Twelfth parades given the institution's declining membership. Concerned about the future of the institution, current Orange leaders want to maintain public interest and build youth participation, and the Twelfth provides opportunities to reach out to the public using familiar practices that are seen by many—if not most—Orangemen as central to their identity.

Public Relations and Branding

Beyond Orangefest and Flagship Twelfths, the Orange Order has become much more aggressive about developing its ability to shape media coverage and public perception or build the Orange "brand" (Kaufmann 2007:301). Orangemen widely acknowledge that they have often failed to appreciate the importance of public relations, assuming that self-evident merits of their fundamental positions would carry the day. Many Orangemen probably felt that public relations work signaled a lack of faith in fundamental principles, which would undermine the very fabric of Orangeism. One can imagine that their assumptions were rarely challenged while Orangeism drew much of its legitimacy from its association with the state. However, there is a growing awareness that a purely teleological stance is not sufficient.

Philip, a spokesperson for an Armagh County Lodge, described a growing interest in public relations during an interview at his home:

The major change that has come about in this past number of years has been the feeling that it's not simply enough for us who belong to [the Orange Order] to know what it's about. We need to be able to project ourselves out to the wider community, to say to people, "Well, this is what we're about." In a way, we would hope that that would get over some of the misconceptions that's held about us. What we even say now is that, "Well, really at least if you understand us, whether you like us or not, at least you've got a better informed opinion." So, if any change has come about, it has been that the Orange Order has been more able to say, "Well, listen, this is what we are. This is what we stand for. This is what we do. This is what we're involved in." Whereas in the past, it was more of an organization that just worked away itself and didn't feel the need to explain itself to others. There was maybe a certain amount of arrogance there. It automatically felt, "Well, because we're the Orange institution, we are almost above question." But that's one of the major changes that has come. We're prepared to say, "Well, this is what we are. Yes, ask us about whatever you want to ask, we appreciate that. It'll be a learning experience for you. It'll also be a learning experience for us, because it helps us to see what way people sort of misconstrue what we're about or maybe have notions about what we're about that we may not be about."

Gareth, an Orangeman and community worker in Portadown, reflected the perception among many unionists that they have simply been outgunned by nationalists in the public sphere. As Gareth put it, "the situation's been hijacked."

The Order as it stands at this minute in time is certainly not where I would like to see it going. I would like to see it being much more aggressive, much more radical in promoting what we are. Instead of people being shy and timorous about who we are, we should be shouting it from the rooftops about how we are doing A, B, C, and D, and how we can be a positive influence in this community. Because [the situation] has been hijacked. We've been demonized, and we're vilified for little or no reason. Therefore, how do we arrest that, and how do we turn that round to our advantage? Because, I believe an ill wind blows nobody any favors. So, therefore, how do we [re-]interpret ourselves such that the world sees us in a positive light? And if we can't do that within our own community first and sell it to our own community, then forget it.

Gareth's remarks are reflected in a number of policy decisions made by the leadership of the Grand Lodge of Ireland. A public relations working party was established in 2000, and a team of media consultants was hired in 2001 for training Orangemen in preparation for the upcoming parading season. Reputation Matters, a public relations firm, was retained in 2002 until Austin Hunter, a former editor of the unionist-leaning *Newsletter*, was brought on as a part-time media consultant in late 2006 (Kaufmann 2007:301).[13] This is not to say that the organization has always excelled in its efforts, and some, such as, the Reverend Brian Kennaway, argue that public relations efforts have limited utility when they amount to damage control for incidents when lodges or individual Orangemen have publicly engaged in disruptive or sectarian actions, often during parades (Brown 2003; Kennaway 2006:261–63).

Dialogue and Negotiation

The Orange Order has also shown a growing willingness to engage in dialogue with parties they formerly would have either avoided or studiously rejected. The best-known example is the Order's official position that it will not negotiate over parades with nationalist residents' committees. The involvement of figures like Gerard Rice (Ormeau Road, Belfast) and Brendan MacCoinnaith (Garvaghy Road, Portadown), who have been involved in the republican movement, has been a par-ticularly difficult hurdle for Orangemen, who feel that to negotiate with anyone connected to republican violence might lend credibility to that struggle and betray victims of republican violence, including fellow Orangemen.

However, following the example of the Apprentice Boys of Derry, which suc-cessfully negotiated alternative arrangements to their annual parades with local businesses and nationalist residents, the Orange Order has become more open to dialogue (Ross 2001). In 2003, Portadown District elected to enter talks with nationalist residents after the City of Londonderry Grand Lodge came to an agreement with residents (Kennaway 2006:189). In 2007, Portadown Lodge No. 1 agreed to take part in a mediation process with the Garvaghy Road Residents Coalition and began direct correspondence (*Belfast Telegraph*, July 2, 2007; *Portadown Times*, November 8, 2007). By 2008, Portadown Orangemen had held meetings with Catholic Cardinal Sean Brady, the SDLP, representatives of the Taoiseach's office, and even Gerry Adams, the president of Sinn Féin (GOLI press release, July 6, 2008; *Kilkenny People*, October 8, 2008).

Community Outreach and Education

As noted in Gareth's remarks, reported earlier, ensuring that their own community sees the Order "in a positive light" is a significant part of recent public relations efforts. Opening the halls to more community access is a recurring theme (*Orange Standard*, August 2006). Robert, a clergyman and Orangeman from East Belfast, described the opening of the hall near Cluan Place:

> For a lot of years, we've become like the churches. We've went in and closed our doors and become Orangemen and didn't engage with our community. Now, part of that was our members dispersed, where years ago one lodge would have been from maybe two streets, but people moved out, and housing changed; not as many people lived [nearby]...and there was a loss of contact with the local people. It probably culminated in the Cluan Place riots in that the hall wasn't open for people to go to in time of need. So, there was a younger leadership moved in or were elected within the institution....and they, from the very first night, took a proactive community approach and have held public meetings in the Orange Hall, and everybody's invited to it. All the political parties, all the bands, all the local community groups, just everybody.

Orangemen at a 2007 Orangefest Christmas party in a hall on the Shankill Road made similar comments to me. They explained that they felt they had lost touch with the local community and were trying to reach out.

The Christmas party featured an art competition with awards to local schoolchildren, who were invited to attend the event. Though the Orangefest party was a district event, the Grand Orange Lodge has also begun to focus on youth with regular visits to schools by a full-time education officer, who talks about the "traditions and values" of the Orange Order. Similar efforts at shaping public opinion have included official representation at the annual Royal Ulster Agricultural Show at Balmoral and increased charitable giving (Kaufmann 2007:301; GOLI press release, 24 November 2008).

Institutional Outreach

In addition to grassroots outreach, Grand Lodge has worked to establish relationships with the state and other prominent institutions. Political relationships have largely been taken for granted given the Order's historical partnership with the Ulster Unionist Party and the gate-keeping role it played for unionist politicians. Even today, one-half of unionist members of the legislative assembly (MLAs) are Orangemen (Tonge, Evans, Jeffery, and McAuley forthcoming). Orange leaders still value the political capital they can garner through public contact with British ministers and unionist politicians. During 2007, described as a "Year of Outreach" in a Grand Orange Lodge press release, Secretary of State Peter Hain publicly opened an exhibition focused on William of Orange at Schomberg House, Grand Lodge headquarters (GOLI press release, November 9, 2007).

However, following the lead of the Education Committee of the 1990s, Grand Lodge has sought to engage a widening range of influential institutions. On at least one occasion, the Grand Lodge's Education Officer, David Scott, represented the Order to local government when he met with Councillors in the primarily nationalist district of Limavady in February 2009 (*Derry Journal*, February 13, 2009). Grand Master Robert Saulters met with Cardinal Sean Brady in 2006 and 2008, and in November 2008, he announced that Grand Lodge was "working closely with government agencies including Ms. Ritchie's Department of Social Development to widen our outreach and take our message to people who do not always hear it" (GOLI press release, November 24, 2008; *Irish News,* March 3, 2008). Margaret Ritchie, the SDLP minister for the Department of Social Development, had come under fire by Grand Lodge only a week earlier for calling the Orange Order "sectional and sectarian" and "deeply divisive" at a Gaelic Athletic Association (GAA) event (*Newsletter* December 9, 2008).

International Outreach and Education

More than ever, Grand Lodge has been trying to secure international interest in the Orange Order. This has primarily taken the form of increasing cooperation with Irish officials and relationship building with organizations in the United States. Grand Lodge has developed closer contact with the government in the Republic of Ireland while working on the development of the Boyne Battlefield site at Drogheda, and the Irish government has awarded grants for the development of Orange halls in border counties. On September 29, 2008, Grand Lodge convened in County Cavan, the first such meeting across the border since partition (*Kilkenny People*, October 8, 2008).

Occasional attempts have been made to influence opinion in the United States and counter popular support for republicanism. The Reverend Martin Smyth, a unionist politician and former Grand Master, appeared on talk radio programs while traveling internationally in the 1970s, and in 1998, the Reverend Brian Kennaway, who was serving as the Convenor of the Education Committee, traveled to the United States also in his capacity as a Presbyterian minister but lectured about Orangeism (Kaufmann 2007:301). Dr. David Hume, a historian, Ulster-Scots enthusiast, and Grand Lodge Director of Services, has made numerous trips gathering information about Ulster-Scots immigration to the United States.

Outreach to the United States was stepped up when an Orange delegation participated in the annual Smithsonian Folklife Festival held on the mall in Washington, D.C. Northern Ireland was selected along with the state of Virginia and the Mekong River Delta to exhibit expressions of culture, traditional practices, and industry. Orange representatives met with members of Congress and they sponsored a banner-painting tent that provided the opportunity to greet and discuss Orangeism with visitors (see figure 5.6). A kind of informal coalition was formed with other representatives exhibiting lambeg drumming, mural painting, carpet weaving, and shipbuilding. Further outreach to the United States took place in June 2009 when an Orange delegation accompanied representatives (also Orangemen) from the Ulster-Scots Agency and the Ulster-Scots Community Network on a trip to New York aimed at developing American tourism. Representatives of Tourism Ireland were also present, and the event was planned in cooperation with British and Irish authorities (GOLI press release, June 28, 2009).

■ A LONG TUMULTUOUS TURN
  TOWARD PERSUASION

These shifts in strategy have taken place amid significant changes on the political scene and within unionist politics. In particular, political opinion within the Orange Order has reflected reticence among Protestants generally about the peace process and the state of the union. The separation of the Orange Order from the UUP in 2005 was a manifestation of declining Protestant support for the Belfast/Good Friday Agreement after it was signed. By 2003, according to one poll, only 16 percent of Protestants wanted the agreement to be implemented in the form that was negotiated amid concerns over decommissioning, police reform, the release of prisoners, and the erosion of the union. Likewise, within the Orange

Figure 5.6 The Orange Order sponsored a tent on banner painting during the 2007 Smithsonian Folk Life Festival in Washington, D.C., July 1, 2007.

Order, by 2004, only 12 percent of Orangemen said they would support the agreement in a second referendum. However, in a 2007 survey of 1,376 Orange Order members, that number more than doubled to 26 percent, still less than one-third of those surveyed (McAuley and Tonge 2007:41; Tonge, Evans, Jeffery, and McAuley forthcoming). In 2001, slightly more Orangemen reported supporting the anti-Agreement DUP over the UUP, and in the following two years, a number of prominent Orangemen shifted their allegiances to the DUP (Patterson and Kaufmann 2007:225, 28, 42). By 2004, more Orangemen were voting for the DUP than for the UUP, a trend that was especially apparent among Orangemen under the age of twenty-five (McAuley and Tonge 2007:43; Tonge, Evans, Jeffery, and McAuley forthcoming). While tension within the Orange Order grew between its traditionalist wing and its growing populist wing, the DUP was gaining steadily on the UUP within the unionist electorate and became the largest party in the Assembly at the 2003 elections.

In separate research projects, Kaufmann (2007), McAuley and Tonge (McAuley and Tonge 2007; Tonge and McAuley 2008) have documented the shift in the makeup of the Orange Order toward working-class "rebels" from "traditionalists," a trend that is reflected in the growing support among Orangemen for the DUP. "Traditionalists" are those who cherish loyalty to the crown and a deep sense of

British identity; they often emphasize the faith dimensions of the institution. "Rebels," on the other hand, tend to emphasize the cultural or ethnic role of the Order, draw from the Scots-Irish tradition of dissenting Presbyterians and Methodists, focus their national identity closer to home, and are more likely to refer to themselves as Ulstermen. Their political roots are populist (and therefore more permissive of paramilitaries and grassroots agitation) compared with the more elite and middle-class model of political loyalty to the Crown preferred by traditionalists.

Does the shift within the Orange Order toward rebels correlate with the Order's emerging emphasis on outreach and public relations? It is tempting to make the link. After all, there does seem to have been acceleration in Orange outreach since the cease-fires. The political and public relations successes of Sinn Féin may have spurred imitation in the Orange Order. It may be that the momentum of the political process made it increasingly clear that devolution was likely to occur. However, we might expect that to contradict the shift, as the Ulster Unionist Party spent its future on advocating for the Belfast/Good Friday Agreement, unlike the DUP, which long maintained a staunchly anti-Agreement position that aligned more closely with opinion within the Orange Order. In one of the strange ironies of Northern Irish politics, the DUP, having won the 2003 Assembly elections, negotiated the St. Andrews agreement with Sinn Féin, and Ian Paisley became first minister on May 8, 2007. The anti-devolutionist party had taken up power sharing with its enemy. Perhaps it is no surprise then that the increasingly DUP-leaning Orange Order would also break script and embrace the politics of public persuasion more fully.

If there is a connection, it is more likely that the Ulster ethnic predispositions of the rebel faction align well with a less religious program of outreach, manifested in the array of Ulster-Scots folk festivals that have been incorporated into Twelfth activities. However, we should be cautious about associating the shift in strategy in the Orange Order with the demographic and ideological shift that Paterson and Kaufmann (2007) and Tonge and McAuley (McAuley and Tonge 2007; Tonge and McAuley 2008) identify. Attempts among prominent Orangemen and committees to develop a more proactive public relations capacity can be traced back to the 1970s when the traditionalist Education Committee, chaired by Canon S. E. Long, advocated media training, and the Reverend Martin Smyth, a former Grand Master and MP, and other leaders, such as, Harold McCusker MP, made it a point to speak internationally and engage the international media (*Orange Standard*, June 1992, p. 6; April 1995, p. 5).

Interestingly, these developments emerged after a new populist leadership in the Orange Order began challenging the more patrician elite leadership of the Orange Order from the mid-1960s (Patterson and Kaufmann 2007:86). Similar initiatives were advocated through the 1980s. The Reverend Brian Kennaway assumed the chair of the Education Committee in 1989, which reached out even more aggressively, producing a range of educational publications, presenting at the

Ulster People's College cross-community events and the Columbanus Community, meeting the Parades Commission on educational concerns, and joining the Irish Association (Kennaway 2006:194–98; Kaufmann 2007:183–84). The late Colin Shilliday, one of the committee's members, was involved in 1990 with the Order's current public relations consultant, Austin Hunter, in the development of a ninety-minute historical and advocacy video timed to coincide with the tercentenary of the Battle of the Boyne and marked a period of introspection and anticipation of the millennium (*Orange Standard*, July 1990, p. 16; May 1991, pp. 1, 5; February 1995, p. 13).

Ultimately, the Education Committee's innovations were taken to task by more militant members, especially the Spirit of Drumcree faction. As it turns out, however, traditionalists' evangelical enthusiasm had staying power and features prominently in today's Orange agenda, albeit in a less religious fashion (Kennaway 2006; Kaufmann 2007:197). Even as the Education Committee was under direct attack within the institution, the necessity of reforming the Order and developing its own public relations capacity was being accelerated by the Drumcree parading crisis in Portadown, the development of the peace process, and eventually the abandonment of the organization's formal political ties with the UUP.

On the broader political stage, the decommissioning of republican weapons, the abandonment of Articles Two and Three in the Republic's constitution, and the formalization of the principle of consent in the terms of the Belfast/Good Friday Agreement have made the defensive positions of unionists less comprehensible while republicans have proven adept at building international and domestic support by constructing a power narrative of victimhood and group rights. The longer the Assembly functions and political power is centered in Northern Ireland, the more important it becomes for the Order to cultivate influence locally, and the Belfast/Good Friday Agreement has encouraged and incentivized the development of ethnic identities within a multicultural framework. Finally, one of the dividends of the peace process is simply a freeing of organizations like the Orange Order to crawl out of the bunkers, so to speak, and think creatively about how they might participate in a new Northern Ireland.

Outreach and image management is also made necessary by declining membership and influence, especially since 1960. Tonge and McAuley (2008) reckon that though the institution's membership was believed to lie between 80,000 and 100,000 in 1999, it had fallen to approximately 40,000 by 2008 (p. 289; Elliott and Flackes 1999:380). Kennaway (2006) estimates that the Order had 70,000 members in 1964, roughly 60,000 members in 1972, just over 40,000 members in 2000, and 36,998 in 2004 (pp. 18, 254–255). Kaufmann's (2007) study of the Orange Order shows that the institution has been in steady decline since 1960 when its membership fell just under 70,000. By 2002, the Order's numbers had fallen to between 30,000 and 40,000 or 60 percent of its 1945 level with membership in Belfast falling from approximately 16,000 in 1961 to just over 6,000 in 1986 (though there was a rise in membership during the early years of the Troubles 1970–1972; pp. 273, 277,

283). For the Orange Order to survive over the long term, it will have to staunch the loss of members, which appears to be a consequence of poor recruitment as opposed to resignations, if Belfast's experience is an indicator. (However, rural areas have fared better than urban ones; pp. 272–73, 277–80). This probably explains why much of the organization's outreach has been directed at youth, especially as working-class youth have increasingly turned to loyalist bands as recreational and expressive outlets (Bell 1990; Jarman 2000; Kaufmann 2007:282).

The decline has been most severe in urban areas, such as, Belfast, while rural areas have fared better, where the Orange Order provides a venue for socializing and organizing for isolated Protestants, especially those in areas with strong nationalist populations (Kaufmann 2007:277–78). Kaufmann compares the Orange Order's decline in Northern Ireland with a previous but similar decline in Orange membership in Canada. He finds that road expansion—and other indicators of mobility—are the most powerful predictors of decline in membership, suggesting that the institution may be suffering from a general loss of social capital or networks like that documented by Putnam (2000) in the United States (pp. 275, 280–82).[14]

Patterson and Kaufmann (2007) describe the changing complexion of the Orange Order as "a social and political earthquake." They summarize, "Unionism's rebel alter-ego has moved into the driver's seat and the traditionalism of a century is shrinking back into the shadows" (p. 255). Yet, interestingly, a strategic agenda to modify its practices and engage in public persuasion has survived the earthquake. Though traditionalists championed the cause throughout the Troubles, it continues to be advanced today. What we see going on within the Orange Order may in some respects parallel the political rise of the DUP, but a longer and much slower development of a strategic agenda can be identified in at least some corners of unionism and loyalism. I have discovered recognition in the Orange Order that engagement and persuasion are powerful activities, though over the course of the Troubles it was usually overshadowed by the institution's commitment to majoritarian unionism and a fixation on republican terrorism and state security policy. Nonetheless, a strategy of public persuasion has gathered momentum since the 1990s.

The rise of the populist rebel tradition among unionists and in the Orange Order led some observers to predict a retrenchment of anti-agreement politics that would make devolution and consociation unlikely (Evans and Tonge 2007:166; Patterson and Kaufmann 2007:94). However, as we now know, Paisley's DUP chose to partner with Sinn Féin in government and wage its fight politically instead of following old ideological scripts. "No" is no longer the predominant strategy. Instead, engagement in the public sphere has grown and holds important implications for Orange, unionist, and loyalist identities.[15] Rebel unionists, including those in the Orange Order, have decided to develop new practices and modify old ones. These are choices that are both strategic and cultural, having been adopted within the structures of political and social circumstances and their own collective identities and simultaneously contributing to the reframing of those identities.

■ CHANGING PRACTICE AND IDENTITY CHANGE

To say that the Orange Order is participating in conflict transformation through the initiatives detailed above is not to say it is promoting radical reconciliation initiatives or fundamentally revising Christian doctrine and unionist ideology. Whether changes in institutional practice reflect and contribute to changes in collective identity is important for assessing contributions to conflict transformation. I have proposed that much of conflict transformation involves the slow reinterpretation of collective identities through the incremental modification of collective activities. Innovations in long-held rituals introduce opportunities for the reframing and performance of group priorities and myths. It can be a challenging process to study as its efficacy lies largely in its reliance on tradition and perceptions of continuity while innovations are developed behind closed doors before they are introduced. The acceptance or rejection of innovative discourses is an aggregated process with outcomes based on contention within and between organizations. Much as astronomers study stars indirectly by observing the gravitational impact they have on neighboring celestial bodies, contention offers sociologists opportunities to observe identity change, somewhat obliquely, as individuals and organizations compete over the adoption of novel activities.

In a remarkably insightful article, Todd (2005) addresses "changes in collective categories of identity" that are possible because identities are not monolithic constructs but are multifaceted, allowing for the innovative combination and rearranging of elements under pressure from changing social pressures. However, she emphasizes "moments of intentionality":

> Identity formation and change is thus a continuous process that involves a considerable degree of intentionality. It takes place by the incorporation of new elements of embodied meaning and value, or the rearrangement of old. New elements may be created, not *ex nihilo* but by the choice to foreground particular practices and relations rather than others, so that over time the meanings embedded in these practices become an integral part of the self, while others fade. (p. 437)

Under conditions of significant social change and shifting power relations, various strategies of identification may be adopted to deal with the dissonance created when new social circumstances no longer align with the old identity schema (see also Ganiel 2008a:15–20). Todd (2005:440) offers six "directions of change in collective identity categories" that fall across a matrix charting the extent of change in identity categories and the degree of coherence or tension between new practices required by the new social order and the dominant identity category (see table 5.1).

Reaffirmation "reaffirms the existing core binary oppositions and welcomes or resists change in their name" (Todd 2005:440). Actors *assimilate* when they "reshuffle" components of their identity to accommodate the new social order by foregrounding elements that are less offended by the requirements of the new

TABLE 5.1 *Direction of Change in Collective Identity Categories*[a]

	No Change	Partial Change	Total Change
Transparence and coherence between practice and category	Reaffirmation	Assimilation	Conversion
Ambiguity and tension between practice and category	Adaptation	Ritual appropriation	Privatization

[a] Todd, Jennifer. 2005. "Social Transformation, Collective Categories, and Identity Change." *Theory and Society* 34:429–463. (p. 440).

order. "They thus find in themselves the dispositions and expectations necessary to succeed in the new order, while retaining a sense of continuity with their older selves" (p. 443). *Conversion* occurs when old categories become "irrelevant" or "absurd" and former identities simply cannot be salvaged (p. 441). *Adaptation* occurs when actors manage to follow new practices without abandoning the essence of their identity. "They are 'sensible' and agree that the new is here to stay, but they 'act' in it while keeping their own values and self-categorizations distinct from this practice" (p. 442). *Ritual appropriation* occurs when "new practices are accepted and assimilated within old narrative forms, and ritual structures that are used to legitimate, appropriate, and redefine the practices, thus assuring continuity of meaning despite change in practice" (p. 443). New practices and old categories impact one another, influencing and resolving the tension between them. *Privatization* requires confining identity to the private sphere, in homes and churches, for example (p. 442). Todd is addressing the way changes in "practices" that are imposed as a result of political processes interact with shared understandings of collective identities, but this can obscure the possibility of changes in practices that are not merely accepted because they are imposed but that are both influenced by changes in the environment and initiated strategically within influential organizations.

It is thus possible to expand Todd's table to capture a wider range of variability in change in practices (see table 5.2). The cells at the opposite corners of the table, in which identity change and changes in practice are inverted in relation to one another, do not, however, add value to Todd's classification scheme. Collective identity and collective practices are so closely related to one another that it is

TABLE 5.2 *Strategies for Negotiating Changes in Practice and Identity*

Practice	Identity		
	No Change	Partial Change	Major Change
No change	Reaffirmation	Justification	
Partial change	Conservation	Ritual appropriation	Metamorphosis
Major change		Innovation	Conversion

difficult to imagine or find instances in which drastic change in one could accompany no change in the other. It should also be noted that the table represents continuums or degrees of change in identity. Individuals, and especially groups, might adapt multiple strategies for action, though in those cases we could expect to find that contention arises over which strategies are most appropriate, fueled by the ambiguity and tension between practices and identity that Todd identifies in her scheme.

Before we delve into the categories that illuminate the shifts among individuals and organizations identified in this book, it is worth noting that among those individuals most committed to ethnopolitical identities, the prospects for drastic identity change are small. Partial change is far more realistic; identifications do not fade easily. Even in cases that might be considered akin to conversion, interviewees often reported persistent attachments to traditions and values from earlier in their lives that continue to shape their personalities and worldviews. I found the scheme in table 5.2 helpful in navigating a complex mix of strategies undertaken by unionist and loyalist organizations and individuals as they worked to adapt to changing political circumstances from within the boundaries of their own ethnopolitical identifications. We will address each mode in turn.

Reaffirmation

Reaffirmation reflects common stereotypes of loyalism and unionism: defensive, dour, and convinced that any compromise represents a step on a slippery slope toward a united Ireland. At one time, we would have turned to the Reverend Ian Paisley for illustration of this category. We might have cited his famous speech at the time of the Anglo-Irish agreement when he spoke at City Hall saying, "Where do the terrorists return to for sanctuary? To the Irish republic, and yet, Mrs. Thatcher tells us that that republic must have some say in our province. We say: Never, Never, Never, Never!" However, since becoming the First Minister of Northern Ireland and working closely with Sinn Féin's Martin McGuinness, the Deputy First Minister, Paisley has become an icon of transformation. No longer the same firebrand evangelical and politician, he has developed close working relationships with republicans in Northern Ireland and the government of the Republic of Ireland.

However, others have taken up the mantle of evangelical loyalism. Jim Allister, who took Paisley's European parliament seat, founded the interest group Traditional Unionist Voice in 2008. Supporters of the Orange Order in its standoff at Drumcree echo the slogan derived from Martin Luther's statement during his defense before the Diet of Worms in 1521: "Here I stand; I can do no other. God help me. Amen." The phrase has often been replicated in reference to the parading standoff.

An Orangeman I interviewed illustrated this category when he indicated that the increasing attention and energy being paid to cultural activities, such as, the development of Orangefest and tourism initiatives, did not fully align with his sense of identity as an Orangeman for whom faith was the highest calling.

> I just see a movement away from the faith-based Order, which would have been very prevalent in the days when I joined into a more politically based organization with right wing political tendencies. Then, whenever that backfired, shall we say, to a certain extent, they have now tried to manufacture this cultural identity, and we have expositions of and comparisons with the Notting Hill Carnival, Spanish cultural events, [with] all of which I have huge difficulty. I can see no relevance whatsoever to the Notting Hill Carnival and the Orange Order.

The founding in July 2009 of a protest group within the Orange Order, called Orange Reformation, also illustrates reaffirmation. Interviewed in the *Newsletter* (August 28, 2009), the group's founder, the Reverend Stephen Dickinson, called for

> a strong, Protestant, biblical Orange Institution to champion the cause of Christ and give a clear lead for others to follow in days when "compromise" and "political correctness" seem to be preferred to truth and principle.... We believe that the Orange Order can only be at its best when it stands firm for the great truths of the Protestant faith.

According to the article, Orange Reformation resists attempts to "soften the Protestant image of the Orange Institution in an attempt to 'rebrand' it and make it more appealing to a wider audience." Reaffirming Orangemen resist movement away from traditional practices or principles.

Justification

In some cases in which there is no interest in changing traditional practices, stasis has been justified with new rationales that deviate from fundamental tenets or ideology. The adoption of human rights discourse to justify the continuation of Orange parades on traditional routes stands out as a prominent example. Rights discourse has long been understood by unionists to be a tool used by nationalists to undermine British rule. The civil rights movement was questioned by many Protestants who felt that if Catholics used the word "rights" to mean employment and housing, then Protestants were equally victims of human rights abuses, but their loyalty to the British state disinclined them from holding it accountable, and once a human rights discourse had been adopted by Catholics, it was considered inappropriate under the totalizing and polarizing logic of ethnopolitical division. Once it was associated with nationalism, it was tainted.

Interestingly, however, in recent years, the language of human rights and civil rights has become increasingly common among Protestant activists, notably in relation to parades. The appropriation of human rights language and even direct appeals to EU human rights law have become common as a defense of the right to parade. Often, rights are claimed in association with the sovereignty of the British state; Orangemen have often referred to the right of British citizens to process down the "Queen's highway," which they point out is kept in good repair by taxpayer dollars. A focus on rights of citizenship kept the focus on the authority of British administration in Northern Ireland.

Over time, the use of a discourse of rights has become more expansive and has tapped into both the moral and ethical high ground of human rights as well as the potential legal advantages that rights legislation affords. By November 1999, the Orange Order had launched a civil rights Web site that signaled a significant departure from the traditional taboo on human rights strategies. On its front page, the site quoted the U.S. civil rights leader Martin Luther King, Jr.: "Somewhere I read of the freedom of assembly. Somewhere I read of the freedom of speech. Somewhere I read of the freedom of the press. Somewhere I read that the greatness of America is the right to protest for right. And so just as I say, we aren't going to let any injunction turn us around. We are going on."[16] The "injunction" to which King refers is equated with rulings by the Royal Ulster Constabulary and the Parades Commission to ban, postpone, or reroute parades. The direct reference to civil rights is surprising given the negative interpretations most Protestants have held of the Catholic civil rights movement in Northern Ireland. In these cases, a new discourse of human rights was adopted to justify a continuation of traditional practices—in this case, parades.

Conservation

Conservation, which nearly matches Todd's "adaptation," is similar to justification in that a rationalization takes place. In justification, an intention not to change a traditional practice is framed by adopting a new position that requires jettisoning previously held beliefs or ideas. In conservation, a change in practice is made to align with familiar narratives, making the adoption of the new practice easier, more palatable.

A news story from Sunday Life (July 16, 2006) illustrates this strategy. The article addresses attempts in 2006 to make the Twelfth in Belfast a "family affair." The article describes the scene in "the Field" at Malone House, just outside Belfast, which had become known for excessive drinking and public urination and was an unsuitable place for children. However, in 2006, Andrew Smyth of the Ulster Heritage Council was tapped to make the activity at the field a more welcoming event by giving it a festival atmosphere. Historical reenactors, dancers, Ulster-Scots music, inflatable slides, a motorized bull, simulated sumo wrestling, and other carnival games were brought in to cater to young people. Smyth declared that the Orange Order wants to include families, and not just Protestant ones. However, instead of talking about these changes as new, he aligned them with a common vision of a bygone era, a golden age, in which Orange parades were not contentious. It is a story I have heard many times over the course of a decade in my interviews of Orangemen and their supporters. They recall when parades were "a family day out," when men wore their Sunday best clothes and waved to their family and friends. I have often heard Orangemen in rural areas tell me that Catholic farmers offered to help with their Protestant neighbors' farm chores on the Twelfth so that they could be free to parade. Bands associated with Gaelic Athletic Association clubs or the Irish National Foresters Club loaned a drum or other gear to local Protestant neighbors.

Smyth describes the new activities as a return to the past, though the range of activities in the field in 2006 were almost certainly never a part of Twelfth events in the twentieth century. "We have a real chance now to make this a family day out and to make the Twelfth more inclusive," he said. "We want the Twelfth to be like what it was 20 or 30 years ago, with entertainment for adults and children—to be much more family-orientated" (*Sunday Life*, July 16, 2006). Conservation is thus a strategy for framing a change in practice such that it aligns with familiar principles and experiences held by those who share collective identities.

Ritual Appropriation

In her scheme, Todd (2005) describes "ritual appropriation" as an interactive process in which new practices are brought into tension with new ways of constructing collective identity. In ritual appropriation, new actions and practices are proposed, often for political, financial, or other pragmatic reasons, and they are carefully chosen, with the knowledge that proposals that are too ambitious and violate a shared sense of ontological security are likely to be rejected and the credibility of those who proposed the change undermined. Thus, the local or indigenous knowledge of grassroots leadership becomes critical.

It is not always easy to identify ritual appropriation/modification because if it is executed carefully and subtly, the reconciliation of identity and new practices happens without creating splits and divisions. Often, the best a researcher can do is identify tension within discourses that do not always erupt into public debates or contention. David Burrows's comment at the Orange art exhibit in Portadown in 2005 indicates these kinds of tensions well:

> It's not a secret that we had to move on as a district, and we got the bad publicity over a number of years. Some of it I have to say probably is our own making and a lot of it not. But yes, we had to move on, and I think we have. The district has been moving on in the last number of years. And I say a district, I mean, a district of nine-hundred people.... And, to be doing some of the things that have been done in the last couple of years, to have been doing ten years ago, if we even talked about them, the district would probably have had a difficulty.... What we had to do was to make people [feel] that there is no threat by opening up.

Burrows is referring to initiatives like monitoring the placement of flags in the town to make sure that they are not up past the parading season. Under pressure of bad publicity, the Portadown District Lodge has introduced new practices in order to "move on," but has not done so without tension within the district. The new initiatives had to be chosen carefully and required a certain amount of framing work to align them with the core components of identification shared by nine

hundred district lodge members. In adopting new practices, such as, flag monitoring or turning Orange parades into festivals, Orangemen have had to wrestle
with the art of making new practices consonant with Orange identity and incorporating new components of identity that are represented in new practices.

Ritual appropriation, while one of the more difficult modes to document, is the
most likely mode of identity change to associate with conflict transformation as
new, less polarizing practices can be introduced and authorized within the tradition, and a less defensive ethos has been folded into the tradition. Gareth, the
Orangeman and community worker in Portadown, described his hopes for appropriation of community development projects into the core of Orangeism:

> Using the analogy of a race, the politicians have just moved off the starting blocks.
> They're 400 meters round the track, and the churches and the Orange Order are only
> getting their kit off. The frustration is, if we went too far ahead, we become disillusioned.
> The last thing we want to do is to be dragged back by the clergy or the Orange, for
> example. We want them to have an injection of energy. To recognize, "Phew, there's
> something of value here. Can we take the core principles of community development
> and tweak them so that they are conducive to what we want?" When I say conducive to
> what we want, [I mean] consistent with the ideology, values and ethos [of Orangeism].
> So, how can we evolve ourselves? So, much like we're talking about paramilitarism evolv-
> ing themselves or reinventing themselves within society, the Orange Order need to rein-
> vent themselves.

Gareth's comment reflects Liechty and Clegg's observation, noted in chapter 2, that
in a process of mitigation, "The tradition works to heal the tradition" (2001:229).

Innovation

What distinguishes innovation from ritual appropriation is that the new practices
in question have not been undertaken before. These are not modifications of
familiar rituals but instances of striking out and developing practices that have
never been associated with an organization or its adherents and supporters. The
Grand Orange Lodge has begun to implement a range of initiatives that are novel
and depart from the Order's insular and secretive reputation. As part of a public
relations push to take control of the Order's public image, the leadership has begun
working with media consultants, tourism officials, and cultural agencies to build a
brand that has historical depth but is also seen as modern and relevant in a society
emerging from conflict. While all of these initiatives are intended to represent the
Order and thus draw on familiar symbols and narratives, many of them are
unfamiliar.

In November 2007, the Order launched a campaign to introduce a new symbol,
a superhero cartoon character designed to reach out to youths. Young people were
asked to submit names for the character, and the winning submission, Diamond
Dan, was announced in April 2008. In one Grand Lodge press release, the character

was described as a new symbol for new times. In another press release, the Grand Lodge explained that this new hero was designed to embody "civic responsibility."

> Diamond Dan will be the kind of person who offers his seat on a crowded bus to an elderly lady. He won't drop litter and he will be keen on recycling. He will also be very committed to the Orange Order and to the Junior movement and will make efforts to know all he can about the history and culture of his community. (*RTE News*, April 3, 2008)

Excerpts from press releases show careful work in situating Diamond Dan alongside (not in place of) King William as an embodiment of Orange "values," and in that sense, this might be considered a kind of ritual appropriation. However, the writer also connects those values to entirely new concerns, such as, recycling.

Metamorphosis

Over the course of field research, I came across individuals who were deeply involved in projects of ritual appropriation and community development. However, they would tell me in confidence that their own political views and senses of identity were significantly out of phase with many in their own families and communities. They were often frustrated with a pervasive lack of leadership in their communities, parochial worldviews, and sectarianism. They saw their efforts as community workers in loyalist communities as an attempt to empower and educate their respective communities. They did not, however, feel that they could openly share their opinions, for fear of losing credibility, or worse, putting their own safety at risk.

One afternoon, only a few days before I left Northern Ireland in 2007, I sat with Adam in a corner of the bar of the La Mon Hotel outside Belfast, the site of one of the most shocking atrocities of the Troubles. On February 17, 1978, the IRA ignited an incendiary device in the hotel restaurant. Twelve Protestants were killed when flames engulfed the restaurant (Taylor 1999:163). Adam and I talked for several hours about the work of his organization, his interest in conflict transformation, and what he saw as the significant challenges loyalists faced in terms of developing the skills and confidence necessary to undermine the feelings of alienation and exclusion that have kept loyalists fractured and have stymied attempts to decommission loyalist paramilitaries. He emphasized the need for new ways of thinking about identity and nationality among Protestants. He identified mural redesigns as one activity that had opened opportunities for discussion within his own community.

During our conversation, Adam revealed that his own sense of Ulster nationalism allowed for a united Ireland but that he could only go so far in revealing his political views.

> I would see myself as a Social Democrat. I believe in democracy; I believe in the social need for some sort of fair system within a government. I would also see myself as an

Ulster nationalist, right? But I do not want nationalism to be my politic because it's such a destructful thing when it comes to power....I want to get away from nationalism, but I retain my right to be an Ulster nationalist....I want to project my identity; I can do that through using words like "Ulster Nationalist" because then people can at least get a starting point....I could live on this island with two parliaments. I could live on this island with one constitution that protects those parliaments. I would live in a constitution and a bill-of-rights that has written in it that [I], as a British-Ulster person, [am] recognized equally....I have to be careful about talking in this tone, or using this language. You know, you go down to Mersey Street where you live and say I was talkin' to Adam, you know, he has no problem with one island and all that, and I'd get fuckin' shot dead.

Despite his position of leadership in a prominent loyalist organization, Adam has adopted a rather unusual political position compared to most of his loyalist neighbors and colleagues. He has a vision for a shared democratic future between Catholics and Protestants, and he is eager to see loyalists engage in public discussion about their culture, their history, and Northern Ireland's future. In another part of the interview, he spoke of how the use of Celtic mythology in a new mural had led to opportunities for constructive dialogue among loyalists about their collective identities. However, he is also aware that while there is some room for debate, there are limits to the ideas or actions that can be proposed in loyalist organizations and communities, leaving him in a position of major change that can only be accompanied by partial change in the kinds of public collective activities he and his organization can undertake.

Conversion

Todd describes conversion as those instances when old categories become "irrelevant" or "absurd" and equilibrium or coherence between practice and identity is achieved. For Todd, conversion is a consequence of changing circumstances that "render irrelevant older categorical oppositions" (p. 441). Structural changes can of course have precisely this effect, and the enormous political changes in Northern Ireland drive many of the changes addressed in this book. However, because drastic identity changes are relatively uncommon, instances of metamorphosis and conversion tend to be individual ones. Converts are those who have to some degree abandoned or rebelled against identities they once held to be central to their sense of self. As one might expect, conversion is essentially an exaggerated form of metamorphosis.

Technically, this category falls outside the scope of the research. Since the research presented here focuses on individuals who continue to work within Protestant unionist and loyalist organizations and communities, they have not entirely abandoned their ethnopolitical identities or at least activities in light of their professional and vocational work. However, they have taken significant steps toward abandoning their identifications as Protestants, unionists, or loyalists.

Jonathan, one community worker with whom I spoke, has become deeply involved in reconciliation work but has a public profile as a voice of grassroots unionism, especially with regard to victims' concerns. His community relations work has provided an arena in which he can withdraw to some extent from his loyalist upbringing, but he finds it difficult to publicly abandon the category because of his family ties.

> I think the first thing I have to say to you is that I'm not a loyalist, while I'm from a loy-alist community. I'm from a strong Protestant unionist community. I myself am not a loyalist and don't know that I've ever really been one either, you know? I mean, I've had that upbringing for sure. My father was a member of the UDA. My earliest memory politically was being taken by the hand with him on the Ulster Worker Strike March in 1974 or whenever that was, and yeah, I mean, I was brought up pretty much to distrust Catholics and all things republican. When I was the age to vote, my father would have told me who to vote for and all that. That's not very different from most people that were brought up in a loyalist family. And it wasn't really until I started to think for myself that I started to realize that I myself really had very little in common with the kind of ideology that was being proposed. I'm probably more closely aligned to an Irish Nationalist mind-set at the minute, although I've never really publicly come out and said that, unless I feel really safe to do so. I certainly haven't done it where I think people could pick up on it, because at the end of the day, my mum and dad still live in a loyalist housing estate. My dad, while he's no longer involved with the UDA, he's still very much of a loyalist/unionist mind-set, and I wouldn't offend him for the world, you know? He knows anyway because of the conversations we've had privately, but that's very different than actually coming out publicly and actually stating that you've no time for that, you know? I honestly believe that economically, and just because of who we are, that we probably are better suited in an all-Ireland framework, simply because I don't think that Britain wants us near the place. I think we're actually an embarrassment to them. Now, that said, I do have an understanding of how Protestants are thinking because I'm from that community, so I can talk about that if you want. But I'm not, myself—and I have to put this on the record—a Loyalist.

All things being equal, Jonathan, like Adam, holds significantly different political views from those in the community they are often seen to represent, and in this sense Jonathan might be considered in a state of metamorphosis. What separates Jonathan from Adam and justifies placing his experience in the conversion category is that he has changed his public actions more drastically than Adam by agreeing to speak at republican events.

> Even though I'm not necessarily a unionist, I'm perceived as that. I mean the number of invitations that I've had to come and speak at things from a nationalist republican quarter have been really surprising, because I would have never had those things going back two or three years. I mean, this year alone, I have given [presentations] in Derry. I have spoken at [an] event up in West Belfast. I have spoken [with republican

prisoners]…and they were bringing me…because I was Jonathan from the Unionist community. I think, in their understanding, maybe I'm a soft unionist, you know, but I'm not a unionist, and they don't actually know that, but even when I do those things within my own community (and this is the big question that I have for myself), I get further isolated where I don't get invited at all to any unionist things. I mean the unionists had a group of victims over at Stormont…a lot of months ago, and I mean there's no way I would have been invited to that, 'cause I would not have been singing from their hymn sheet.

As a consequence of Jonathan's decision to engage with republicans publicly, he has begun to actualize his hidden identity as a nationalist. He is converting his collective identity, and he may eventually be pushed out by more committed loyalists.

■ CONCLUSION

In chapter 2, I asserted that conflict transformation involves changes in identity and the ways in which conflict is carried out. In chapter 4, we looked at the way in which symbols and rituals, short of being abandoned, may be mitigated by removing some of the more polarizing aspects. We looked in particular at bonfires, murals, and flags. The current chapter has followed in much the same vein by examining how another ritual, Orange parades, which have a particularly long history and in recent years have become a surrogate arena for ethnopolitical conflict, can be mitigated. Attempts to modify Twelfth celebrations reflect a larger shift within the Orange Order as it tries to adapt to social, political, and demographic pressures by trying to redefine its role from staunch defenders of unionist rule to participants in a shared civil society and grassroots politics.

Despite a tumultuous shift in the ideological makeup of the Orange Order, the Grand Lodge has increasingly undertaken a range of initiatives to improve public opinion and build institutional credibility and political capital. Examining the Orange Order's efforts provides one opportunity to observe whether and how innovations of core rituals are aligned with and incorporated into collective identities. The relationships between collective identity and collective action are recursive ones that can contribute to conflict transformation by integrating less polarizing rituals and activities into collective identities. Examining the relationship between change in practices and identity is important for understanding how each informs the other. New activities, such as, Orangefest and public relations initiatives, can be authorized by the tradition but can also be incorporated into the tradition, incrementally shifting collective identities in less exclusive directions. The process is almost always contentious and does not necessarily move in the direction of conflict transformation. In the chapter that follows, we will look at ways in which notions of heritage and the narration of historical identities are used to reframe collective identities among Protestant unionists and loyalists.

■ Notes

1. Tonge et al. (forthcoming) point out that the Orange Order's membership surpasses the combined memberships of all of the political parties of Northern Ireland.

2. Additional events include church parades, arch banner and hall parades, and the Royal Black Preceptory's gathering at Scarva on July 13 and the Orange gathering at Rossnowlagh, Donegal (in the Republic), on the Saturday before the Twelfth. For a full accounting of the types and annual cycle of parades, see Bryan (2000:183–84). Parades are not limited to the Protestant community; nationalist and republican communities also hold parades, and while they are far less frequent, they have grown in number. Nationalist organizations, such as, the Ancient Order of Hibernians (AOH) and the Irish Nationalist Foresters, have represented constitutional nationalist political views for most of this century, but they have, in recent years, been eclipsed by republican parades commemorating events such as, Bloody Sunday, the Hunger Strikes, and the 1916 Easter Rising (Jarman and Bryan 1996).

3. Arches are said to demonstrate the exclusive character of Orange traditions in the way that they mark out territory, and Loftus (1994) claims their origins lie in the Roman practice of erecting arches through which victorious armies would return.

4. For an excellent overview of the loyalist and nationalist parading traditions, see chapters six and seven in Jarman's (1997) *Material Conflicts: Parades and Visual Displays in Northern Ireland*.

5. "Other" parades include youth groups, Royal British Legion, trade unions, and so on (Flanagan 1999:33). The rise in the frequency of loyalist parades corresponds with the widespread view that Protestants express heightened anxiety about the political situation through parading. However, the increase may be exaggerated by the way the figures have been compiled by the RUC (Bryan 2000).

6. Off-licenses sell alcohol in blue plastic bags.

7. Since the 1970s, loyalist bands have become independent from Orange lodges, which they accompany during parades, raising questions over the Order's responsibility for disorder and sectarian incidents connected to bands. The Reverend Brian Kennaway (2006) has launched a stinging criticism of Orange Order leadership for its lack of decisive action in disciplining members with paramilitary ties and those who have engaged in unbecoming behavior. He also criticizes the Order for failing to hold bands accountable for their behavior during parades despite the institution of contracts between bands and Orange lodges since 1986 (pp. 44–73; see also Kaufmann 2007:286–88, 92).

8. The Downing Street Declaration stipulated that any action to alter the sovereignty of Northern Ireland required the consent of a majority in Northern Ireland and was particularly divisive for unionists since UUP politicians took a generally moderated stance toward the document while Ian Paisley and hard-line unionists were outraged.

9. At the time of writing, under the terms of the Hillsborough Agreement of February 5, 2009, a new regulatory body is being developed to replace the Parades Commission.

10. Disputes over parades in Portadown date to the late nineteenth-century origins of the Orange Order and were renewed more recently in connection with protests in support of republican hunger strikers in the early to mid 1980s (Bryan, Fraser, and Dunn 1995; Mulholland 1999:6–8, 18; Ryder and Kearney 2001).

11. For detailed descriptions of the practice, paraphernalia, and history of parades, see work by Bryson and McCartney (1994), Loftus (1994), Jarman and Bryan (1996), Jarman (1997), Jarman and Bryan (1998), Edwards (1999), Bryan (2000), Fraser (2000), and Jarman (2000).

12. The Ulster Bands Association has taken similar steps to improve the public experience of band parades that are unrelated to the Orange Order (*To the Beat of the Drum,* vol 5, issue 1 and 2; vol 6, issue 1).

13. Please see Kaufmann's (2007) endnote for 2001 as the correct year for the Orange Order media training (pp. 301–54).

14. Putnam was invited to address the Orange Order about social capital trends in 2005 (Kaufmann 2007:284; Tonge and McAuley 2008:293).

15. Gladys Ganiel (2006) has documented a similar process among Protestant evangelicals in Northern Ireland.

16. According to *Ulster Loyalism and Unionism Online*, "By September 2005 the Web site had moved to the new URL below, dropped the 'Civil Rights' part of the title and been transformed into a straightforward Orange Lodge site." http://cain.ulst.ac.uk/loy/local.html Archived copies of the site are available at http://web.archive.org/web/*/http://www.orangenet.org/civilrights.

6 Heritage, Memory, and Identity Work

We may not know who we are, but we know who we're not.
—David Ervine, MLA (PUP), interview, July 5, 2006[1]

The past is never dead. It's not even past.
—William Faulkner, *Requiem for a Nun*

In July 2006, I sat across the kitchen table of a loyalist paramilitary leader in East Belfast as he described the determination among many loyalists to persevere in remembering the Troubles.

> Our war of thirty years isn't going to be like the Vietnam War. It's not going to be people trying to sweep it under the carpet and say it never happened or it shouldn't have happened. Now, the war in this country happened, and the people that fought it didn't fly in from another country. They were born and bred here. They fought and defended what they thought was their cause, whether it be republican or loyalist, and it's not something that's going to be swept under the carpet.

Interestingly, this interviewee, in this particular interview, did not emphasize a loyalist history of the Troubles but insisted that the war would be remembered by both loyalists and republicans. His comment raises important questions about the role that collective memory and the construction of collective identities play in conflict transformation. Conflict in Northern Ireland has long been perpetuated by mutually exclusive memories and identities. The compulsion to create shared memory is ubiquitous, and one can hardly expect the Troubles to fade silently into the mists of the past. Nationalists have established a myth of an ancient Gaelic heritage, and unionists have claimed the mantle of modern democracy, which they proclaim was born of William's Glorious Revolution. These and other exclusive myths are unlikely to give way quickly to a new shared Irish, British, or Northern Irish identity. Memories of the Troubles are not likely to be swept under the rug soon, which leaves us to ask: What can be done with memories? What *is* done with them? Are they fundamentally divisive, or can they be mitigated? Do the popular activities through which memory and identity are constructed offer opportunities for introducing new interpretations and diminishing their heavy-handed and politically expedient use?

In the previous two chapters, I focused on public artifacts and rituals, but much of the work of constructing memory and sustaining identity takes the form of texts and narratives. In this chapter, I examine projects that are more overtly historical or narrative. This is not to say that murals and parades do not fulfill similar functions but that some projects seek not only to symbolize the past in a condensed form but also to "explain" the past through storytelling or historiography, what I will call "historical identity work." These are initiatives that narrate a shared past among unionists and loyalists.

Leaders in staunchly unionist and loyalist organizations perceive a deficit in historical knowledge among members of their organizations and communities that leaves them feeling insecure and unprepared to engage in cross-community dialogue and political debate. Yet, they also recognize the need to make the case for their place within Northern Ireland. They note the adept ways in which nationalists have developed political and social capital through the advancement of Irish historical and cultural activities including genealogy, language, dance, music, and history. Increasingly, historical activities among unionists and loyalists are accompanying the kinds of mitigating initiatives that were covered in chapters 4 and 5. They provide opportunities to engage publics domestically and internationally, improve public relations, and develop political efficacy.

Unfortunately, the construction of historical narrative always holds the potential to generate divisions and prejudices, as has often been the case in Ireland. However, since conflict transformation involves a shift in conflict methods from coercion to persuasion, we may welcome the shunting of conflict into the symbolic and political realm, largely because, as I argued in chapter 2, persuasion is more amenable to dialogue and relationship building than violence. The development of historical consciousness may hold the potential for moves toward coexistence by enhancing the quality of cross-community dialogue and providing grounds on which dialogue can take place and on which a more diverse, sophisticated, and shared historical narrative can be developed.

I often encountered unionist and loyalist activists who believed historical and cultural activities offered opportunities to build confidence in Protestant/unionist/loyalist (PUL) communities and to open doors for improved community relations. David Jones, spokesperson for the Portadown District Orange Lodge, described his hopes for initiatives such as, the 2005 art exhibit at the Millenium Court Arts Centre:

> I feel that there's a lot of people in my own community, if they were aware of the actual history of Orangeism, why it's there, where it came from, what it's trying to do, what it has been involved in over the years, if they understood that better, they'd have a much better understanding of our own culture and then wouldn't feel as threatened by an opposing culture.

Undermining threat is central to conflict transformation, and unionist cultural activists I interviewed often cited overcoming fear and insecurity as a central goal of their work.

This raises a difficult dilemma. Groups that share an uncertain collective identity, that are unsure about their status and security, can be prone to turn to violence.
Cultivating a historical narrative that legitimates the group can be used to justify
discrimination and even violence. Conflict transformation requires both a shift to
nonviolent conflict, which diminishes the fear and threat that contributes to intractability, and a reorientation in which collective memory and collective identities are
brought into line with new, less-violent circumstances. Thankfully, memory is malleable, and both remembering and forgetting are important facets of changing identities and peace processes (Brewer 2010:146–54). How unionists and loyalists go
about remembering and forgetting is the main concern of this chapter.

■ MEMORY AND COLLECTIVE IDENTITY

The relationships between historical memory and contemporary identity are close.
Since Maurice Halbwachs (1980) undertook his work on collective memory between 1925 and 1945, and especially since his work, *Collective Memory,* was translated into English in 1980, a great deal of sociological theorizing has followed
around the construction of collective memories through public discourses. At the
root of much of this theorizing is the view that shared schemata of historical events
are constructed by those who gather or "collect" the narratives that interact to constitute what is perceived and feels like a common experience or "heritage" (Young
1993). This may take the form of formal historiography, and O'Keeffe (2007)
reminds us, "To my mind, then, collected memory is always historical (or narrato-
logical) and is always the product of some programme of being-reminded. However,
and at whatever scale a collective is constituted, we have no collective capacity to
share memories that are not in some way externally programmed for us" (p. 5). Our
memories are not our own. They are not an undifferentiated mass of recorded or
remembered stimuli but are filtered and preserved through the mnemonic influence
of our social and physical environments. We are socialized by our families, teachers,
government officials, and other authorities through school curricula, memorial
holidays, and religious rites that provide mnemonic hooks on which we hang
preferred narratives, leaving others to fall away. That is, we remember together or
"co-memorate" (Zerubavel 1996:294). We can experience memories of events that
occurred long before we were alive to participate in them.

Thus, Protestants today remember, in mental images and with emotion, the
Siege of Derry, or young nationalists can conjure in their minds the narrative arc
of the Battle of the Bogside punctuated with its iconic elements of banging trash
can lids, Molotov cocktails, and Saracens. Conversely, even events in which we are
participants become directed by narratives that distill the experience down to
selective and essential facts and claims. Such programming can be introduced
through historical scholarship, literature, mass media, historic preservation of buildings and landscapes, public art, and sites of commemoration, all valuable cultural real
estate over which battles to shape collective memory and thus collective identity are

waged (Barthel 1996; Schwartz 1996; Wagner-Pacifici 1996; Zerubavel 1996; Olick and Robbins 1998; Olick 1999; Moore and Whelan 2007; Graff-McRae 2009).

Heritage, a form of collective memory, is a shared sense of connection with forebears and their experiences (usually victories and accomplishments) and often becomes made material through reenactments and performance, preservation of landmarks and landscapes, and museum curation (Claval 2007). As Anderson (1991) asserts, the modern formation of nationalist identities was closely related to the development of printing technologies that allowed for the dissemination and adoption of historical narratives and has led to the democratization of memory collection, taking the work out of the hands of the educated classes and blurring the distinctions between high-brow and low-brow culture, leading to a growth of vernacular activities (Claval 2007). Irish nationalism offers a prominent example of this process during the Irish Gaelic revival during the last decades of the nineteenth century that was incubated in cultural, literary, athletic, and historical clubs and societies outside of the institutions of the British state. With the ever expanding availability of means to publish and receive information, through mimeographs, desktop publishing, and now the Internet, the advancement of heritage projects and vernacular history is alive and well.

■ HISTORICAL TRADITIONS WORK IN NORTHERN IRELAND

Historical projects that focus on Protestant experience including migration, industry, military battles, and political struggles are playing an increasingly prominent role in the activities of a range of unionist and loyalist organizations. Amateur historical and cultural organizations have sprung up in working-class East Belfast and the Shankill Road, though these types of organizations are not limited to urban areas. Loyalist paramilitary organizations have built historical education into their transformation schemes, and ex-combatants have integrated history programming with community development work. The Orange Order, as part of its attempts to improve its public image, has placed historical work front and center. Flute bands, a popular and growing recreational activity among young male loyalists, have incorporated historical work into their activities.

Community-level historical organizations have become increasingly common in Northern Ireland since the mid 1980s and 1990s, though some prominent organizations emerged earlier. In 1985, the Ulster Society was founded and made its mission "To preserve the heritage and culture of Ulster and the Ulster-British people" and to promote "wider acceptance of the Ulster-British heritage and culture throughout Northern Ireland and the Border Counties." The society has specialized in publishing pamphlets, articles, and other manuscripts about regional historical events, literature, and aspects of Ulster-Scots culture, such as, music. Public events have included exhibitions and lectures on topics such as, the battles of the Boyne and Aughrim, Ulster emigration to North America, the Ulster Unionist

Convention of 1892, and the Battle of the Somme. On their Web site, the society identifies a range of organizations on both sides of the border with which it has worked, including other local historical and cultural associations, the Ulster Bands Association, and prominent institutions, such as, the Linenhall Library, the Ulster Museum, and BBC Northern Ireland. The Ulster Society is staffed by individuals with history degrees and appears to operate largely with other professionals, but it also serves as a bridge between the academic world of professional historiography and more popular formats, such as, community lectures and museums.[2]

Grassroots organizations that undertake similar work, though usually without the same resources or expertise, are of particular interest because they are situated within local networks where friends, neighbors, and relatives signal their beliefs and priorities to one another. This is perhaps especially true in working-class "hard to reach" areas or in close-knit rural areas.

Local Historical Organizations

Amateur history organizations produce pamphlets and organize classes on historical topics (often for youth), organize public events, and commemorate victims and historical figures through the erection and maintenance of monuments and other public displays, such as, murals, sculpture, and public art works. The number and variety of organizations and activities I encountered in my research make it impossible to describe all of them in rich detail, but I can offer a representative selection.

The East Belfast Historical and Cultural Society (EBHCS) illustrates the kind of grassroots organization that operates within its own community to build awareness of shared heritage. According to its Web site, "The Society aims to promote unity amongst the people of east Belfast, educate our children and the many visitors to our city, remember the fallen and celebrate our history and culture." Robert, a local Presbyterian minister and prominent Orangeman, described the organization as unaffiliated with paramilitaries and distinguished between "academic" historical work and contemporary unionist and loyalist culture.

> It was very much a grassroots start-up. Like, "Our culture's not being recognized; nothing's being done about it. There's no cultural group." There's the East Belfast Historical Society, but that was almost an academic or layman's traditional culture [organization]. It wouldn't have been interested in loyalist or unionist culture as such. It was more social culture and social history.

Robert's comment signals a perceived need for organizations and activities that address the political dimensions of Protestant history and experience, the mix of unionist, religious, ethnic, and social influences that many Protestants perceive as central to their individual and collective identities. The group formed in 2002 and began its work by building and unveiling a memorial garden on the Newtownards Road on June 28, 2003, in memory of victims shot by Republican snipers over June

27–28, 1970, as riots spread across Belfast. A firefight was waged on and around the grounds of St. Matthew's Chapel in the Short Strand neighborhood that borders on the lower Newtownards Road, where the garden stands today (Taylor 1998:75–77, 1999:79–80). Two Protestants were killed, and twenty-eight others injured when IRA volunteers opened fire from the grounds of the chapel that interfaces with the Protestant Lower Newtownards Road. One IRA volunteer was killed and another wounded in the fight.

The society next erected an exceptionally large mural in Thorndyke Street that, according to its Web site, "was targeted at countering the argument from the Republican community that as a community we have no history." The wall features twelve panels, each representing an important event or theme in Ulster Protestant history. The society offered historical detail and interpretation through the publication of pamphlets (with the Ulster Society in one case) that accompanied the opening of both the memorial garden and the Thorndyke Street mural. When the mural was unveiled in September 2004, local community members dressed up in period costumes like those worn by many of the figures in the murals. The society employed increasingly familiar repertoires of historical interpretation, murals, reenactment, and music to rally the local community and frame and make tangible a particular rendition of Protestant history.

Similarly, the Ballymacarrett Arts and Cultural Society (BACS), founded in 1996, has undertaken to raise awareness of Protestant culture and history, especially in East Belfast. BACS emphasizes the arts, making explicit connections with youth and addressing social problems, such as, alcohol abuse, anti-social behavior, and broader issues of social and economic exclusion among working-class Protestants, including educational underachievement, housing, unemployment, and a sense of disempowerment (Ballymacarrett Arts and Cultural Society 2000:4). BACS' (2000) mission statement illustrates the very intentional way in which the organization sees cultural activities as an avenue for addressing social problems and improving community relations.

> To offer the community of East Belfast a means of expression in art and culture using exploration in Dance, Drama, Music, Poetry, Debate, Fine Arts and Education. To educate through social interaction with other communities and address questions of Division, Diversity, Pluralism, Heritage and Allegiance in order to enhance understanding of such issues. (p. 8)

A selection of BACS activities listed in the organization's (2000) report, "Prods Can't Sing Act or Dance" include

- Somme Remembrance Parade and Educational Nights
- Nineteen weeks of Irish history program
- Visit to the Battle of the Boyne site
- Ballymacarrett Community Festival
- *In Titanic's Wake* play produced by Brian Ervine

Arts-oriented events also figure prominently:

- Production of *Grease* musical with young people
- Community program with creative writing
- Ten-week art workshops
- Music into schools project

Partnership projects:

- Murals project replacing paramilitary images with historical ones
- Preparation for Ulster Scots Festival
- Planning for shared St. Patrick's Day event
- Meeting with Newry Protestant group to develop cultural exchanges. (p. 9)

BACS has succeeded in securing funding from external agencies, such as, the Northern Ireland Voluntary Trust, Arts Council, Belfast City Council, Cooperation Ireland, Community Relations Council, Irish government, and the National Lotteries Charities Board (Ruddy undated:4).

The extent of intentional reflection on collective identity work is revealed in a Community Think Tank project in which BACS partnered with the Farsett Think Tank project and produced several reports in Michael Hall's *Island Pamphlets*, a long-running series of short publications documenting ethnopolitical perspectives on the Troubles and community relations initiatives that often presents the views of Northern Ireland's working class. BACS produced three pamphlets as Ballymacarrett Think Tank: "Puppets No More," "Orangeism and the Twelfth: What It Means to Me," and "Beyond King Billy," each documenting an emerging interest among working-class loyalists to develop a greater awareness of history and heritage and address what they perceive as an inability to act effectively in the public sphere, both in dialogue with nationalists and in the political field.

Ex-combatants and Conflict Transformation

Historical and cultural initiatives have become a prominent activity among ex-combatants and figure into conflict transformation programs undertaken by paramilitary organizations. East Belfast's Gae Lairn (associated with the UDA and translated as "go learn" in Ulster-Scots) and the West Belfast Athletic and Cultural Society (WBACS) on the Shankill Road (associated with the UVF) were founded by loyalist ex-combatants and incorporate arts and historical activities into their work.

As its name indicates, the West Belfast Athletic and Cultural Society has focused on fitness, an interest developed by many ex-combatants in prison, but the organization has incorporated cultural and historical work in a manner one contact identified as being similar to the Gaelic Athletic Association (GAA), a cornerstone of Irish nationalism that organizes Irish sports as well as activities in music, dance, and language.[3] According to interviews and online promotional materials, WBACS has organized photographic exhibitions at the Spectrum Centre (a local community center) on "the modern social history of the Shankill," exhibitions of World War I memorabilia and artifacts, "seminars on local history and cultural identity," and "assistance with family history research and the tracing of local soldiers in two World Wars."[4]

I visited the West Belfast Athletic and Cultural Society, which is on the Shankill Road at the corner of Wilton Gardens, just behind the memorial garden honoring local residents who lost their lives in the world wars and the Shankill Road bombing of 1993. I was first given a tour of the garden before we went inside. The first floor looked like any well-run, small gym that houses exercise and weight-lifting equipment. I was invited into a conference room on the second floor for an interview with one of the organization's staff members. The room contained few obvious references to the contemporary Ulster Volunteer Force (UVF), but it was lined with framed pictures and glass cases displaying posters, documents, and artifacts from the second decade of the twentieth century, when the 1912 Ulster Volunteer Force was formed to dissuade nationalists and the British government from negotiating Home Rule, an independent parliament for Ireland. Only one year after its formation in 1913, Sir Edward Carson placed the UVF in the service of the British Army as World War I erupted. Contemporary members of the paramilitary UVF, having adopted the older organization's name, often consider themselves a reconstituted force. Thus, one is not surprised to find such a prominent display of World War I artifacts in a UVF ex-combatants' organization.

The collection included UVF and World War I–era British Army recruiting posters, bits of uniforms, sketches and paintings depicting World War I battles, worn documents, such as, a copy of Ulster's Solemn League and Covenant and orders for "Ulster Special Service Force" members to muster for inspection by Sir Edward Carson in 1914. Though the room was dominated by historical artifacts, I was asked not to photograph one wall with more recent pictures featuring events such as, the planting of a tree by the Shankill Somme Association to commemorate World War I veterans from across the border. The tree planting coincided with an exhibition of memorabilia at a local community center and parallels the work of a similar organization in East Belfast, the 36th Ulster Division Memorial Associations.

In most such cases, ex-combatants work alongside other community activists and are associated with paramilitary organizations by dint of their past or current memberships. The organizations themselves are not technically part of paramilitary organizations, though informal connections exist. That said, the incorporation of historical and cultural activities has also been formally taken up by paramilitaries as part of their effort to negotiate new roles that avoid the kind of stigma that might undercut support for decommissioning weapons and standing down their organizations from active service.

The Conflict Transformation Initiative (CTI) or "Loyalism in Transition" project that the Ulster Political Research Group (the political arm of the Ulster Defence Association [UDA]) negotiated with authorities is based firmly in a single-identity and cultural traditions work model, according to the project's director, Frankie Gallagher (2007):

> While the emphasis in society is always on community relations work it is important for the communities to firstly address issues surrounding their own Loyalist identity. Leading theorists have suggested that in society, no meaningful engagement can occur unless individuals can satisfy universal needs, such as, security, development, and most importantly identity and recognition of that identity. We aim to reinforce individual and community identity in our constituencies as an essential pre requisite to any community development and relationship building work. (p. 18)

In pursuit of the "recognition" that the UPRG feels is essential, they have developed a historical collection of stories about life in loyalist communities and sent a group of young people on a cross-border trip to the Republic of Ireland to "reinforce their identity and develop their understanding and confidence" (p. 18).

Though it has not received the same government support that CTI has enjoyed, a similar program, "Beyond Conflict," has been developed as an alternative to CTI for the South East Antrim Brigade, which was expelled from the mainstream UDA in 2005. Tommy Kirkham, who formerly served as the manager of the Fernhill House Museum, a museum of Protestant and Orange history until it closed in 2007, serves as the organization's primary spokesperson. According to policy position documents on the organization's Web site,

> Beyond Conflict [is] an amalgamation of ten community associations from the South East Antrim area, from Whitewell right through to Ballymena. The purpose of the group is to assist the transformation of one section of Loyalism, namely, the South East Antrim Brigade of the Ulster Defence Association, from conflict into an organization that uses community development as their tool.

Like CTI, Beyond Conflict focuses on issues of social and economic development, but it incorporates cultural awareness, Irish history, cultural diversity, Ulster-Scots, local history, and World War I history through visits to the International School for Peace Studies at Messines, the development of an Ulster-Scots museum and crafts center, and guided Ulster-Scots tours.

Ulster-Scots

One of the most prominent forms of Protestant identity work falls under the rubric of "Ulster-Scots." A growing number of unionists and loyalists have turned to historical and cultural links with Scotland as a reservoir of unique cultural practices and a place of origin. It is often pointed out that the stretch of Irish Sea between the coast of Northern Ireland and Scotland served not as a barrier but as a thoroughfare for immigrants, trade, cultural exchange, and kinship ties. One community worker quipped that Protestants in Northern Ireland were essentially "Scots who were good swimmers."

Much as the Ulster Society has worked to advance "Ulster-British heritage and culture," the Ulster-Scots Heritage Council and the Ulster-Scots Agency, among other organizations, seek to build awareness of Ulster-Scottish heritage and culture. The Ultach Trust was formed in 1990 to promote the Ulster Gaelic language and was followed two years later by the Ulster-Scots Academy and the Ulster-Scots Language Society for the promotion of Ulster-Scots culture and language or "Ullans" as it was dubbed by Dr. Ian Adamson, one of the language's most energetic advocates.[5] The academy, a voluntary organization, successfully lobbied in 1999 for formal classification of Ulster-Scots as a European Regional Language. A similar project, called the Ullans Academy, supported by a coalition of Ulster-Scots enthusiasts, envisions a center modeled on the Fryske Akademy for study of Frisian in the Netherlands. The school would build grassroots cross-community interest and support for a range of Ulster-Scots and Ulster-Gaelic activities that could eventually lead to incorporation in school curricula, as one Ulster-Scots activist explained,

> We would be anxious to promote [the dialect] but not by trying to codify it and standardize it as a language and stick it into the curriculum and, you know, say to people, "you must learn this, and that's part of our identity and so on." I think we just want to make sure that we understand our history and we understand our heritage and that we understand, you know, how we are culturally unique and look at the literature that's in Ulster-Scots and preserve it. And if that develops an interest in speaking Ulster-Scots and people want to learn that, fine. But the Ullans Academy is dedicated to just the preservation of our culture, our heritage, our history as a unique part of Ireland and a unique part of the British Isles.

The Ulster-Scots Academy, by contrast, tends to focus on the language and its formal inclusion in school curricula alongside other modern languages.

The Ulster-Scots Heritage Council, now called the Ulster-Scots Community Network, was formed in 1995 and was directed from 1997 to 2003 by Nelson McCausland, a DUP MLA who, at the time of writing, serve as minister for Culture, Arts, and Leisure in the Northern Ireland Executive. The network operates as a hub for community organizations pursuing a range of Ulster-Scots cultural and heritage activities. According to Paul of the Ulster-Scots Agency, the council was formed in the wake of the 1994 cease-fires:

> The Ulster-Scots Heritage Council was formed in 1994 by a group of activists on the ground who realized that we were now pulling out of a terrorist conflict or war-type zone, and our people were now looking for social entertainment, looking for social interaction within their own communities, within their own areas, and when these [Orange] halls were opening their doors again, and the shutters was coming off the windows, and the steel bars was coming off the doors, and these halls were very much a vibrant central place of usage for our people. Several activists came together and formed the Ulster-Scots Heritage Council, which in essence lobbied government and persuaded

government that there was a need to address the inequality of structures currently on the ground for people to be able to come together to capacity-build, to create groups that could further the whole re-structure, re-movement, and regeneration of an identity of a people that was almost lost.

The emergence of many of those grassroots organizations corresponds with the cease-fires and, as Paul describes, were initiated at the grassroots level.

Historical and cultural activities have also been officially encouraged. Moves by the Irish and British governments to frame the cultural aspirations of the two main communities into the political peace process can be traced to the Anglo-Irish Agreement in 1985 and was reiterated in the Downing Street Declaration (1993) and Framework Documents (1995; Nic Craith 2003). In 1995, the UK committee of the European Bureau for Lesser-Used Languages endorsed Ullans as the Scots language in Ulster (Jones 1997:617; Nic Craith 2001:25; Radford 2001:53). The Belfast/Good Friday Agreement of 1998 set in motion government policies to further awareness and use of both the Irish and Ulster-Scots languages. Commitments to "enhance and protect" the Irish and Ulster-Scots languages were reiterated in the setting up of the North/South Language Body overseeing the Ulster-Scots Agency and Foras na Gaeilge under the terms of the North/South Co-operation (Implementation Bodies) (Northern Ireland) Order 1999 and the St. Andrews Agreement. For its part, the Ulster-Scots Agency aims to "promote the study, conservation, development and use of Ulster-Scots as a living language; to encourage and develop the full range of its attendant culture; and to promote a wider awareness and understanding of the history of the Ulster-Scots" (Corporate Plan 2005–2007). The British and Irish governments in their Joint Declaration of 2003 pledged to establish an Ulster-Scots Academy, though the project has been plagued by internal disputes over how the language should be taught and how much money should be made available relative to funding for the Irish language.

As in most identity or nation-building projects, language offers a distinctive marker as well as a historical link to former generations of speakers, and it has been a cornerstone of the Ulster-Scots movement; though many linguists consider Ulster-Scots a dialect, not a fully fledged language, debate continues among scholars about its status (Herbison 1992; Kirk 1998; Nic Craith 2001; Gallaher 2007:94–95). Ulster-Scots has nonetheless received recognition under the Belfast/Good Friday Agreement and the European Charter for Regional or Minority Languages guaranteeing it state recognition and support and giving Ulster-Scots activists leverage with which to lobby for programming time on the BBC and inclusion in school curricula. The dialect is still used in some rural communities, and enthusiasts are quick to point out the linguistic roots that appear in place names and geographical features. Poetry by figures such as, W. F. Marshall, John Hewitt, James Orr, and Rabbie Burns has commonly served as vehicles for the use and appreciation of the language by enthusiasts.

Statistically speaking, the full use of the Ulster-Scots language or dialect is rare, but a significant minority values it. The Northern Ireland Life and Times (NILTS) survey incorporated a series of questions in 1999 about Ulster-Scots, and among those who did not identify Ulster-Scots as their main language,[6] only 2 percent reported that they spoke Ulster-Scots, while 12 percent of Protestants had never heard of it (10 percent of Catholics reported they had never heard of it). When asked whether the Ulster-Scots language is a vital part of Northern Ireland's heritage, 15 percent reported some level of agreement while 56 percent disagreed, figures that were nearly identical for both Protestants and Catholics (ARK 1999). In short, many Protestants remain skeptical about the value of the language, while approximately one in seven values it. With Ullans under heavy scrutiny and often ridicule from both unionists and nationalists, some enthusiasts (especially those from working-class communities) have emphasized other expressions of Ulster-Scots identity. Activities by which participants express their Ulster-Scots identity include reenactment, Ulster-Scots and Scottish dancing, music (often performed by Willie Drennan and the Ulster-Scots Folk Orchestra and the Ulster Scots Experience), quilting, cooking, and displaying tartan plaids (McCall 2002:205–6).

Among Ulster-Scots activists, the search for a narrative of ethnic origin, a legitimate homeland, and relevance on the international stage takes several forms. Over the course of the Troubles, Dr. Ian Adamson, a former UUP Lord Mayor of Belfast and author, along with Michael Hall, who is perhaps best known for the Island Pamphlets series, wrote books and papers claiming that immigrants from Scotland settling in Ireland were not in fact only colonial settlers but were returnees to their land of origin. They argued that the Pretani or Cruthin were a unique and distinctive pre-Indo-European non-Celtic group that migrated from the region now known as Scotland and settled in the Down and Antrim areas around 700 B.C. before fleeing to lowland Scotland in A.D. 637 after their defeat at the Battle of Moira (Hall 1986; Buckley 1989; Adamson 1991; Hall; Adamson [1974] 1995, [1982] 1987). The theory has met with criticism in academic circles with archaeologists, anthropologists, and historians arguing there is little evidence to support it (Buckley and Kenny 1995:49–51; Gallaher 2007:96–97). The historian Jonathan Bardon (1992), for example, claims that the Cruthin, without "a language, social structure or archaeological heritage" were not sufficiently distinct from the Irish Celtic population. Instead, there was a "constant blending" over time, making Ireland notably homogenous in cultural terms (p. 14).

Nonetheless, the Cruthin theory has been adopted by loyalists and Ulster-Scots enthusiasts to preempt nationalists' claims to indigenousness or at least to pursue cultural parity (Nic Craith 2001, 2002:93–95). The case for the Cruthin became influential with Ulster nationalists and members of the UPRG and UDA, who advocated for an independent Northern Ireland in 1978 before proposing a devolved consensus government accompanied by a written constitution and Bill of Rights (Taylor 1999). Parity of culture and recognition of a unique identity that is both Ulster Irish and Scottish played prominently in these initiatives. In a 2007

LIVERPOOL JOHN MOORES UNIVERSITY
LEARNING SERVICES

interview, an influential loyalist with ties to the UDA willingly entertained the prospect of a united Ireland as long as his Ulster-Scots identity could be fully recognized:

> I don't need borders; borders are the borders of my mind. I can do away with the borders of my mind. But if I could get national recognition from the Irish, because I do not see myself as Irish, I am not Irish in any way, shape or form. I'm an Ulsterman, part of the Ulster people, those very ancient Celtic people who have never been part of United Ireland in over two thousand years of contemporary history. What I would like to do is say to the Irish... [I] would recognize your Irish right to national self-determination, but you also have to recognize me as an Ulsterman and my people and recognize us firstly as a people unto our national self-determination, and then we can make a new Ireland.

He later questioned why nationalists would not allow him both Irish and Scottish identities if he had cousins in both countries. He went on to emphasize Scottish heritage, drew on the Cruthin theory, and identified the UDA's Conflict Transformation Initiative as providing opportunities to discuss issues of origin and identity.

> I would be more of the Scotia or the Scottish than I would be of the Éirinn or the Irish, because the name Scotland came from the Scotia, who left Ulster to go there. That's where the name from Scotland came. It was the Ulster people who gave Scotland its name, and it was Anglicized by the English, the Land of the Scotia, Scot Land and all the rest. So, [nationalists] don't even want to get into this debate... CTI and Loyalism in Transition gave us a vehicle for establishing debate in and around all these things.

Identification with Ulster as a nexus of both Irishness and Scottishness thus forms the basis for a highly localized claim to cultural parity of esteem.

However, for most Protestants interested in Ulster-Scots, these discourses and practices exist alongside celebrations of Britishness. Ulster-Scots activities are understood to enhance the legitimacy and confidence of Protestants who remain citizens of the United Kingdom and need not jettison their familiar allegiances to the crown or the British State, especially with regard to state security forces, the Williamite saga, and the plantation of Ulster.

This kind of hybridization was on full display at the fifteenth annual Broadisland Gathering in Ballycarry on a beautiful weekend in September 2007. The festival was first organized in 1992 by Valerie Beattie and David Hume, who serves as the director of services for the Grand Orange Lodge of Ireland and is a prominent Ulster-Scots activist and historian (Hume 2007). The festival featured dancers and traditional Ulster-Scots music by seventeenth-century reenactors in armor bearing lances, lambeg drummers, and practitioners of spinning and other traditional crafts. Vendors hawked the usual fare of Orange pins, band CDs, flags, and football scarves as well as tartan scarves and hats. Local history was emphasized through the parading of banners representing local townlands, which was discussed in chapter 4 (see figure 6.1).

Figure 6.1 Townland Banners at the Broadisland Gathering. Ballycarry. September 1, 2007.

Though the festival is billed as an Ulster-Scots event, there were prominent displays of British militarism and reverence for British security forces and the Royal Ulster Constabulary (see figure 6.2). Vintage military vehicles paraded. An armored British Army vehicle, weapons, riot gear, and operational manuals were exhibited alongside reenactors, who displayed World War I British Army gear and demonstrated life in the trenches, including cooking and how to react during a gas attack. The parade of vintage military vehicles was marshaled by an actor playing the part of General James Steele, a native of Ballycarry who signed the mobilization orders that committed the British Army to action against Nazi Germany in 1939.

Presbyterian heritage was also on display during a service in Old Presbyterian Church at which the Reverend Jim Mattison, an Orange Order District Chaplain and Ulster-Scots cooking enthusiast, delivered a sermon. The sanctuary was festooned with floral arrangements featuring tartan plaids and designed around themes such as, Scottish culture, beekeeping, farming, art, Highland bagpiping, the Scottish poet Robert "Rabbie" Burns, and the Ulster poet James Orr.

Five flags were displayed at the front of Old Presbyterian Church: American, Australian, Union Jack, St. Andrew's, St. Patrick's, and the Ulster-Scots flags. The common theme of Ulster-Scots immigration (from Scotland) extends to emigration, especially to the United States, where enthusiasts are quick to point out that

Figure 6.2 Police and military equipment on display at the Broadisland Gathering. Ballycarry. September 1, 2007.

the genealogy of "at least a dozen" U.S. presidents can be traced back to Northern Ireland (Webb 2004:10; Reid [1912] 2005; Zito 2008). More than once I was encouraged to read U.S. Senator Jim Webb's (2004) book *Born Fighting: How the Scots-Irish Shaped America* about Ulster-Scots immigration to the United States, a book that has been praised for its engaging narrative and criticized for its romanticism, historical inaccuracies, and racial undertones (Newton 2006).

Loyalist bands have also taken up historical interests, as indicated in "Know Your Culture" essays in the magazine of the Ulster Bands Association, *To the Beat of the Drum*. Most issues since the magazine was launched in1999 contain a brief article on an event or individual in Protestant-Ulster, British, or Irish history, such as, the Siege of Derry, Sir Edward Carson, the Cruthin theory, the 36th Ulster Division, St. Patrick, and the Battle of the Diamond. The association has worked with the Ulster Society and the Ulster-Scots Association, and as Kyle, an officer of the Ulster Bands Association in 2007, pointed out, the leadership of the association feels a responsibility to improve youth appreciation of Irish and Ulster history since it is not covered in schools, and participation in bands has become popular among young people (Nic Craith 2003). According to Kyle, "There's a void there, and people are trying to fill that void. I mean there is an identity crisis. There's no question about it; young Protestants have an identity crisis."

The Orange Order

The Orange Order has long nurtured its members' interests in Protestant and unionist history and sees itself as the protector and steward of the legacy of King William of Orange as well as Irish Protestant ethnicity, which is sometimes referred to generally as "Orangeism" (Kaufmann 2007:2–3). Parades, for which the Order is best known, are themselves ritual commemorations of the Battle of the Boyne. In the *Orange Standar*d, the Order's newspaper, one often finds articles similar to those in *To the Beat of the Drum*, as well as the creation of commemorative memorabilia, such as, medallions and pins. The Order grants charters to a limited number of special purpose lodges, such as, the Lodge of Research, which focuses on the study of Protestant, unionist, and Orange Order history.

As Kaufmann (2007) notes, part of the Order's moves to raise its profile, to staunch declining membership, and to take advantage of new funding streams associated with devolution (especially through the Department of Culture Arts and Leisure [DCAL]) has moved historical and cultural activities to the forefront of the institution's agenda, especially as its political role has diminished since its disaffiliation from the Ulster Unionist Party in 2005. A Historical Committee has been in place since 1922, for "archiving of documents, constructing memorials, re-enacting events, producing pamphlets, and lecturing to the rank and file." An Education Committee followed in 1948 to take up the work of the Historical Committee and address legislation around educational concerns (Kennaway 2006:192–93; Kaufmann 2007:7–8). Kaufmann (2007) traces advances in the Order's "cultural heritage" work to Canon S. E. Long's efforts via the Press Committee in the early 1970s to improve public relations and correct misinterpretations of the Order in the media. The work continued into the 1980s in partnership with the Ulster Society and was accelerated under the modernizing leadership of the Reverend Brian Kennaway in the Education Committee from 1990 (pp. 183–84).

We will return to media relations in the next chapter, but here it is important to note that part of the new secular yet, outwardly "evangelical" approach included "our historical and cultural heritage" (quoted in Kennaway, p. 184). Though Kennaway and the rest of the committee resigned en masse in 2000 under pressure from more conservative brethren, historical and cultural work remains front and center, even if it has taken on an increasingly Ulster-Scots cast, in contrast to the Anglo-Irish tastes of the leadership of most of the twentieth century (Kaufmann 2007:213–15). My research revealed many informal connections between the Grand Orange Lodge leadership and Ulster-Scots organizations and activities.

Numerous initiatives have been launched that trumpet the Order's long history in increasingly public ways, through media coverage, cultural tourism, and education. A Grand Orange Lodge press release on April 27, 2009, reports a speech at a conference of the County Grand Lodge of Central Scotland by the Order's director of services, Dr. David Hume (a historian and prominent Ulster-Scots enthusiast), in which he bemoans "agendas which have attempted to downgrade the national identity of the UK." Hume rallies Orangemen to the task of preserving Protestant and British identities:

> Our challenge in this modern world is to preserve our heritage, but to do much more than that. Our heritage is built on our culture. Our society. Our ethos. The history that has shaped us. And our faith. What we need now in this Kingdom is a revival of our identity, for all the best and all the right reasons, a cultural, social and religious revival for the 21st century. There are people who have tried to take the Great out of Great Britain, to bring disunity to this United Kingdom. Our legacy for the future should be to take the lead in making people rightfully proud of who and what they are. We are the very organisation which can take that lead, the very people who can hand down that legacy. (GOLI press release, April 27, 2009)

Another press release in December 2007 declared a "Year of Outreach for the Orange Order" and relayed Grand Master Robert Saulters's assessment that "the Order had undertaken a mission to explain its traditions and cultures and as a result many more people now knew and appreciated what the Institution stood for." He detailed projects by which the Order had undertaken to engage the public:

- Sending representatives to the Smithsonian's Folklife Festival on the mall in Washington, DC during the summer of 2007;
- The development of a new cultural tourism site and Orange Lodge at the Boyne;
- A Williamite Archive exhibition in GOLI headquarters, and the distribution of 20,000 Orange history booklets to schools across Northern Ireland. (GOLI press release, December 12, 2007)

Other initiatives have included a "Thistle Trail" and "Williamite Trail" to guide tourists to sites of Scottish influence and along the route traveled by King William and his forces in 1690 before and after the Battle of the Boyne (*Orange Standard*, June 1995, p. 2). A new glossy and illustrated history book, *Beyond the Banner*, was designed to introduce readers to the history and culture of the Order beyond the parades with which most people are familiar; and an exhibition in 2008 of Orange "Heroes from History" featured influential individuals, such as, the humanitarian Thomas Barnardo and William Ferguson Massey, a former prime minister of New Zealand. Even the name of the Order's new cartoon superhero, Diamond Dan the Orangeman, refers to Dan Winter, in whose cottage the decision to form the Orange Order was made. In short, the Order increasingly seeks to present its own narrative in public through lectures, reenactments, and participation in popular public events such as, the Balmoral agricultural show held each year at King's Hall in Belfast, not to mention incorporating reenactments, music, and dance into Twelfth events, as discussed in chapter 5 (see also Kaufmann 2007:303).

■ FUNCTIONS OF PUL HERITAGE WORK

As political and ethnic commitments have increasingly come into alignment over the course of the twentieth century in Ireland, Protestant identity has been based on simple propositions about allegiance to Britain and doctrinal contrasts with the Catholic Church. Without narratives that provide historical perspective and tie together religious beliefs, political ideologies, and cultural practices, many Protestants can feel alienated and even intimidated, especially as issues of culture and identity have become central in the outworking of the political peace process. They feel that Catholics have cornered the market on culture, history, language, and the arts both in Ireland and internationally.

Consequently, one constantly encounters expressions of frustration among grassroots unionists over a lack of awareness of Irish and British history within their own networks and communities. Many of my interviewees feel as if Irish history has been unfairly framed in ways that favor nationalist interpretations, and they fear that moves to incorporate Irish culture more fully into the public sphere may go too far and overshadow expressions of British identity or "de-Britishize" public spaces, such as, the workplace and schools, as one of my interviewees put it.

The obstacles have not been exclusively related to education policy. Protestants' proclivities to cling to the patronage of the British state have preempted the development of the political and popular space in which anyone might venture to articulate *local* historical narratives because they might be seen as questioning allegiance to the union, especially during the Troubles. Presbyterians' involvement in the 1798 United Irishmen rebellion against British rule, for example, has been publicly explored only in recent years.

The political and economic environments have also changed, making the shift from civic to cultural orientations easier. The availability of new funding streams and the centrality of cultural development in the political peace process have incentivized the work, as we will address in the next chapter. Some of my interviewees asserted that only since the cease-fires have they had the time and freedom to explore historical interests. They claim that throughout the Troubles, their time was spent defending their communities through participation in paramilitaries or the British security forces, such as, the UDR. Besides the international political and economic attention that Northern Ireland has garnered from the United States and the European Union, globalization and especially affordable travel have created new opportunities for enthusiasts to both facilitate cultural tourism in Northern Ireland and become cultural tourists themselves by traveling to the United States to study Scots-Irish heritage or to France and Belgium to visit World War I battlefields.

Having established the growing prevalence of historical and cultural identity or heritage work among a range of Protestant grassroots organizations, we can ask what kinds of concerns and interests motivate participation. The incorporation of historical narratives and activities is thought to provide a sense of pride and assurance that the grounds for Protestants' presence in Ireland is not merely a byproduct of British colonialism but is sufficiently rich, long, and unique to compete with nationalists' irredentist claims to Ulster (Nic Craith 2003:59–60, 65–68). The Ulster Society's Web site articulates well the concerns that underlie nearly all of the historical initiatives I encountered.

> It has been demonstrated that the passive approach to culture and history has not been beneficial to our country's interest. As a result, many feel that a concentrated effort to deny the validity of Ulster-British heritage is on-going. Therefore, it is the Ulster Society's aim to set the record straight by promoting the long and proud tradition of the Ulster-British people.

The East Belfast Cultural and Historical Society (2006) expresses the same sentiments in a foreword to a pamphlet about the Thorndyke Street Mural project that was described in chapter 4:

> The Society is of the opinion that our culture requires a higher and much more positive profile. We decided to demonstrate to all that as a community we have a rich and varied history and culture. A culture, which offends no one and a history, which demonstrates that we are not just implants who have no rights in our own country and a history of which we should feel very proud.... We are often accused of having no history, of having no culture; Thorndyke Street dispels that myth, which is pedalled by republicans. Education of our own and more importantly the wider community was one of the drivers behind the scheme. (p. 1)

The reference to republicans illustrates the sense of insecurity that many loyalists feel when they compare nationalist claims to heritage with their own. Heritage activities aim to instill a sense of interest and pride, mobilize group members, and build skills that can contribute to social uplift and improvements in basic living standards and quality of life. The slogan of the East Belfast Historical and Cultural Society captures at least four basic functions of heritage work: Celebrate – Remember – Educate – Unity.

Celebrate

Celebration entails selecting and highlighting positive narratives that can be ascribed to the group. However, what is considered acceptable or positive can vary widely within and outside the group. Honoring local paramilitary organizations or security forces can cause offense, and many such activities have contributed to deep divisions. Indeed, expressions of ethnopolitical identity have been best known for their capacity to intimidate and alienate one group or another. However, many organizations have tried to identify historical themes that celebrate but avoid drawing stark political lines in the sand. Emma, a community worker at a women's center, described how she felt heritage work should be developed in the Shankill Road.

Not many people on this road would know at one time Shankill was the biggest parish in Northern Ireland, went right away down past Sandy Row, you know. Shankill, this road, has a tremendous history. I was asked recently by someone in the media if the Shankill (because we're quite close to the city center) could become part of the city center. What would we actually lose? We would lose the whole working-class history of Belfast. This is where it started. People traveled in and lived on the Shankill to get a job in the docks, in the shipyards.... That was being lost. Young people know nothing of the history of their own road. Peter [a community worker and amateur historian at the local community center] is trying to reinvent that and bring it back and say, "Do you know for instance we've the oldest thatch cottage on the Shankill?" It's not there. It's a shop now. That was the oldest one. And do you know why it's there? Up in one of our churches here, we have a large dome in the grounds of it, and many people believe it has supernatural qualities about it. Do you know why the church up the road is built in the shape of a shamrock? Do you know why? So there's a whole history there that we need to be getting through to our young people, to take a pride in their own area. And I know there's a lot of areas, Laganeele, for instance, they have their own village cultural history; we need to be doing more of that.

The statue and murals in honor of C. S. Lewis in Ballymacarrett or plans to honor William Connor, a local painter in the Shankill Road, represent similar attempts to claim a legacy without agitating political fault lines that lie close under the surface.

Remember

Remembering or commemorating victims or others who have died in the service of a group highlights a figure or narrative around which to signal solidarity and can be especially emotive and meaningful. Stuart, a UVF ex-combatant and Somme enthusiast described a World War I commemoration event in a local pub that was designed to evoke and shape collective memory:

> It gives them something to be proud of. You know, if they haven't anything to be proud of in their area, they have things to be proud of in their history and their culture, and it gives them a sense of pride and that there. In the Welders [Club] last night, we had a remembrance ceremony where we had guys who marched round in replica First World War uniforms, then lectures, and we had young kids doing poems, and the piper from the Royal Irish Regiment was there and played the pipes, a bugler playing the Last Post and things like that. And you see the people that were there, you know, it gave them ones a pride, it brought back to them just [a] reason to be here and the reason is so, so strong in people because their forefathers went out and fought and died so that we could have these, these freedoms and things that we have today.

Commemoration can often come much closer to disputed and sensitive territory. Murals or pamphlets that detail attacks on a community inevitably conjure up feelings of animosity and fear that become associated with the "other" community

Figure 6.3 Victims mural. "We owe it to the future and the victims never to forget the past." Derwent Street, East Belfast. September 25, 2007.

from which the attacks were supposedly launched. When the deceased are honored for their service in paramilitary or military organizations, the activity may still serve the purpose of unifying the commemorating group while reinscribing division (see figure 6.3).

Educate

Heritage activities are often characterized as an alternative form of education, as a partial remedy to gaps in formal history education and as an extracurricular means of developing learning and social skills that build capacity in a local community. The Ballymacarrett Arts and Cultural Society, for example, lists as one of its aims, "To develop educational programmes which will empower the local community to address issues that affect their daily lives" (Ballymacarrett Arts and Cultural Society 2000:8). Emma, the community worker on the Shankill Road, described the role that educational courses play in the center's attempts to empower local women. Trips to Messines, Belgium, the site of a major World War I battle in which the 36th Ulster Division and the 16th Irish Division fought alongside one another, have proven popular, and she compares them with adult education courses available through a local community college.

Capacity building and the more knowledge someone has, you know, the better and the more knowledge they have of their own history and their own identity the more that they can relate to others. That's the way we see it. It wouldn't be just Messines, you know, the Ulster People's College would maybe e-mail me with something, "We run this course free," and I'd go "Ah, that'd be good," and we'd look into that, and if that sounds good, we'd bring it on, you know?

Similarly, Craig, a loyalist and community worker in the Upper Ardoyne area of North Belfast, connected heritage and mural redesign work with building youth skills.

I want young people to become involved in mediation classes, history classes. They need to understand first what they're about before they can go and argue on behalf of their own community for improved life for that community. And I think what I'm trying to do is give them that information to qualify themselves and make them confident to articulate the background of their own community.

Craig describes a process of building local leadership. Others take a more modest view that at least involving people in heritage activities helps reduce anti-social behavior. The Grand Orange Lodge's "Educating Ourselves" program, which offers user-friendly materials on Orange history, was designed to address the lack of history curricula in schools and to transform local conflicts, which have been known to become violent on occasions. Curtis, a Grand Orange Lodge officer described the intention behind the program:

Our view is that, particularly working-class communities in Belfast, . . . the Whiterock riots and things like that, the difficulty is that those people don't have the educational answers. If somebody says to them, "You know, a certain thing happened in history, you know Presbyterians were united, they were the first republicans, and you know, you're denying your heritage," well, they don't know how to answer that, because it hasn't been addressed with them . . . and if people don't have the answers that they can argue back with, then unfortunately some of them will throw a brick instead of trying to answer that [question].

When asked about the centrality of historical and cultural work to community developments on the Shankill Road, Kevin, a long-time community activist and director of a community center in a loyalist neighborhood, rated it highly in relation to paramilitary organizations.

Well, it's central, because paramilitary organizations are a part of the community. That's number one, and as I've been describing, they have tremendous capacity to wreak mayhem and inflict damage. Counter to that is that a lot of the people who have been in paramilitary organizations have tremendous potential to contribute towards fulfilling that vision, and it can't be fulfilled unless they're engaged in a positive way. So, the West Belfast Culture and Athletic Association is an example of where people with a paramilitary background are actually contributing positively, as are other projects and some of the projects I mentioned like Alternatives.

Heritage activities are widely believed to help replace violent activities by encouraging participants to redirect their energies and empower them to engage in debate and other persuasive forms of contention.

Unity

Interestingly, unity, the final component in the EBHCS slogan, is rarely addressed directly, perhaps reflecting the cherished ideas of individualism and citizenship among Protestants in contrast to the values of community solidarity that are often associated with nationalists. However, the subtexts of community development and empowerment would seem to imply if not require a certain degree of solidarity and unity. Attempts to reach out and awaken an American diaspora, such as, the Ulster-Scots Agency's Web site, www.ulstervirginia.com, and the Northern Ireland contingent's trip to the Smithsonian Festival in Washington, D.C., in 2007, could be classed as building international unity. In the next chapter, we discuss in more detail how heritage activities are believed to build social capital and organizing skills.

Community Relations

Finally, some assign cross-community potentials to heritage work, suggesting that historical themes and narratives that avoid direct reference to the Troubles or violence can be used to replace or mitigate some offensive practices much like the modification of public displays of ethnopolitical identity covered in chapters 4 and 5. More direct and ambitious cross-community efforts have been undertaken around World War I history, since large numbers of both Catholic and Protestant soldiers served in the British Army. Joint trips to European battlefields have become an increasingly common vehicle in the search for a shared history, though other topics are being employed to similar ends.

One community worker, Paula, who works primarily with women in a staunchly loyalist area, described cross-community trips to the walls of Derry and the site of the Siege of Derry.

> We brought the two sets of women together...and they went to Derry's Walls and they did the tour and they went into the Apprentice Boys [hall], they opened it up especially for them, and they were getting the history of the Apprentice Boys, and apparently I'm hearing that the women in The Falls said, "I didn't know that, that's where that came from," and the Protestant women were going as well, "I didn't know that, that's where that came from," so the Protestant women were learning about their identity, and the Catholic women learned about what the identity of the Protestant women was. They're going on a trip again in November, the same women, and they're going to the [Boyne] battlefield and...are going to be told about the battle and all the rest of it, and then come January onwards, we have secured some funding for seven trips throughout the year, and we are bringing women from the Falls, from the Shankill, to...seven different places to show

each of them their different cultures and build confidence up. And it builds a friendship up.

Stuart relayed a similar belief in relation to music, poetry, and World War I history:

> You know, in my young days, there was only two songs I knew as a loyalist. One was "No Surrender," and one was "The Sash," you know, and there's many more songs and poems and things out there pertaining to all sorts of things that people can understand and which can be shared by the other community. The one thing that both people, both sides, are looking at and have done recently is we have a shared history within the First World War, and if we start from there, well then God knows where it will end, if you know what I mean.

The belief among community workers in loyalist areas that heritage work can improve the environment for community relations and even serve as opportunities for cross-community dialogue brings us back to the debate over cultural traditions work and whether it can be said to contribute to the transformation of ethnopolitical conflict or whether it hardens problematic divisions.

▣ HERITAGE WORK AND CONFLICT TRANSFORMATION

The Belfast/Good Friday Agreement was negotiated on the basis of a range of issues including power sharing representation, policing, security arrangements, and cultural recognition. With the Anglo-Irish Agreement, the British and Irish governments agreed that the recognition of ethnic identity would have to figure prominently in a negotiated settlement, thus formalizing a "politics of identity" which frames Northern Ireland in bifurcated terms, often described as "the two communities." The framers of the agreement could hardly be blamed for addressing the obvious connections between Protestant or Catholic ethnic religious affiliation and unionist or nationalist political ideology, and they should probably be congratulated on having recognized that identity and its expression would have to be addressed. However, concerns have been expressed about the oversimplification of lumping all Protestant unionists and loyalists together and all Catholic nationalists and republicans together. From this perspective, the adoption of a cultural traditions approach only serves to deepen the problem by actively *encouraging* people to develop unifying ethnic narratives. The fear of course is that Northern Ireland has suffered enough from sectarian bipolarization, and surely the way forward requires exploring the overly simplistic mantras of the past to find areas of overlap and complementarity in what is in fact already a rich and diverse ethnic landscape.

In two insightful and comprehensive books, *Plural Identities—Singular Narratives: The Case of Northern Ireland* and *Culture and Identity Politics in Northern Ireland*, Máiréad Nic Craith (2002, 2003) warns us about the dangers of reinforcing a bi-cultural "politics of difference" based on simplified and homogenized myths that fail to retain enough nuance to allow the kind of critical reflection on the past that would serve contemporary peacebuilding. One community worker in East Belfast expressed the view to me this way:

> You know, you talk about celebrating the U.S. presidents [from Ulster] and whatever, who have been born here, and whose homesteads are here...my sense [is that they are] reaching after a culture in the same way that [John] Hume and so on reached after a Gaelic culture from way, way back, that there is something going on now that's about the creation of a myth and a story that's true for all time, to do with all sorts of people, [but] it doesn't really exist, excepting the fact that people have the sense that "we need something. We need something that can be as robust and as compelling as the Republican myth."

Similarly, Nic Craith (2003) quotes Waldron, "To *preserve* a culture is often to take a favoured 'snapshot' version of it, and insist that this version must persist at all costs, in its defined purity, irrespective of the surrounding social, economic, and political circumstances" (pp. 18–19). Cultural traditions work is thus characterized as narrowing the field of vision and excluding alternative inter-pretations. According to Nic Craith (2003), "The identity model fossilizes com-munities.... It is a paradigm which places great emphasis on boundaries rather than similarities between groups" (pp. 12–13). Steve Bruce (1994a) offers a sim-ilar warning,

> Put simply, there is a gamble at the heart of the Cultural Traditions programme. To encourage people in a deeply divided society to value their history may change their relationship to the past and politically neuter it by making it "heritage." Equally well, it simply reminds the committed protagonists on each side why they are still on different sides and make them more committed and better informed protagonists. (p. 23)

Nic Craith's and Bruce's concerns over bi-cultural identity politics are certainly warranted. Nic Craith (2002) does not propose that the "identity model" that has been adopted in the peace process should be jettisoned but wisely reminds us that it is important to appreciate the heterogeneity of cultural life in Northern Ireland. "This means that traditional group boundaries have to be recognized as flexible and open to questioning. Ethnic identities are neither pure nor static. 'Rather they change in new circumstances or by sharing social space with other heritages and influences'" (Modood 1999: quoted in Nic Craith 2002:201).

The question that concerns us here is how that change might take place at the grassroots level within traumatized and hard-line communities, that is, whether cultural traditions work in fact leads to further bifurcation of monolithic and opposed identities or whether it can lead to the kind of cultural diversification for which many are calling. John Paul Lederach (2005) describes a process by which memory in the present can be constructed with a view to a just and democratic future.

To restory is not to repeat the past, attempt to recreate it exactly as it was, nor act as if it did not exist. It does not ignore the generational future nor does it position itself to control it. Embracing the paradox of relationship in the present, the capacity to restory imagines both the past and the future and provides space for the narrative voice to create. As such, the art of imaging the past that lies before us holds close the deep belief that the creative act is possible. To live between memory and potentiality is to live permanently in a creative space, pregnant with the unexpected. But it is also to live in the permanency of risk, for the journey between what lies behind and what lies ahead is never fully comprehended nor ever controlled. Such a space, however, is the womb of constructive change, the continuous birthplace of the past that lies before us. (p. 149)

"Restorying" both acknowledges the power and ubiquity of memory in social life while reminding us that it is malleable and can be shaped in constructive if often unpredictable ways. Nic Craith and Lederach offer different assessments of cultural traditions work, and both have merit.

Is there any evidence that historical and cultural traditions work can encourage cross-community engagement, dialogue, and cross-fertilization? Does it at least accommodate the possibility of cultural diversification? The picture is predictably complex, but there is compelling evidence that many, though not all, of those engaged in this kind of work do so because they believe it enables them to break out of old and narrow worldviews and provides useful opportunities for building relationships that were formerly forbidden or difficult. The common use of the word "beyond" in unionist and loyalist documents and initiative titles (e.g., *Beyond* the Banners, *Beyond* the Fife and Drum, and *Beyond* Conflict) at least suggests a desire to address division and conflict in new and forward-looking ways. There is reason to believe that the work may in fact lead to more, not less, dialogue and cross-fertilization with Irish nationalists, though it is a process that is (sometimes frustratingly) slow and presents a number of pitfalls.

Brian Walker's (2000) tracing of commemorations of the 1798 rising shows that both academic and popular readings of historical events evolve over time. Wolfe Tone's memory has been appropriated by republicans of various stripes to help legitimize their agendas over the twentieth century, and loyalists have attacked his grave and a statue on St. Stephen's Green in Dublin, but the bicentenary celebrations of the rebellion introduced a new interest among Protestant unionists and loyalists and Catholic nationalists and republicans in a shared history. Walker attributes the shift to the efforts of intellectuals and "interested members of the public" over two decades to articulate an increasingly detailed and inclusive reading of events (pp. 66–77).

Over and again, I encountered Protestants engaged in cultural work that they described as questioning and testing the already fossilized shibboleths of Protestant history bound up with loyalty to the British state and defense against an encroaching nationalism. They refer to a Protestant identity that is not fully synonymous with a loyalist, unionist, or British identity but is mediated through an interest in local, Ulster, and Irish history and culture. Tim, a muralist who grew up in loyalist East Belfast [to protect the identity of this contact just a little more.] described the logic behind replacing paramilitary murals with historical ones that are more apt to encourage questions about collective identity and memory:

> It's about getting people to question themselves, "I agree with that. Was that wrong or was that right?" even though it was before their time, nothing that they could have ever had a sphere of influence on. Questioning it is always a good thing. Questioning who you are and why you are [who you are] is a good thing.

The idea is that people are enticed or encouraged to take a greater interest in history that leads them to more sophisticated interpretations of history that overlap with those usually considered exclusively nationalist. One could discover, as did Roy Garland, the unionist columnist for the *Irish News*, that one's own family does not pass the litmus tests of ethnopolitical orthodoxy.

> I had always had a desire to know my roots and to be Irish without qualification. I loved Irish music although I was ambivalent because, to be Irish seemed to mean being Catholic, Gaelic, and republican. I was deeply Protestant, had no knowledge of Gaelic and as a child was fascinated by monarchy. Despite this I persisted and the more I investigated the more fascinating history I uncovered. Instead of—in the words of the Orange song—fighting for King Billy on the green grassy slopes of the Boyne, the family fought for King James. They also took different sides in many historic conflicts and suffered from and inflicted suffering upon their Old Irish neighbors on the borders of the northern Pale.

When asked whether and how the Ulster-Scots movement has contributed to the peace process in Northern Ireland, Simon, of the Ulster-Scots Agency, replied that its influence had probably been minimal but that it had the potential to make a contribution in persuading people to widen the scope of their worldview.

> If it can help people here, sort of, become more outward looking rather than constantly keeping themselves within the goldfish bowl of, you know, "I don't like you, and you don't like me." If you can just, sort of, pull your head up out of that and look around the world and just say "Look, see all the things that happened in Scotland, they have an effect here, and the things that happened in the States, a lot of it was driven by people who left here, and then one-hundred years ago, Belfast was a city with a real global vision. You had the biggest shipyard in the world, the biggest tobacco works, the biggest road works and the biggest linen industry. It was immense." People kind of need to rediscover that it's not just a historical story, but the story creates opportunities for them to think outside of this place and outside of the goldfish bowl.... [There is] navel gazing, a lot of history that is in the past, and we're trying to look to the future.

Simon's comments sound remarkably like Lederach's restorying of "the past that lies before us." Serious consideration should be given to how new unionist and loyalist histories are interpreted by Catholics and nationalists and whether they have been developed in cross-community collaboration. We will return to those concerns shortly, but we can say that there is at least an intention among many Protestants engaged in heritage work to stretch the boundaries of Protestant, unionist, and loyalist worldviews.

Keeping in mind that conflict transformation entails building relationships even while they might remain conflicted, historical and cultural work offers several ways in which new contacts can be made and cooperation initiated. There is a prevalent, though not universal, view that cross-community and cross-border dialogue should be a central element of heritage work to offer opportunities for cross-community interaction and to spark interest in dialogue.

One UDA leader in East Belfast relayed a story about a meeting with republicans in which the 1798 United Irishmen rebellion provided a basis for constructive dialogue.

> We went up to [a local peace center]…[Michael] was taking the chair, [and he said,] "I don't know what way to start this off," and I stuck my hand up…"How has these guys become the men of '98, and *we're* the men of '98?" Here's Joe [a republican], "What?" I said, "Well, you walk up around our place, and by the way, you see [a commemoration of] a member of '98. We're the people of '98. I'm a County Down man."…Joe said, "Well, this isn't going to be difficult at all now." And it just shows you, if you take their theme and turn it and say, "No, this is our theme," it makes common ground, because they're going to ask, "Why is it your thing?" And we say, "Here's why it's our thing." So, it starts talking.

This use of historical exploration and cultural activities turned out to be a recurring theme over the course of the research as common interests in activities, such as, language, dance, or history, were identified as bridges for contact and cooperation, established common ground, and undermined division[7] (Hall 1993, 1994b:9–10, 2007).

In 2007, contacts among a group of Ulster-Scots enthusiasts invited me to a rather unusual Saturday morning breakfast meeting. One of the men picked me up at a local coffee shop and drove us to the offices of a civil service agency in East Belfast. When we arrived, a conference room was set up with service for coffee and tea and a full Ulster fry breakfast. After a while, two leading figures in the Irish language movement in West Belfast arrived. It seemed an unlikely gathering given nationalists' resistance to the development of Ullans (Nic Craith 2001:24–25); at least three people in the room had been ranking officers in the UDA or were closely connected to it, and at least one of the visitors from West Belfast was deeply involved in the republican movement and Sinn Féin and had once been under threat by the UDA. Nonetheless, they discussed how they might develop a collaboration and jointly plan shared cultural events in west and east Belfast in which each would travel to co-host evenings of cultural performance, such as, Irish and Ulster-Scots poetry readings, dancing, and music. The Protestants in the room were modest in expressing their desire to learn from Irish cultural enthusiasts and voiced some concerns about their own ability to move as quickly as they expected their better-resourced partners in West Belfast to do. This same group of amateur historians and Ulster-Scots enthusiasts have taken up planning annual St. Patrick's Day breakfasts, to which they invite both Catholics and Protestants and discuss the history of the saint, to whom they feel a historic connection, though Patrick has been most commonly associated with the Catholic Church and Irish nationalism.

Similarly, the Ballymacarrett Arts and Cultural Society has been explicit in incorporating cross-border collaboration into their programs, having conducted ten cross-border exchanges in 2000 (Ballymacarrett Arts and Cultural Society 2000:4). Vinnie Blyth, of the Sligo Inner City Cultural Project, with whom BACS has cooperated, states, "We feel that the discovery of shared interests in historical reenactments is a form of 'cultural politics' which opens up whole new areas of non contentious cross border cooperation" (Ballymacarrett Arts and Cultural Society 2000:12). Gareth described with great satisfaction his trip to Dublin with other community development workers, where he discovered that the Lord Mayor's gold chain of office was presented to the city by William of Orange in 1698.

World War I commemoration has become an increasingly common vehicle for cooperation. Though remembrance of World War I veterans is most enthusiastically practiced by Protestants, many Catholics fought in World War I in the British Army. Nearly half of the 10,000 soldiers who died during the Battle of the Somme were in the 16th Irish Division. Many nationalists have downplayed or minimized these parts of their family histories, but these stories have been resurrected in recent years. Since 2005, Glenn Barr and the International School for Peace Studies have organized services of recognition at the cenotaph at the historic Diamond in the Bogside of Derry to commemorate soldiers, including nationalists, who lost their lives at the Battle of Messines in Belgium. On the ninetieth anniversary of the Battle of the Somme, the West Belfast Athletic and Cultural Society rededicated a historic tree on the Shankill Road in memory of men from the south who served in the war. In both of these instances, World War I commemoration facilitated new cross-national and cross-border identifications.

In September 2002, Alex Maskey, as Lord Mayor of Belfast, laid a wreath at a ceremony in Belgium to remember men from north and south who lost their lives at the Battle of the Somme in France. On July 1 of that same year, he had laid a wreath at the cenotaph at City Hall in Belfast in what has traditionally been an exclusively unionist ceremony. In an indication of how state rituals can remain highly sensitive for unionists, they expressed outrage in November 2008 when Sinn Féin Lord Mayor Tom Hartley was out of the city during the annual Remembrance Sunday commemoration, even though he had laid a wreath at the cenotaph in Belfast in July. Unionists' protests at Hartley's absence could easily be interpreted as a dogmatic attempt to force him to imprint Britishness on the Lord Mayor's office. The interpretation would probably be accurate, but at the same time, we should also note how extraordinary it is for unionists to be upset that a Sinn Féin politician is *not* taking part in a sacred rite of British identification!

One of the most incongruous instances of political theater played out at the site of the Battle of the Boyne as Northern Ireland's first minister Ian Paisley and Bertie Ahern, in his final day as the Taoiseach, used gleaming swords to jointly open a new visitor center alongside representatives of the Orange Order, one of whom spoke Irish to Mr. Ahern. In his address, Ahern declared,

> The fact that we have come here together shows us once again that our history need not divide us. Your history is our history too. We need to understand our shared history if we are to build our shared future. In the future, let us be reconciled with each other. Let us be friends and let us live in peace.

The Irish government's Office of Public Works (OPW) has teamed up with a consortium of Orangemen to develop the site of the battle, including a heritage trail, an Orange lodge, and a rebuilt obelisk to replace one blown up in 1923. It should be apparent from these examples that historical and cultural work can provide opportunities for experimentation with the traditional boundaries of collective identities, by claiming new narratives (sometimes others' narratives) and adopting new cultural practices, thus making old divisions porous.

In an interview, Nigel, a civil servant remembered, as a child, picking through the rubble of his local corner shop for sweets after the IRA blew it up and his father joined the neighborhood defense association. He became a youth worker in loyalist areas of inner city Belfast as a young adult. Now, in his early forties, he has taken up the uillean pipes and the Irish language. When I asked him why, he said he wanted to depoliticize the language and challenge stereotypes. Interestingly, he feels it was his historical "community" from the early twentieth century that challenged him:

> There's no reason for [republicans] to take the language if the UVF in 1912 had as its headline, "God Save the Queen, and Erin Go Bragh," which is "Ireland forever." You know, I suppose that phrase really gave me a lot of confidence in being challenged by my own community to say, "Hold on a wee second; you know, in 1912 the UVF had as their saying 'Ireland Forever,' but they didn't say that in English, they said it in Irish. So, why would you be challenged now by the Irish language when it was culturally part of your identity in 1912, you know?" ... There are so many fantastic events in our history that we can draw on. We don't have to draw on the bad stuff or the stuff that divides, you know. I think this is, again, where the whole nationalism thing, the whole twentieth century-political viewpoint has skewed and clouded vision, you know? I wanted to take those glasses off and see things in a different way.

Nigel felt bloodshed had simplified mentalities, and the end of violence had opened doors for political and cultural experimentation. He even imagined a point at which unionists and loyalists could be persuaded to abandon the union, given the opportunity to maintain their own value sets, which deviate from those in the United Kingdom now.

> While they say they're British, they're not British because they don't behave as loyal citizens of the British State. They behave as Citizens who are loyal to their own culture and their own identity. It just so happens that the British State allows them to do that, and therefore, they show allegiance to the British State. But, when the British State stops them doing that, then they change, and they decide to do something else and, and to some extent that's why it's a very fantastic time and a very dynamic time within the community. We have many, many possibilities . . . the big issue that you're dealing with will probably be challenging those cultural identities and allowing the community to make a step in the right direction, that is, recognizing that "I'm not British, but actually I have an allegiance to a political structure that allows me to behave as I choose, and I actually don't care what that political structure is colored in? I don't care if it's a Crown, and it's red, white, and blue. I actually don't really, at the end of the day, care if it's green, white, and gold. If it allows me to do what I want to do, then I'll probably support it, and if it doesn't allow me to do what I want to do, I'll not support it." So, the issue is, will the community recognize what it wants to do by having those things challenged? In other words, by somebody saying to the community, "Actually, you don't need the red, white, and blue to be a Protestant in Northern Ireland and to be an Ulsterman. You actually don't need that. You can be a full blooded, you know, true blue Orangeman not within the British State, within some other structure."

Nigel decouples ethnic identity from political identity and claims that the former takes priority. His perspective mirrors the basic approach of the Belfast/Good Friday Agreement in which parity of culture is promised in return for participation in democratic politics. Unionists insisted on the principle of consent, believing this would sustain the union, and nationalists were reassured that they would enjoy full cultural and political rights and opportunities. Nigel foresees a situation in which it is unionists who could theoretically be persuaded to become citizens of the Republic of Ireland or an independent Northern Ireland as long as they could retain some core of their unique identity as Northern Ireland Protestants.

Over and again, I encountered unionists and loyalists who were notably undogmatic when talking about their identities as Protestants, unionists, and loyalists. They were certainly not indifferent and were often defensive, feeling that cultural expressions with which they identified were undervalued and even undermined, especially in comparison to the successes of the Irish culture industry. What is remarkable is the way in which heritage and cultural activities were identified as gateways to contact and cooperation and in some cases even the development of shared memory and history. This is not to say that historical narratives and cultural displays have become noncontentious, only that there is evidence that cultural and heritage activities may constitute a dimension of grass-roots conflict transformation.

■ PITFALLS AND CULTURE WARS

The potential of cultural and historical identity work to introduce new interpretive schemes and to challenge old ones is apparent, but it would be naïve to overlook the many potential pitfalls of such contested terrain. Seventy percent of respondents to the Northern Ireland Life and Times Survey between 1998 and 2000 either agreed or strongly agreed that "living in Northern Ireland means that we are influenced by several cultural traditions." Half (50.7 percent) agreed or strongly agreed that "having different cultural traditions in Northern Ireland means that there will always be conflict between them" (n = 4780). Nearly half (43.5 percent) agreed or strongly agreed that "having different cultural traditions in Northern Ireland enriches us all" (n = 4770), and these respondents were less likely to feel that there will always be conflict between cultural traditions. Those who agree that different traditions will always be in conflict with one another are more likely to also disagree or strongly disagree that "having different cultural traditions enriches us all" (ARK 1998–2000).

Unionists have been more suspicious than nationalists about the future of their cultural traditions. When asked from 2001 to 2003 whether they are "confident that your cultural tradition is protected in Northern Ireland these days," only 28.4 percent of unionists (n = 2,012) agreed or strongly agreed while 71 percent of nationalists (n = 1,428) agreed or strongly agreed. Their suspicions also seem to be reflected in a question asked from 1998 to 2000 about whether "at some time in the future the viewpoints of all cultural traditions will be accepted by everyone in Northern Ireland"; 30.6 percent of unionists (n = 2,342) agreed or strongly agreed, but 54 percent of nationalists (n = 1,446) agreed or strongly agreed (ARK 1998–2000, 2001–2003).

Parity of culture is a cornerstone of the cultural traditions model, and while reassurances that collective cultural rights will be protected has been helpful in moving the peace process forward, in its simplest form (separate and equal), it falls short of the transformative potentials that have just been presented. A resort to cultural parity slips into an otherwise highly reflective comment by the Reverend Jim Rea at the Orange art event at the Millenium Court Art Centre in Portadown.

What we should do is to have a look at each other's culture, and I think that this exhibition has been an attempt by the Orange Order to say to people across the community in Portadown, to some degree, come and have a look at what we're about! And I think people in the Nationalist community should also be saying: "Let's look at our culture." And that's not saying to everybody: "Everything about us is great! Everything about us is right!" This is about us saying: "This is how it is, this is what we are, and this is how we got here." You know? And to some degree, you know, we want to go forward into the future in a way that we can coexist with our neighbors and have what Sinn Féin often quote, "parity of esteem."

The Reverend Rea is proposing a cultural coexistence in which two traditions stand as monoliths beside one another. Similarly, in a speech to the bi-annual conference of the County Grand Lodge of Central Scotland in Motherwell, Dr. David Hume claims an Orange heritage of pluralism but then invokes majoritarianism in nearly the same breath with equality.

> The heritage which the Orange Order propounds is a heritage of civil and religious liberty. This means that we support a pluralist society as part of the legacy of the Glorious Revolution of 1688–90. But, equally, it means that we expect to have our majority views and ethos respected and taken account of. (GOLI press release, April 27, 2009)

The temptation to protect the older accepted and institutionalized frames of reference remains, as these comments reflect. Oliver, a UUP political activist and a member of the Apprentice Boys of Derry, interprets multicultural heritage work as a potential threat.

> If there's a threat at all to the Apprentice Boys, it's that the Roman Catholic nationalist community are now open to the siege [of Derry] and now want to claim their part as well. So, there's a trick now for everybody to manage.... Everyone can put their slant in it. I mean, there was three main writers came out of the siege, and each one of them wrote a slightly different story, put a different emphasis on it. So, there is the trick where we try to manage the fact that everybody's now interested in the siege, and it's not just our stories that have to be told.

The dangers, which critics of the identity model have raised, is real and can prove more severe than the comments by the Reverend Rea, Dr. Hume, and Oliver.

"Fossilization" or the maintenance of zero-sum mentalities by claiming historical ground in exclusive ways represents the antithesis of Lederach's process of restorying and merely looks backward, lacking the creative tension that incorporates a constructive and democratic vision of the future. Web sites such as, PULSE (Protestant Unionist Loyalist Social Education, formerly Calton Radio), based in Glasgow, Scotland, exemplify the revanchist quarters of loyalism where zero-sum mentalities are perpetuated. PULSE caters to bands, paramilitaries, and their supporters, hosts online discussions, publishes newsletters, and streams a radio broadcast of loyalist and Orange tunes. The materials available on the Web site typify the defensive and studiously anti-republican views of working-class Protestants who feel "under siege" and question whether the war is truly over. Paramilitaries figure prominently in the music that the site broadcasts, and the newsletters detail republican and Catholic conspiracies and stories of attacks on Protestant homes and neighborhoods. Some historical pieces appear, such as, one titled "The Words and Wisdom of Oliver Cromwell" that compares Cromwell's disdain for the Parliament of his day with the author's distaste for Paisley and all other pro-agreement (B/GFA) politicians (*Pulse Newsletter,* February 2009, pp. 2–3). These are the representations of loyalism that tend to dominate public perceptions, and they should not be discounted (though it may be worth noting that PULSE originates in Scotland and not Northern Ireland).

How can the experience of the Troubles be represented in ways that do not encourage fossilization and automatically redraw old fault lines? Commemorating victims is surely an improvement from celebrating paramilitaries, and it has figured prominently in the work of many organizations, but how can victims be commemorated without immediately and implicitly conjuring bitterness toward the perpetrators and the communities who are believed to have harbored them? The East Belfast Historical and Cultural Society has made commemoration of victims central to its work, and the Orange Order has made much of the more than three hundred Orangemen who lost their lives in the Troubles, launching a "Murdered Brethren Appeal" in 2007.

How can loyalist paramilitaries be accepted as agents of cultural conflict transformation? Some argue that they are nonetheless members in standing of their communities while others resent that they maintained positions of influence through a contradictory mix of intimidation and service. The UDA's use of Remembrance Day (in honor of British armed forces veterans) for parades has raised consternation, for example. Oliver explained:

> I have no doubt, that the key government policy now is getting a unionist community that is free of paramilitarism, by throwing money at the paramilitaries the way [Irish President] Mary McAleese is doing. I don't think it is helpful because it's still giving those people this veneer of peer leader for the community. And those people should have earned that right without it being given to them by another council or something like that.

Gareth, the community worker in Portadown, expressed a similar sentiment:

> Government is about reinventing paramilitarism into community where, as far as I'm concerned, paramilitarism today is criminality. Agents of law and order should be going after them, apprehending them and giving them to the courts. Now, those who were "cause men" and who were in it for the cause, who have divorced themselves from that, they should be lifted and supported to reintegrate into communities. But they should be reintegrating into our community as opposed to our community reintegrating into that reinvention of paramilitarism.

The paramilitaries' legacies are especially difficult to overcome when the pace of decommissioning weapons has been slow and occasional unrest is connected to paramilitary infighting.

Even after decommissioning, the specter of violence can be renewed through activities that valorize armed struggle or defense. Representations in murals or reenactments of medieval or seventeenth-century battles might cause offense, even if swordplay and single-shot muskets are less likely to induce fear than automatic weapons or scarves and balaclavas. Some cases, such as, a republican parade through the center of Belfast on August 12, 2007 that included replica weapons (at least one of which was carried by a masked gunman), have provoked outrage. One can imagine that the display of police and army gear observed at the Broadisland Gathering in Ballycarry could evoke similar feelings among many nationalists.

Finally, there is a need for both critical and strong historical reflection. A willingness to be critical about the past is discernible, if not fully developed, in the field of cultural traditions work. As the Reverend Jim Rea proposed at the Orange art panel discussion at the Millenium Court Arts Center in 2005,

> I think that what we need to do is to become self-critical of our culture. You know, it's important that I hear David say and, I think, others say, "You know, there are things about Drumcree, when somebody in one hundred years writes a history of Drumcree, there are things about Drumcree that are very, very bad." And it's good that people are prepared to say that there are things, let's hold our hands up, things that we have done in this community that are very bad. I want to hear republicans, and I want to hear loyalists say: "We have done bad things." That, I don't hear. What we always hear is people who are apologizing and become apologists for what they've done: "We did it because they did this, and what about you? About such and such?"

The will to be critical must be continually encouraged, but we must also acknowledge that basic historical skills are often missing, largely because of the lack of Irish and Ulster history in state schools, and partly because of the way the conflict has forged a divided society. Amber, a community arts worker who has worked closely with loyalist community groups in North Belfast, shared her experience working on mural redesign projects with historical themes:

> A lot of the people here putting these up are not 100 percent sure of the history themselves. They know some of it, but it's probably something that's been passed on from maybe their own parents or, you know, something they've heard. It's not necessarily factually correct. And I think that's a massive problem, is that people are told things, and they think it's the gospel truth—that's the truth, and it may not be the truth. It may not be how things actually happened. And it's a problem here, because we do not do our own history in school. We didn't do it. I didn't do it. Did you do history in school? [to a colleague at a desk nearby, who replied "no"]. No, none of us—it's not taught here.

Under these circumstances, the prospects of revisionism loom as they do in most historical projects. It is important to remember that the potentials of historical and cultural work to advance conflict transformation are realized when a dialectical *process* of dialogue and exchange helps produce increasingly nuanced historical narratives. As Edna Longley, a founder of the Cultural Traditions Group, states in an undated article on the Ulster Society's Web site,

Peace Process politicians constantly preach "Forget the past." I agree that it is not so easy to do that, nor do these politicians themselves always practice what they preach. Really "to forget" is to accept the challenge of remembering in more complex and less divisive ways.

Longley's challenge should be taken up across the ethnopolitical divide but also between amateur enthusiasts and professional academics.

The Cultural Traditions Group that was formed in 1988 drew from "universities, museums, Irish-language and other cultural bodies" (Fitzduff 2002:61). Significant disconnects exist between academic historical work and working-class grassroots work. As the historian R. F. Foster (1983) said to the Royal Historical Society in 1982 with regard to Irish historiography, "The point should also be made that the triumph of revisionism in Irish academic historiography is a particularly exact instance of the owl of Minerva flying only in the shades of nightfall: events in the island since 1969 have both emphasised the power of ideas of history, and the irrelevance of scholarly revolutions to everyday attitudes" (p. 191). The Ulster Society and the Cultural Traditions Group have helped bridge the gap by partnering with amateur historical societies and organizations of the sort covered in this chapter, but there remains a mutually reinforced detachment, with academics decrying the politically selective and inaccurate use of historical narratives and amateur heritage enthusiasts finding professional academics unapproachable and detached from the realities of working-class life. The arrangements are not conducive to the advancement of historical and cultural work in either domain.

■ CONCLUSION

One of the fundamental tenets of conflict transformation is that intractable conflict is not resolved in the short term as much as it takes on new forms. Particular grievances must be resolved, and new policies must be established to help ensure that justice and equality can be sustained and to facilitate the continuation of conflict through institutional politics. However, even as violence ends, the relative proportion of contention can shift to the symbolic realm. There, social and psychological legacies of discrimination and violence can remain embedded in mutually exclusive cultural schemata that are sustained by memories of trauma and injustice. A shift to symbolic conflict can be welcomed as a merely less-violent surrogate for armed struggle, but I have argued in this chapter that it contains its own transformative potential even as it could be said to sustain ethnic and social-psychological divisions.

Heritage and cultural activities maintain shared memories and identity and sustain ontological security. It is true that the selective process of creating mythologies, memory, and identity can obviously contribute to violent intractable conflict. The republican movement in Ireland was largely built around literary, arts, and athletic clubs that celebrated the myth of a free Gaelic nation. Fundamentalist Protestants and Ulster-Scots enthusiasts have cast themselves as protectors of a light on a hill where reformation Christianity and democracy were saved from tyranny by King William of Orange and subsequently exported by Ulstermen (women are usually overlooked) to another great democratic nation, the United States. These myths can exhibit remarkable continuity, but they are also open to reinterpretation, and in order for former enemies to coexist, they must reframe their core narratives in less exclusive ways that accommodate new political and social arrangements.

The kinds of activities addressed in this chapter, such as, amateur historiography, music, language, and commemoration, constitute opportunities for two seemingly divergent functions. In a period of transition, heritage activities can channel insecurities and fears into activities that maintain continuity with the past but also introduce new frames for navigating the future. We have seen how local history education, commemoration, and Ulster-Scots language and literature activities have helped to reassure some Protestants. Even more interestingly, these practices have provided opportunities for cross-community engagement, be it sharing commemorative events or cultural activities or engaging in dialogue about historical figures and events, such as, the relevance of St. Patrick to both Protestant and Catholic traditions. However, most important are the ways in which unionists and loyalists begin to reconsider and reframe their identities, not merely as subjects to a patron state but as people with a rich and even checkered past and a democratic future.

Ethnopolitical conflict is no doubt still being played out through these activities as unionists and loyalists seek to build cultural and political capital by laying claim to legitimacy through historical arguments and Irish, British, Scottish, and American connections. As we will see in the next chapter, heritage work and mitigating cultural activities can serve pragmatic political, social, and economic functions as many unionist and loyalist organizations seek to adapt to new political circumstances and become more adept at organizing and building public support.

■ Notes

1. The late David Ervine formerly served as the leader of the Progressive Unionist Party until his sudden death on January 8, 2007. He had served on active duty with the Ulster Volunteer Force and was jailed for transporting munitions in 1974. Ervine worked for the negotiation and implementation of the Belfast/Good Friday Agreement and became one of two MLAs with close links to a loyalist paramilitary organization when the Assembly opened.

2. http://www.ulstersociety.org/; accessed May 16, 2009.

3. The combination of athletic and cultural interests is unusual within Protestant communities, but I also identified the East Antrim Athletic and Culture Group, part of the East Antrim Conflict Transformation Forum, which has developed a protocol for the removal of UVF and YCV (Young Citizens Volunteers) flags and emblems after the summer marching season.

4. http://www.mygroupni.com/shankillpartnership/directory/; accessed October 9, 2007.

5. According to Ian Adamson's Web site (http://ianadamson.net/notes/ulster-scots.htm), "Ullans" is a combination of the words "Ulster" and "Lallans," Scottish for "lowlands" or the language spoken in southern and central regions of Scotland. It can also be interpreted as an acronym, Ulster-Scots Language in Literature and Native Speech (cf. Gallaher 2007:88–89, 92).

6. Only 1 percent of males reported Ulster-Scots as their main language.

7. For a contradictory view, see the Reverend Brian Kennaway's commentary, "Mardi Gras culture no answer for Orangeism" in the *Irish Times* on August 31, 2006. Kennaway is the author of the book, *The Orange Order: A Tradition Betrayed.*

7 Strategy, Pragmatism, and Public Relations

> East of the Lagan lies Ballymacarrett, a staunchly Loyalist working-class community in East Belfast. "Lies" is far too passive a word; since the 18th century, activity in Ballymacarrett has had enormous impact on Belfast, the UK and the world. It's noisy too: in the past century one could hear the groaning and screeching of massive machinery used to make not only rope and linen but also colossal mechanical achievements (and more notably—failures), the giggling and singing of the children who would swing around lampposts, boys' mischievous moaning from behind old gravestones, the craic and laughter spilling out from the pubs, the explosions caused by Hitler's Luftwaffe intent on wrecking Ballymacarrett's industrial capacity, and the gunshots and peal of thrown glass bottles shattering onto the street-these sounds distinctive and frequent during the Troubles. And from the cacophonous environs have arisen Voices—words proclaiming truth and wonder, songs expressing fondness, melancholy and mysticism—which have resounded throughout this past century. C. S. Lewis was born and grew up here in East Belfast. Van Morrison was nursed on American jazz music fed to him by his father's record player on Hyndford Street. Playwright Marie Jones listened to her aunt's and mother's chatter in an East Belfast kitchen.... It's an inspiring place, filled with fascinating people...
>
> —Skainos Web site[1]

The opening selection has been excerpted from the Web site for an impressive new community development project in the Ballymacarrett ward of East Belfast. The East Belfast Mission (EBM), a small Methodist congregation, is opting to replace its church building with a much larger new complex that will facilitate local business, voluntary organizations, education, and affordable housing. A modest sanctuary for the congregation will be incorporated toward the rear of the complex. The *Skainos* project is designed to tackle inner-city social and economic problems, but its organizers understand that a sustainable community must have a sense of solidarity and ownership in its future. At a minimum, it must recognize any vision of the future as its own, and thus, a sufficient consonance with the past must apply.

The mission is fully integrated into the Ballymacarrett Ward and is committed to its regeneration. Space does not allow me to detail the many projects of social and economic uplift that the mission sponsors, such as, a chain of eight thrift stores, a twenty-two-bed homeless hostel, and the Inner East Forum. The forum brings together representatives of local community organizations, loyalist para-militaries, and civil service organizations such as, the Housing Executive, Health Service, and the Police Service to consult and pool resources to best deal with local concerns. The forum has proven instrumental in dealing with interface tensions, especially at the interface between the Catholic Short Strand neighborhood and a short row of houses in a side street, Cluan Place. EBM has incorporated local cultural expression, recognizing that the community's sense of identity is an important component of its development. The Reverend Gary Mason and the forum have worked with loyalist paramilitaries in the area to redesign several murals, which have attracted considerable press attention and were mentioned in chapter 4. What should we make of this intersection of community development work and cultural activities?

In this chapter, we focus on whether the kinds of cultural initiatives covered in previous chapters can be said to contribute to community development in ways that in turn help transform conflict and diminish division. We also turn to questions about the *strategic* dimensions of cultural traditions work to examine what benefits stand to be accrued besides the social psychological ones that we have already discussed, and we consider whether pragmatic concerns and collective self-interest can contribute to conflict transformation. Do pragmatic concerns, such as, funding, public influence, and community development capacity, underpin cultural traditions work and the modification of cultural expressions? How do such concerns impact the prospects of collective identity change that is central to conflict transformation?

Much of the energy and motivation behind the voluntary cultural activities addressed so far derives from social psychological sources, such as, the satisfaction people derive from music or the exploration of history, the fellowship of socializing with peers, or a sense of reassurance that comes from signaling solidarity. However, as we know, culture also serves political and pragmatic purposes (Kertzer 1988). It is important, when studying conflict transformation, to consider what incentives and pressures could encourage the mitigation of divisive cultural expressions. While we can and will analyze the costs and incentives that influence decision making about cultural activities, it is worth noting that in the flow of everyday life, people do not fully distinguish between their material or economic circumstances and their culturally elaborated worldviews; it is difficult to disentangle one from another.

Goals and strategic interests develop within all groups. Agendas become systematized in ideological schemata with which group members identify, becoming emotionally and psychologically charged and resistant to change. Actions or tactics that are understood to advance group goals become incorporated into familiar repertoires and perform collective identity, reinscribing the canon of beliefs and ideas that form the group's ontological boundaries. However, as group needs and the political environment change, actions that were once effective and that could be justified within the group's ideological schemata start to lose their efficacy. A dilemma emerges. Repertoires of collective action that have been adopted over long periods of time no longer effectively address group needs, yet, they remain iconic and representative of group identity. The challenge becomes adopting new tactics that meet group goals and continue to sustain a sufficiently coherent group identity. The process can be fraught with internal dissension and external skepticism as new tactics and their justifications are developed. In this chapter, we will examine how basic Protestant/unionist/loyalist (PUL) interests, such as, community development and political capital, have generated incentives and pressures to adopt new activities and reconcile them with the prevailing narratives with which members identify.

Among working-class loyalist organizations, cultural traditions work has become increasingly intertwined with community development concerns, such as, building political influence, and accumulating social capital, funding, and organizing skills. With the institutionalization of cultural traditions activities, first through the Community Relations Council and its Cultural Traditions Group and later the political peace process, political and monetary incentives have become attached.

■ COMMUNITY DEVELOPMENT

Over the course of the Troubles, community development work, which aims to strengthen community infrastructure and capacity, has often been conducted separately from community relations work, which focuses on challenging cultural and social psychological barriers through contact schemes and facilitated dialogue (Neilands 1997). The Community Development in Protestant Areas Steering Group (CDPASG), formed in 1991 to address concerns about the lack of community development work in Protestant areas, adopted a definition of community development penned by the Community Development Review Group (CDRG) in 1991:

> Community development in Northern Ireland is a process which embraces community action, community service, community work and other community endeavour—whether geographical or issue-based—an emphasis towards the disadvantaged and powerless within society. Its values include participation, empowerment, self-help, [sic] community development challenges prejudice, sectarianism and the unequal distribution of resources (cited in CDPASG document, p. 8). Examples of community development include: housing action groups; women's groups; community business and co-operation environmental groups; welfare rights and community planning and campaigning; history; research; community education community action in general. (p. 8)

Among the issues raised in the 1992 report of the Community Development in Protestant Areas Steering Group were deficiencies in organization capacity and skills, overdependence on the patronage of politicians, interference by paramilitaries, and a perception that addressing social issues is "anti-state" and communal or "Catholic" and thus contradictory to Protestants' individualism and work ethic

(p. 7). Participants noted the reluctance of Protestant organizations to make their needs public or to aggressively pursue charitable funding, especially compared to their Catholic counterparts.

In his opening address, Paul Sweeney, a Catholic from Derry/Londonderry, who served as director of the Northern Ireland Voluntary Trust from 1987 to 1994, noted several important factors that can often inhibit effective community development work in Protestant areas, including the differing needs of urban versus rural communities and inner versus peripheral urban areas, the economic environment, the "brain drain" effect (by which upwardly mobile Protestants tend to move away when they are able), and the extent of community infrastructure through which community development goals can be pursued. He also focused on cultural dispositions that can foster a state of "communal intransigence" and mitigate against community development: a work ethic that frowns upon accepting charity or being able to acknowledge that one's circumstances are structurally conditioned.

> There is an innate resistance on the part of Protestants to declare themselves in need. This strong sense of pride inhibits groups from approaching charities for help. Catholic groups on the other hand are very conscious of where they stand on the league table of deprivation and have no problems in declaring themselves in need. I have direct experience of this as a charitable trust administrator, however, I recall an anecdote by a key civil servant responsible for promoting the ACE [Action for Community Employment] scheme in the early 80's. A Ballymena (Protestant) group whom he visited to promote ACE subsequently telephoned to say that they might take one secretarial post on a part-time basis, whereas a group from Newry (Catholic) telephoned to say they would take 100 initially with a view to expansion in the near future. This reluctance towards charity and deference towards potential benefactors is a real issue in Protestant communities. I notice this in the Northern Ireland Voluntary Trust where there is often a marked difference between applications from Protestant and Catholic groups. The former exhibit:
>
> - A real reluctance to come forward
> - Meticulous adherence to the details of their request
> - The constitutionality and representative nature of the groups will be well established.
> - The request will be modest and seldom commensurate with the level of need.
> - Strong emphasis on accountability and propriety.
> - Patrons and testimonials to support the request.
>
> The net result of this is that there are whole areas (Protestant) of Northern Ireland who seldom approach organisations, such as, charitable trusts or charities, for help. A number of funders quite deliberately target certain areas and adopt a certain liberalisation of their grant-aid criteria to encourage applications from the Protestant community. When initiatives such as, the Belfast Action Teams

> commenced, this reluctance on the part of Protestant groups to come forward was
> marked. Thankfully this has been redressed in the recent past. (p. 12)

One must always think carefully about assigning generalized cultural predispositions to any group, let alone large populations, as they might be misinterpreted as
somehow determinative. Yet, as we academics are in the business of generalizing,
given convincing evidence, I will venture a few broad statements regarding what
one might call characteristic "mentalities" among Protestants. These are much
more subtle and persistent than fully formed ideological positions or ethnopolitical identities. Followers of the French sociologist Bourdieu might refer to these
dispositions as habituses, deeply socialized expectations or lenses for interpreting
and interacting with our social worlds. We must be careful not to fall headlong
into stereotyping, but there seem to be some recognizable tendencies, such as, val-
uing individualism and embracing a work ethic, that can inhibit community
development activities.

For example, community activities that could be interpreted as circumventing the
state's authority or questioning the state's competence can be cast as anti-state and a
threat to the union, which one can imagine is not popular among unionists. My contacts often referred to a lack of confidence in their leaders and their own abilities to
articulate rationales and justifications for their political positions and cultural legitimacy. Consequently, community development goals tend to be limited and intermittent, and activists find it difficult to challenge persistent cynicism about community
development. Ultimately, the culture of skepticism negatively influences the
development of organizing skills and social capital. Sweeney's comments return us to
questions about how reconsidering identities and worldviews can make way for new
practices, including community development activities, and reciprocally, how new
practices can inspire further reflection on identities and worldviews.

■ COMMUNITY DEVELOPMENT AND CULTURAL WORK

Community development work can contribute to conflict transformation, but
since it can be inhibited by cultural values and ideological commitments, we return
to the central question of how attitudes and beliefs can be changed and by whom.
I have taken the position that such work is most effectively undertaken within
groups and communities, on their own cultural turf, and I am especially interested
in those quarters that are often considered ideologically rigid. Yet, many people
I interviewed expressed the need for their fellow Protestants to find ways to adopt
new expectations about both cross-community and community development
work. The expressions of frustration I encountered signaled hope for improvement. However, even if community workers in PUL areas can identify ways in
which community development has been hindered and could be improved,
collective change presents its own challenges. New expectations are not merely

adopted, en masse. They are developed through experimentation and public discourse, and the kinds of intentional efforts at experimenting with new versions of old identities and practices addressed in previous chapters can overlap with community development efforts.

In the field, I often found it difficult to disentangle historical identity work from concerns about the capacity to address social problems or the ability to be politically effective. I recall sitting in a conference room in a loyalist community development center in East Belfast interviewing two loyalist ex-combatants. In my fieldnotes, I commented that although one of the gentlemen insisted on the importance of learning Irish history, I found it difficult to assess the importance of the historical identity work to the rest of the center's work because the conversation did not naturally turn toward identity issues. Instead, the conversation veered toward unemployment, ex-prisoners, social housing, drugs, the black market, and decommissioning of paramilitary arms. Yet, we were surrounded by posters on the walls (published by the *Belfast Telegraph*) about Irish history. A poster of Cúchulainn (a mythical figure considered by some loyalists to represent the defense of Ulster against invading Irish clans) adorned one wall, and before I left, one of the men gave me materials about the International School for Peace Studies in Messines, with which he has been involved.

Cultural traditions work and community development work interpenetrate one another. Their linkages can be traced in part to their similar origins in concerns about solidarity and well-being. One also finds a widely expressed belief that cultural traditions work can help build skills and outlooks that are "empowering" and conducive to community development. Paul Sweeney, who delivered the opening address at the Community Development in Protestant Areas Steering group conference, asserted:

> Cultural exploration is the fifth column of community development. Cultural development provides a vehicle through which people can explore their heritage and identity, their art and politics. This process can be extremely liberating and empowering and is very much alive in the nationalist community. I wonder to what extent has a similar process begun in the Protestant community. Culture is the process that unlocks potential and could be the key to the Protestant community awakening from its "sleeping giant" status.

Cultural traditions work is thus seen as a precursor to community development work by "unlocking potential" or building ethnic pride.

Ultimately, development concerns take priority over cultural traditions work among loyalist community workers. Several times, I was reminded that cultural traditions interests and activities are important, but they are secondary to addressing social problems, as Darren, a unionist political consultant and history enthusiast explained:

> It's peripheral to the reality of everyday life. We happen to have a specific interest in that and a specific desire to support Ian Adamson, whose analysis of things we support in

terms of language and language development. But, coming down to the way we would see the world, you know, that's nothing in relation to getting the fundamentals in place to lift our society up and build it up.

Dean, a loyalist community activist and history enthusiast who has been deeply involved in cultural traditions work in East Belfast, echoed this sentiment but then equivocated.

> [Cultural traditions work is] important, but housing and jobs come first.... In Northern Ireland, every morning we wake up and ask, "Am I Irish or am I British? Have I changed countries overnight?" 'cause it could happen. When I say culture is below all that at the same time, in the back of your head, it's probably their first priority for a lot of people. I want my culture to be strong, my identity to be strong, my nationality to be strong for to remain part of the UK. So, the constitutional position is important.... I mean, they're all out there linked, but for most people it's having a roof, having enough money to buy children food.

"Bread and butter" issues are important for many loyalists with whom I spoke, but I also encountered a great deal of interest in the ways in which cultural traditions work could enhance the quality of life in local communities.

Protestant cultural activists and community workers have increasingly begun to connect cultural activities and community development. The Ulster-Scots Community Network (formerly the Ulster-Scots Heritage Council [USHC]), for example, explicitly links their cultural traditions work with economic development, "The USHC strategy is to enable the Ulster-Scots cultural community to re-engage with its history, heritage, folklore, language, crafts and arts, and to create economic opportunities, procure resources, and remove barriers to development."[2] The prospects of economic development are perhaps the most direct pragmatic justifications for cultural traditions activities, but cultural work is often seen as a vehicle for building skills and social capital.

Economic Development and Tourism

On the economic front, the production of cultural artifacts and the planning of events are expected, if developed properly, to create jobs. Museums, tours, workshops, and media production, to name a few activities, require expertise, organization, and administration to which wage-paying jobs can be attached. Protestants often look to the economic successes of Irish cultural activists in promoting the Irish language, dance, music, and theater, both locally and globally. The West Belfast Festival or *Féile an Phobail* (the Community Festival) was originally developed to channel tension around the August 9 anniversary of internment and has become an internationally recognized event. Successful cultural projects can foster other spin-off projects such as, Féile FM radio, which began broadcasting during the festival in 1996, offered college accredited training in radio production, and was awarded a full-time broadcasting license in 2005. It is now located in a studio in the Conway Mill center in West Belfast and broadcasts seven days a week (Nic Craith 2003:157–60).

Attempts to develop social economy projects with Protestant political and cultural emphases have also been tried. Fernhill House Museum and restaurant in the Glencairn area of West Belfast, was developed as part of the Glencairn People's Project that was established in 1991. The museum, which presented the local history of the Shankill Road (especially during the first half of the twentieth century) and displayed Orange and unionist memorabilia, was intended to generate jobs and "educational and recreational opportunities" to "advance education and to provide training facilities to promote economic regeneration in the area." However, the site closed its doors in 2006 after ten years. The Gae Lairn Centre in East Belfast similarly aims to address "social and economic regeneration to the wider population, business, employment and training" in addition to its work reintegrating ex-prisoners.

Like any widespread hobby or recreational activity, a certain measure of economic stimulus is generated. Ethnomusicology Ph.D. student Jackie Witherow at Queens University in Belfast has identified 681 bands across Northern Ireland, of which 631 are Protestant bands and 35 are Catholic ("Protestant Marching," BBC 2005). The number of Protestant bands in particular seems to be growing. Kyle, of the Ulster Bands Association, made a case for the economic benefits of the growth of bands:

> There is a lot of money spent here, which people don't see. We are producing an economy here. In relation to bus hire, you're averaging between £200 and £300 per week, not even per week, per night, that you're out and some of them are working maybe a Friday night and a Saturday night, but not all the time would they be hiring a bus, but there is large bus hire companies within the country who are up and down the country most weekends between March and literally two weeks ago [at the end of September] when we had finished.... Uniforms are being [made] and I mean 600 odd bands; I'm not saying 600 odd bands get their uniforms at one time, but on average I have to say most of the marching bands, their uniforms are lasting four seasons, maybe five seasons, so you're talking four to five years where that economy is being boosted again. You got that, the buses, you got the bands, and plus you got the instruments.... There is a drum manufacturer in Rathfriland who's charging upwards of about £350 per drum. I mean, we have twenty side drums.... Again, the flutes [cost] within the region, I think it's about £40.... [Many bands] basically have to pay for their uniforms themselves, so what they would do is they would start in September and say, "Right, were going for a uniform next year. The cost is £400. Start saving."

One observer writing in the magazine of the Ulster Bands Association estimated that approximately 200 bands inject at least £500,000 into the busing trade annually. Other expenses include instruments and their maintenance, rent for halls, organization of fund-raising events, recreational equipment rental, insurance payments, printing costs, and food.[3]

Cultural tourism is perhaps the most often-cited vehicle for economic development, with murals, festivals, museum exhibits, band competitions, and loyal institution parades presented as means to draw local and international tourism revenue. Tour buses and taxis regularly ferry tourists around the streets of Belfast on mural tours, and Simon Calder, the senior travel editor for the *Independent* (August 3, 2007), declared West Belfast's murals to be "the UK's top attraction" in 2007. The Northern Ireland Tourist Board sponsored a trip for Dutch travel agents in 2007, who expressed interest in bringing tourists from cruise ships in Belfast harbor to the Shankill Road. The West Belfast Athletic and Cultural Society has staked out "helping to harness the immense potential of the Shankill to develop its cultural tourism on a grand scale" as one of its central goals.

Paula, a community worker on the Shankill Road commented on the *potential* of murals for local economic development through tourism but also noted that the potential has been unrealized:

> [The redesigned murals are] far better than watching these gunmen standing with these balaclavas on, so I see attitudes changing, and I think for tourism, you know, they keep some of the [old] stuff up, because it's bringing tourists here, you know, its bringing money and all the rest of it. It's not bringing money onto the Shankill Road, you know, because we're not all that well organized. It is bringing money onto the Falls Road, because they have (and I think it's wonderful that they have it) like a shop [where] the bus loads stop, or the taxi loads stop, and they go and buy things. We're not that organized over here. I can't see anywhere where, you know, they can stop and buy anything.

Debates have also arisen about the wisdom and sustainability of conflict tourism and the prospects of building tourism around activities and material culture, such as, bonfires, parades, and murals, that have records of contention and even intimidation (Lisle 2006; Graff-McRae 2009). In the case of parades and bonfires, antisocial behavior remains prominent, even as organizers are working to cut down on excessive drinking (especially among minors), and sectarian displays, such as, burning tricolours and posting hate speech on bonfires.

In Northern Ireland, cultural tourism can quickly become difficult to distinguish from conflict tourism, and some fear that accommodating the prurient curiosities of international tourists may constrain attempts to escape the Troubles as the definitive social narrative (Graff-McRae 2009). An editorial in the *Newsletter* on August 6, 2007, raised warnings and articulated the dilemma well.

> The conflict cannot and must not be airbrushed from history, and it is a sad fact of life that there are those who will be drawn to our shores to see the sights associated with it for themselves. The Northern Ireland Tourist Board has a fine judgment call to make on how far its officials go in using the events of the last 40 years as a selling point internationally. There is something distasteful about the notion of so-called "terror tours"; we must ensure that those who do come to learn about the Troubles are given a rounded view and not subjected to propaganda. Thankfully, when our tourist representatives

speak with movers and shakers in the travel industry, they now have a much better story to tell.

Mary, an arts worker in Derry/Londonderry, also expressed her concern over the way in which conflict and division can dominate the public sphere:

> I also worry greatly, particularly in the Derry area, about our culture of conflict. It's our sole identity. And within that, there are very few roles to play. You're either a victim or a perpetrator. And, you know, neither of those sits comfortably with those people. And it works right the way down to the way that city council promotes the city. And if you look at the images that they use for the city, they're largely conflict-based images. Although they wouldn't necessarily acknowledge or agree with that, but it's cannons and walls and hands across the divide; it's historical conflict and modern conflict. And so it's very difficult to change your culture or your self-identity when that is even how you've been marketed and how you [interpret] funding, you know, deprivation areas and conflict and anti-social behavior and, you know, graffiti and grime, you know, which is part of the reimaging community [program]. You have to show how dilapidated and how rundown everything is, how low everyone's spirits are within an area to get the money.…They think conflict tourism is a positive thing, and although they've changed its name to "insight tourism," to give people an insight into the history, you know, of conflicts. But we have other very positive histories in relation to immigration, in relation to industry, in relation to art and culture—writers, music. We have the most fabulous scenery and walks. We have the river that is just basically used [for parking] at the moment. Other countries turn their waterfronts into these amazing places, and ours is just a series of car parks.

Mary's concern was reflected in recurring comments I encountered about pressure from the tourist industry to maintain many of the public trappings of the Troubles. According to an interview with Drew Nelson, grand secretary of the Orange Order, on Radio Ulster's *Inside Politics* program on January 28, 2008, "The Tourist Board says tourists don't *want* a dressed-up commercialized event. They want an authentic event." Edward, a community worker on the Shankill Road, who often works with ex-combatants, spoke from firsthand experience about the dilemma of balancing tourism and reimaging loyalist areas.

> At one level, we are being encouraged to paint out these murals to, you know, reimage them, but then they will not be such a tourist attraction if they don't portray the conflict and the scars of the conflict the way they once did, so that's a big challenge for these communities and how they balance those two, the balance of change and also preserving the conflict or the tourist attraction with the murals because I think the Germans tell you they regret knocking down the Berlin Wall because there is not enough of it to come and see now.

In short, the debate over the kinds of public displays that are desirable for community regeneration or tourism reveals the economic and political advantages that must be weighed up against tradition and collective identity. Caught between incentives to produce noncontentious displays and to maintain contentious ones, local organizations must consider which activities they will maintain and which they will change. Those decisions bear directly on how the group identifies itself and how people identify with the group.

Housing and Regeneration

Redesigning murals and downsizing bonfires and making them more environmentally and community friendly offer social benefits and promise to help improve community relations around interfaces, but such actions also help improve the local environment, impacting on trade, housing values, and the delivery of services. Government agencies, such as, local councils, the Department of Social Development, and the Northern Ireland Housing Executive, offer incentives that encourage community organizations to mitigate the roughest edges of cultural expressions. Luke, in East Belfast, described the way residents near Pitt Park at the bottom of the Lower Newtownards Road traded tradition for housing.

> I think there's definitely a greater pragmatism emerging. For instance, at the bottom of this street you have Pitt Park, and part of the plans for the regeneration of this area includes the building of public housing in Pitt Park. But the implications of that is the loss of waste ground down there for the gigantic bonfire every year. But the community did a trade-off with the Housing Executive and so on. [They became] willing to see regeneration and willing to see community facilities going in like play facilities for children, young people, and community facilities, and a much reduced piece of purpose-built ground for a small bonfire. So, this year is likely to be the last of the enormous three- or four-story-high things.

Local organizations, including paramilitary organizations, also agreed to have tattered flags and graffiti removed from the neighborhood, and Luke pointed out that the enormous Titanic Quarters business and residential development going up across the motorway was convincing community leaders that they must be prepared to take advantage of impending commercial and environmental changes or else be passed over or bought out, very real threats to the working-class community that currently resides in Ballymacarrett ward.

■ FUNDING

Monetary support has been a prominent feature of peacebuilding in Northern Ireland, and funding has been made available by local government, the British and Irish governments, and international sources. It would be impossible to account for all of the funding initiatives that have supported peacebuilding and conflict transformation, but the EU and International Fund for Ireland (IFI) streams deserve special attention. Since the Anglo-Irish Agreement of 1985, the IFI, established by the United Kingdom, United States, Canada, Australia, and New

Zealand, has distributed funds within disadvantaged local communities in Ireland and Northern Ireland, including border areas, "promoting economic and social advance and encouraging contact, dialogue and reconciliation between nationalists and unionists throughout Ireland" (International Fund for Ireland 2005:6). As of the publication of the IFI's 2008 annual report, the fund had committed £628 million (€803 million) over twenty-one years but would stop seeking international contributions in 2010 (International Fund for Ireland 2008).

The original Peace I program (1995–1999) of the European Union Special Support Programme for Peace and Reconciliation in Northern Ireland and the Border Counties of Ireland was established following the 1994 paramilitary cease-fires; it committed €667 million and focused on economic development and social inclusion. Peace II (2000–2004) leveraged €995 million, funding over 6,000 applications, and continued its primary mission while enhancing reconciliation work. Peace II was extended with €160 million in support of the ongoing political peace process in 2005–2006. Peace III, which is most likely the final phase of EU funding at €33 million, covers the years 2007–2013 and is to be implemented as a cross-border program (Special EU Programmes Body 2007). More than sixty reconciliation projects were funded with Peace II money in 2006 and the Community Relations Council (CRC) has served as an important mechanism for disbursing EU and IFI funds. The CRC received £3.1 million from the Northern Ireland government in 2007 for "inter-community work" and disbursed £2 million to forty-eight victims' support organizations on behalf of the Office of First Minister and Deputy First Minister (Northern Ireland Community Relations Council 2007:11,15,19).

Studies that have gathered information from community group leaders, program development officers, and civil servants identify potentials for aid to bypass state bureaucracies and offer important boosts to local economies, undermine exclusion and despair, regenerate ownership in community life, and *eventually* improve the context for cross-community dialogue, though there is little consensus on how efficient aid has been in promoting dialogue and reconciliation (Byrne and Ayulo 1998; Byrne and Irvin 2001, 2002). Nevertheless, the work of grassroots peace and conflict resolution organizations (PCROs) has been assessed as playing an important, if often indirect, role in preparing the ground for the political peace process and moderating the extremes of an already devastating conflict (Byrne and Irvin 2002; Cochrane and Dunn 2002; Gidron, Katz, and Hasenfeld 2002). Since the Anglo-Irish Agreement, state governments have invested heavily in grassroots economic development and community relations work in hopes of taking full advantage of the cease-fires to undercut the socioeconomic and social psychological pillars of conflict. Funds are disbursed through agencies such as, the Arts Council, the National Lottery, the Irish government's Department of Foreign Affairs, Belfast City and District Councils, the Ulster-Scots Agency, the Community Relations Council, Department of Social Development, Department of Culture Arts and Leisure, Rural Development Council, the Community Foundation for Northern Ireland, and Partnership Boards.

In short, economic development and community regeneration are well-established facets of the peace process within the voluntary and community sector. Funds for making bonfires more socially and environmentally safe, organizing Ulster-Scots lectures and exhibitions, and repairing Orange Halls represent the kinds of initiatives for which staunch Protestant unionist and loyalist organizations have sought and received funding. However, Protestants have been more suspicious and less likely than Catholics to take advantage of funding resources, a trend that was reflected in a 2006 public opinion survey of over a thousand adults that found Catholics (57 percent) more likely than Protestants (43 percent) to approve of the positive role of IFI-funded projects in promoting their own community's socioeconomic development (Special EU Programmes Body 2007:30).[4] Similarly, Catholics were more optimistic than Protestants that EU and IFI funds supported the Belfast/Good Friday Agreement, which may also reflect displeasure among many Protestants with the agreement itself (Byrne, Fissuh, Thiessen, and Irvin 2008:12,17,19).[5]

Protestant unionists often have political qualms with the IFI in particular because of its association with the Anglo-Irish agreement and have considered it a kind of bribe to pacify unionists who oppose the agreement—"blood money" as it is sometimes described. Faith-based organizations may choose to pass over National Lottery funds to comply with religious prohibitions against gambling. Across the board, there is some evidence that funding has tended to flow toward moderate established middle-class organizations, compounding the deficit of resources among hard-to-reach working-class organizations, which have been wary of pursuing funding (Byrne and Irvin 2002:78; Gidron, Katz, and Hasenfeld 2002:165, 67).

As Paul Sweeney noted in his comments in the 1992 report of the Community Development in Protestant Areas Steering Group, "There is an innate resistance on the part of Protestants to declare themselves in need" (p. 12). However, there is an emerging and growing willingness to pursue and accept external funding, which Curtis described in relation to the Orange Order:

> It's not happening in some areas, and I suppose in some areas, depending on the age groups and so on, an older age group within lodges will not have the sense of, you know, getting grants and applying for grants. In fact, they'll probably look at that as like a handout.... They're too proud to accept that, and that's part, I think, of the Protestant ethos and identity and all the rest of it too. But I think the younger people are looking at that and saying, "Well, you know, hey, if we don't apply for these grants, somebody else is gonna get that grant, you know, and we're gonna be poorer because we didn't." I think it will catch on, and I think as the older members see the benefits of things like that, they'll understand too.

Often, the pragmatic incentive to apply for funding is attached to the dawning perception that nationalists have become adept at acquiring funding and thus benefit in significant ways. One contact, who is a member of the 36th Ulster Division

Memorial Association, compared republican and Orange Order organizing capacity and attributed the difference to funding disparities.

> The biggest problem is resources. There's no doubt about that. I'm also a member of [a local World War I commemoration association]. At a meeting on Sunday of the committee, we discussed the way forward and how we're going to take it forward, and one of our biggest problems is funding, having the time to get things done, because there is a lot we want to do. The simple fact is that in a republican area of Newry, there's fifteen full-time people funded to do a project.... Whereas, the Orange Order in total has three people funded. Now, the Orange Order brings more tourists to Northern Ireland than some organization in Newry, but that's not recognized anywhere.

Mary, a community arts worker in Derry/Londonderry related a similar story about a loyalist community worker she knew who developed a theater arts program:

> [Protestants] looked across and said, "Well, hang on a minute, they're getting all this money. How come they're getting all this money?" And that's 'cause they're asking for it and putting [applications] together, you know. So, they were kind of behind on that... [A worker at] one of the community centers where we did a project on the siege [of Derry] said that they started a drama group, and they had nowhere to compete to get their young people an opportunity to present. And so, he decided that he would put his kids into the *feis,* which is basically like a big Catholic dance-fest for mothers, and he says, "We were the worst ones." And I thought, "How come they're all so good?" and when I went and looked, they'd been getting money for people to come in and train them and do this.

As they come to recognize the benefits, Protestant organizations have become increasingly open to funding opportunities, particularly when the resources can be used for single-identity work or community development, a trend that has mirrored nationalists' funding preferences (Byrne and Irvin 2002:75–77).

The pursuit of international funding represents a departure from traditional Protestant ideas about charity and social work, which have been perceived as different from the kind of state-based political patronage that majoritarian governance represented between partition in 1921 and the establishment of Direct Rule in 1972. James, a community development officer in East Belfast, described the cultural obstacles to utilizing funding resources and efforts to overcome them:

> The International Fund for Ireland, you'd be aware of them? What happened was that one of the first projects that I was trying to develop, and [my organization] was very much about trying to start things from scratch, to try and get people to think about regeneration, about businesses, the look of businesses, private business, but also social businesses as well. The first one, Dee Street Community Center, it was going great until they heard it was [being built with] IFI money, because the International Fund was set up after the Anglo-Irish agreement. Paisley said it was blood money and all that as well.

And then [after] four or five years, that project collapsed. People just wouldn't take [the money], so it was quite difficult, but about four or five years after that, the International Fund approached me [about twelve years ago] and said "Look, we're finding it hard to get projects in Protestant areas. Could you...work with them?"...In Tullycarnet Estate, we received, well, we have been offered, £950,000 from the International Fund. Another big project in Ballybeen,...the International Fund put up £400,000. So, it shows you the sea change. At one stage, people wouldn't have touched it with a barge pole. Sorry, I can say Protestant businessmen had no problem going for it. They'd have got money to refurbish their premises, but [not] in working-class Protestant areas....One of the things I did, I went to [now First Minister] Peter Robinson away in the 1990s and said to him, "Peter, look, I've been involved in some regeneration things." I said, "This is madness. Here's millions of pounds from America, Europe, Canada, and company, and we can't get any money, or they won't take any money." And the result of that meeting was he organized meetings with councillors and IFI and all that, so things have changed. You get the odd wee area still in rural areas that wouldn't touch it but [it's now acceptable] in the Shankill and all round the place.

Prohibitions about funding have not entirely disappeared. Few would still adopt Paisley's old rhetoric about blood money, but pursuing funding can still be disparaged as crass, greedy, or unearned. Initiatives that make use of external funding can be vulnerable to charges of mere resource acquisition. One common criticism of Ulster-Scots projects is that they are "grant based," "simply a balancing of the books against the Irish language," and thus merely instrumental, without authenticity. Similarly, funding for its own sake, without acknowledgment of parity, can offend, according to Oliver, a community worker in the Derry/Londonderry area:

I've got [nationalist community workers] coming here saying, "You know, do you want me to take your kids away this summer? I can get you some money, you know, money we haven't spent here." We've also had calls here from organizations over the town that have applied for money, applied for our funding program, and they've been successful, but there's a cross-community element to it, so some that have been successful have allocated £30,000 for this or that or the other [for which they] must have six Protestants on it, so that phone rings [pointing to his desk], "I've got some funding here; there's an opportunity here for six young Protestants to go away on a residential to Scotland, into the Highlands or wherever," and I say, "No, no. You sit down and plan and dream with us together, that we're all part of it, and we will go together." But just to think that I'm gonna be turned on, or this community's gonna be turned on by an offer like that. It's not going to happen. And I think this is slowly, slowly getting through.

A similar critique of funding arose several times in relation to the Orange Order as the use of Ulster-Scots activities have increasingly been incorporated with Orange activities. Those whom Kaufmann (2007) refers to as traditionalists resent what they see as a compromise of British and Christian emphases, while "rebels," such as, Curtis, consider interest in Ulster-Scots culture a natural extension of the Order's heritage.

> I think in more recent times things have happened. First of all, grants have become more available, and I think the Ulster-Scots revival has assisted because about . . . 55 percent of our members are Presbyterian and ergo Ulster-Scots, but there is another percentage of them that may not be Presbyterian but are Ulster-Scots as well. So, grants have been available to them, and we've seen a flurry of, I suppose, Ulster-Scots groups based around Orange Lodges or Orange Halls, and some, you know, general grants have been drawn down on as well.

This kind of overlap can lead to confusion and further charges of opportunism when the argument is made that the Order should be able to access funding streams for Ulster-Scots activities as well as funding for Orange activities on the basis that, according to Curtis, the institution is "an Ulster British organisation rather than just an Ulster-Scots organisation."

In short, many Protestant organizations have hesitated to pursue external funding, a practice that, during the first decade of the Troubles, could be interpreted as a weakening of fidelity and trust in the British state but that later registered dissatisfaction with the Anglo-Irish agreement. It was not until the 1990s and the ceasefires that Protestant community workers and leaders began countenancing wider use of external economic aid for community development and cultural traditions work. Despite the availability of funds, a culture of independence and a deficit of skills for pursuing funding have left Protestant, and especially working-class loyalist, organizations underdeveloped.

■ HUMAN AND SOCIAL CAPITAL

The need for organizing skills, social networks, and leadership, often referred to as "capacity building" or "empowerment" constitutes another pragmatic incentive cited for undertaking cultural traditions work. Indeed, capacity building or human capital far and away constitutes the most common rationale offered for how cultural heritage activities might contribute to conflict transformation, by challenging prevalent attitudes about leadership and coalition-building while building important organizing skills that can enhance and accelerate grassroots community development (Becker 1964; Cochrane and Dunn 2002). Robyn, a community worker from the southeast Antrim area, who has worked extensively with loyalist organizations and communities in East Antrim, explained by comparing organizing skills in republican and loyalist communities:

> The Catholic community would have been different because you would've went to small community organizations, and they would have a solicitor sitting on the board; they would have a doctor; they would have the local priest; they would have professional people. Whereas professional people, you know, where I come from, got up, went and

never came back, and some of them would tell you they didn't even come from there [laughs].... So, that's the difference, and that's how community development happened so long ago in nationalist areas.... First of all, [external funding] wasn't blood money to them, so they were able to take the money. They had the people who could drive and plan, and so they learnt the [necessary] skills. So, you know, when people say to you, "So how come, the likes of Gerry Adams and all the Sinn Féin ones are so well educated and political?" That's how they did it. They did it through the community development stuff, you know, where our people weren't engaged in that at all.... You know, somebody said to me the other day, ... "What's your woman, [Caitriona] Ruane [a Sinn Féin politician] like? What's her background? Gerry Adams was a barman, was a barman! What gives them a right to sit as a minister and tell people [what to do], you know what I mean? But the thing is, they are so good because they cut their teeth down in the communities. That's where they learnt their politics and how to speak and all of that. They learnt it all down there, whereas our lot are not really interested. "Go and get a proper job" is what I was told a lot. "Go and get a proper job!" instead of working in the community.

Adam, a loyalist with connections to the UPRG and the UDA, expressed a similar frustration with the "deficit" in "social development" skills.

Here's the reason why we're so poor at social development and social skills and all the rest of it. Ian Paisley told us for years that if we take part in community development, at least social initiatives, that will break down the union. That's against the state. And our people said, "Don't get involved with community development. Don't get involved in education. Don't get involved in human rights. They're another IRA-Irish Republican plot, so don't run to them." So, for thirty-eight years, we haven't. But it's left us with an awful deficit. It's left us, I would say, on a playing field where we're not even in the dressing room yet, and all the other teams are on the playing pitch.

Responses such as, Robyn's and Adam's were common as interviewees expressed frustration about a lack of social capital.

Social capital theory has become enormously influential in discussions of community development in Northern Ireland. It has become widely adopted among sociologists and other social scientists, though its various strands have not been fully reconciled with one another. Fulkerson and Thompson (2008) have identified two main camps: *normative social capitalists*, who are interested in the features of social structure that are conducive to social cooperation in the pursuit of the common good, and *resource social capitalists*, who conceptualize social capital through a conflict lens as a convertible resource, which can be accumulated and spent for individual or collective gain, depending on prevailing circumstances and tend to lead to inequalities. The latter derive their work from Bourdieu's (1986) theorizing of social capital as the institutionalization of relationships that facilitate the asymmetrical accumulation of economic and cultural capital by some groups over others. Some resource social capitalists argue that calling for deprived strata of society to solve their own problems merely frees public expenditures to benefit middle and upper classes. In other words, focusing on the development of social capital at the grassroots can divert attention from systems of power and privilege that perpetuate inequality and deprivation (see also Bacon in Appendix C in Cairns, Van Til, and Williamson 2003:52; Hillyard, Rolston, and Tomlinson 2005).

Social capital theory has most often been applied to Northern Ireland from the normative perspective, which is usually associated with the work of James Coleman, who introduced social capital as a means for bridging rational action and socialization models of collective action. For Coleman (1988), social capital constitutes factors in *relationships,* in sufficiently bounded groups, such as, expectations of reciprocity, diffusion of information through networks, and prescriptive norms of cooperation and sacrifice. The political scientist Robert Putnam advanced Coleman's work when he published *Making Democracy Work* in 1993 (Putnam, Leonardi, and Nanetti 1993) on correlations between effective governance and levels of social capital across fifteen new regional governments established in Italy in 1970. Putnam and his colleagues concluded that social capital makes significant contributions to the practice of effective democracy. In 1995, Putnam published a short article on social capital in the United States that was followed in 2000 by his popular and similarly titled book, *Bowling Alone: The Collapse and Revival of American Community* (Putnam 1995, 2000). The book provoked an avalanche of academic inquiry into the many social, economic, and political benefits of social capital. Putnam argued that despite enormous advances in other areas, Americans "have become remarkably less civic, less politically engaged, less socially connected, less trusting, and less committed to the common good. At the dawn of the millennium Americans are fast becoming a loose aggregation of disengaged observers, rather than a community of connected participants." According to Putnam, Americans seemed to be losing the "norms and networks" that de Tocqueville (2004 [1835]) felt facilitated cooperation, collaboration, and thus democracy. Quality of life is diminished when the ability to solve problems creatively and collectively has eroded. Networks and organizations built on trust and reciprocity serve crucial roles in ensuring that meaningful political discourse is sustained, governments are held accountable, economies are productive, and social problems, such as, crime, are mitigated by minimizing alienation. Even measures of health can be influenced as individuals embedded in close social networks experience lower levels of stress, improving health outcomes (Putnam 2001).

Faced with the challenges of coming out of more than thirty years of violent conflict and many more decades of ethnic and political contention, the normative model of social capital theory predominates among those in the community relations, community development, and voluntary sectors who are deeply concerned about replacing the abnormality of life in a war zone with a stable economy, social safety nets, and working relationships across the ethnic divide. "Asset-based community development" and "appreciative inquiry," which focus attention on the strengths and capacities communities can mobilize are increasingly common (Bacon in Appendix D in Cairns, Van Til, and Williamson 2003:57; Hillyard,

Rolston, and Tomlinson 2005). Terms such as, "empowerment," "infrastructure," "capacity," and "networks" are common. Social capital is often categorized as bonding (level of in-group cohesion), bridging (connections with out-groups), or linking (connections with advocates and benefactors in positions of influence; Morrissey, McGinn, and McDonnell 2002:69; Morrow 2006). Underlying these approaches is the belief that a growing infrastructure of networks and information sharing will lead to a democratic vision of creative and participative problem-solving.[6] Duncan Morrow (2006), executive director of the Northern Ireland Community Relations Council, asserts that bridging capital, civic engagement, and trust-building through the political peace process must be encouraged. In social capital terms, the transaction costs of cooperating across the communal divide must be lowered through the cultivation of trust as both horizontal (cross-community) and vertical (political) relationships develop. He points out that Ireland has a long history of building in-group bonding capital stretching back to the early nineteenth century that corresponds with growing mistrust between Protestants and Catholics and the labor demands of the industrial revolution.

Yet, despite deep divisions between Protestants and Catholics in Northern Ireland that would seem to suggest high levels of intra-group cohesion, one also encounters recurring complaints about the extent to which Protestant communities are fragmented and suffer from apathy, "weak community infrastructure" (low levels of inter-organizational cooperation), and the tendency for people to identify in highly localized ways with neighbors on their street as opposed to their ward or district. Protestants' individualistic work ethic and religious beliefs are often said to undermine community development work and the accumulation of social capital, especially in contrast to Catholic solidarity. Gareth, a community worker in Portadown, expressed the trend:

> Community development doesn't sit very naturally with the Protestant ethos and ethic in that community development is about collective action. So, it's about coalition-building. It's about seeing how you can bring people together, bond people together in a common issue to bring about that change. You look at our worship. Our worship is not based on a collective; it's based on an individualism manifesting itself in a spiritual way. Our teaching would suggest that it's individuals and individual acts and their own conscience and how they impact on issues of salvation particularly.... Whereas, if you look at Roman Catholicism—the foundation of Roman Catholicism in terms of their worship is a collective worship, so therefore it comes naturally that people will then gel together into spheres of life, and I think that's one of the dilemmas that we have in terms of community development, as to how we ensure there are people that have skills, or are assets to the local community, and they acknowledge that they have some role to play.

Gareth attributed poor community development to low levels of social and human capital that are cultural (influenced by a Protestant religious ethos), and then he echoed Robyn's structural concerns about the migration of middle- and upper-class Protestants from communities that need their skills.

Robyn said that the progress made in building community development skills has often been achieved because funders required training. She described most small, localized and uncoordinated groups as unprepared to deal with structural community development issues that affect larger areas:

There aren't enough people in there with the skills, driving people to learn about the skills, because small groups are saying, "Why do we need our people to learn all of that? We just want to look after our street," and you go, "Okay, but you want to deal with housing, and you want to deal with environmental, and you'll need somewhere for the kids," but they don't see things in a bigger picture. They see it very localized. They want other people to come in and work with the kids because when you say to them, "Well, where are they gonna work with them? There's no community center," and they go, "Well could you not get one?" Sure, yeah [laughs]. They've no idea…they want it to stay localized.

Regardless of comparisons with nationalists' capacities and infrastructure, problems in mobilizing voluntary action and building coalitions is a common and long-standing complaint (Shirlow et al. 2005b:14).[7]

Some respondents, however, report progress in building capacity and cooperation around cultural traditions work, because while it requires similar organizing skills, it avoids the cultural dissonance that surrounds community development work in Protestant and especially working-class areas. Gareth followed his comment about Protestant deficits with an illustration of how cultural traditions work can offer pragmatic opportunities for coalition building:

Daniel [a co-worker] done a powerful piece of work around bonfires. Bonfires are traditionally managed by some of the paramilitary circles. Some of them despise, loath, and reject each other, some of them like each other, and some of them tolerate each other. In Portadown, he has been able to achieve a roundtable. We don't have a bonfire meeting in the month of June for July. We have bonfire meetings in July, August, September, October, November, December, January, February and March, April and May—all year round. So we're constantly looking and saying, "How can we change this? How can we do that? How can we do the other? Keep relationships and all those tentacles and conduits going?" We have the management agents coming round that table who previously wouldn't even have been sharing a room together. And that is huge in terms of development competencies, development capacity and people recognizing that the greater good of Portadown is the common bond, right? Those five areas might not see how there's a common approach in achieving that, but through [our organization], we can be that conduit and that vehicle to deliver that common approach,…the common vision, which is the greater good of Portadown.

From Gareth's perspective, modifying bonfires has provided an opportunity to build coalitions among those in "paramilitary circles." This was reflected in Byrne and Wilson's (2007) study of community-level discussions that were undertaken as part of Belfast City Council's bonfire mitigation program: "Furthermore, the conversations created a catalyst for building relationships within communities. It was acknowledged on a number of occasions that there was a degree of conflict and friction surrounding the bonfire, along with other issues, in the community and this program brought people together who normally would not interact" (p. 45). Dealing with issues related to cultural expressions can hold the attention of ideologically committed Protestants because they consider them so important, which actually frustrated Lauren, an East Belfast health worker:

> They're obsessed with the interface and marching and, you know, all those political things, and yes, I mean, the remit of that group was to try and iron out a lot of that stuff. But there's so much more potential that that group could have in terms of really making a change to people's lives in terms of, you know, their health. I mean, again, I'll go back to the whole lobbying thing and using their politicians a lot better. But maybe that will come.

Gareth's comment and Sweeney's claim that "Cultural exploration is the fifth column of community development" suggest that projects that focus on symbolic expression and collective identity can empower communities, but Lauren's comment and others' express frustration that progress on the community development front is slow.

■ PUBLIC AND MEDIA RELATIONS

One of the most prominent benefits that can be garnered through careful strategizing is political capital, in its institutional (big "P") and popular (little "p") forms. The former encompasses access to the mechanisms of government and the leverage that can be applied to shape policy and maintain influence while the latter entails the cultivation of popular support and favorable public opinion through framing efforts in the public sphere, and importantly, through mass media. Persuasion becomes a more attractive inducement in conflict situations in a world inundated with mass media, and I found wide agreement among my contacts that whoever wins the public relations war makes the most progress. As one elderly gentleman from the village of Loughbregan put it when I interviewed him during research pseudonymous in 1999, "The answer's up there, you know, in the satellite, satellite television." He also informed me that the first rule of propaganda is to get one's opponent using one's own terminology; then, the battle is half won. Others I interviewed also recognized the growing importance of "gaining the moral high ground."

The growing prominence of public relations work is one of the most important features of the shifting political environment in Northern Ireland. In the United States, we often equate successful politics with an ability to manipulate public opinion. However, during the many years in which unionism could rest assured of political supremacy, it was not required to develop the skills and organizational structure necessary to deploy the kind of nuanced public relations associated with modern democratic politics. Indeed, during the period 1988–1994, the voices of

Sinn Féin and other republican spokespeople were banned from broadcast. Actors' voices were overdubbed instead (Elliott and Flackes 1999). Yet, unionists' political messages were not well suited to external audiences in Britain or abroad as they relied on the demonization of republican violence and overly complicated political analysis that could not appeal to the average British reader. Consequently, unionist propagandists have come to acknowledge that they lost the propaganda war to nationalists and republicans (Parkinson 1998).

Republicans in particular have developed a well-oiled movement and political machine. The development and use of persuasive tactics initiated since the blanket and hunger strikes[8] has become a familiar element of nationalist politics. Many interviewees commented on how adept Republicans had become at public relations—"light years ahead." Michael, an Orangeman from the Loughbregan area, referred to nationalism as "sexy to the media," and while he expressed pessimism about the ability of unionists and loyalists to catch up, he also acknowledged a new mentality, a need to capture world opinion:

> We all know Sinn Féin are great propaganda people. Sinn Féin are so community orientated and know how to [operate], while the unionists are more independent minded, you know, and believe in doing things for themselves. I think now they've caught on that the world media are important. Before, they sort of just ignored world media, but Sinn Féin never did, and Nationalism never did. They see the world media. [They] show they can get their message very much across.

In the realm of popular politics, unionists have been signally unsuccessful in conveying their beliefs and political positions in ways that could mobilize British and international public opinion. Many outside of the United Kingdom might be surprised to learn how unfamiliar Northern Ireland is to most citizens of Great Britain. Media studies have shown that all but the most rudimentary knowledge of Northern Ireland has failed to penetrate public awareness and public opinion across the relatively narrow Irish Sea that separates Ireland and Britain. They may also be surprised to find that despite the enormous military and monetary investments by tax-paying Britons, nationalists and republicans have been far more successful than unionists and loyalists in conveying their political positions. Parkinson (1998) found that British media coverage during the Troubles featured programming on republicanism more often than on unionism. The media's failure to present unionism and loyalism in sophisticated ways, combined with its tendency to focus on allegations of state injustices, such as, internment, that cast republicans in a more sympathetic light, meant that unionists and loyalists were never able to overcome stereotypes that were established early in the Troubles. As he notes, "In general, the media played mainly on unionism's negative features and by selecting certain features of the Irish conflict at the expense of others which might have created greater understanding of the unionist position, a one-dimensional portrait of the Irish conflict was painted for an undiscerning British public" (p. 165). Poor media coverage has been shown to have limited unionists' political capital, but to what extent has poor exposure been a byproduct of poor public relations strategy? Is there evidence of changes in the public relations acumen of unionists and loyalists at the grassroots, especially as the rules of engagement now favor political persuasion over militarism?

Organizations like the Orange Order and loyalist paramilitaries, whose fortunes were tied to the state and the playing out of the armed conflict, find themselves without the partnerships on which they formerly depended for political influence. For some unionist and loyalist organizations, public relations efforts are now required to ensure their longevity in the face of declining participation. In either case, improving public relations can become an important incentive to establish new priorities and agendas. Given the preponderance of support in Britain, Ireland, and internationally for the terms of the Belfast/Good Friday Agreement and the devolution of governance to Northern Ireland, organizations that are seen to contribute positively to working politics and improved community relations stand to accumulate public support. Initiatives designed to improve community relations or that demonstrate a willingness to work across cultural and political divides can capture the moral high ground and thus develop political capital.

■ THE ORANGE ORDER AND PUBLIC RELATIONS

Media Strategy

The Orange Order provides a useful case study in public relations and media strategizing among grassroots unionists and loyalists. The institution has historically been closely related to unionist politics and Protestant elites from which it drew much of its political capital. The Order's staunch commitment to the ascendancy of both Protestantism and unionism in Ireland has provoked charges of sectarianism, and their image as "bigots in bowler hats" has been exacerbated over the decade since the Drumcree crisis began in 1995. One Grand Orange Lodge officer acknowledged in one of our conversations that to develop popular political capital, the Orange Order must work to overcome the legacy of violence that became more closely associated with parades during the years of the Drumcree crisis, but efforts to construct a new public image are relatively recent, and they remain a delicate issue both inside and outside of the institution.

In 1999, prominent unionists and loyalists outside of the Orange Order articulated their beliefs that the institution was failing to win public opinion. George Newell and Michael Hall describe the consensus of six unionists who participated in a panel discussion on the topic of "Orangeism and the Twelfth: What it means to me," organized by the Ballymacarrett Arts and Cultural Society in the Harland and Wolff Welders Club:

> What most of those present—panelists and audience alike—agreed upon was that the Orange Order was losing the "PR" battle, and the institution's inability, or unwillingness, to take adequate steps to rectify this was something which caused a great deal of frustration at the grassroots level. As if to underline this situation the organizers of the

cultural evening had to admit that no one from the Orange Order could be inveigled to speak at the event. At one stage it had seemed that a representative of the Orange Order had agreed to attend, but he failed to turn up on the night, with no subsequent explanation forthcoming. The complete absence of an Orange Order representative, during an evening devoted to Orangeism, only served to compound that sense of frustration.

Tom Elliott, assistant deputy grand secretary and now UUP party leader, acknowledged in a July 12 speech in Killyleagh in 2009 that the Order has performed poorly with regard to public relations:

> One of the things that we haven't been very good at is putting our case across. We have, as Orangemen, at times failed to do that. Sometimes we think that because we are right we have no need to explain to others why we think we are right, and that is not a good thing. That is why we need to take every opportunity to put forward the Protestant and Orange point of view. We must get across to people both within the Order and those who are not what we are basically about; that we are not red face bowler hatted bigots who want to walk over the top of people. That has never been my experience of Orangeism.

Some in the leadership of the Order were aware of the problem or at least appreciated the merits of media relations as far back as the Reverend Martin Smyth's tenure as grand master. In 1988, as a UUP MP, Smyth founded the Ulster Unionist Information Institute, and in 1996 the Unionist Information Office was established in London in order to disseminate favorable information to the British public (Cochrane 2001). Under the Reverend Brian Kennaway's leadership, the Grand Orange Lodge's Education Committee became convinced that the Order must become more adept at presenting itself publicly and made special efforts to improve the Order's outreach. When Ruth Dudley Edwards (1999), a Dublin journalist, was researching her book on the Order, the committee became sensitized to the potential for strategic public exposure to open doors to those with influence, even in the Republic of Ireland. A former member of the committee explained to me that Edwards corresponded and encouraged them to be more proactive about public relations in the Republic of Ireland:

> [She wrote,] "Look, I come from Dublin. I come from the republican tradition there. You need to make yourself *known* to the southern constituency." As a result of that, we got an invite from the Irish Association to go down and to speak at a meeting in Dublin in Boswell's hotel. Quite a large selection of people [attended]. The British Ambassador turned up, and we thought, "Oh, this is a more powerful meeting than we ever thought it would be." And, as a result of that, doors opened, and we made friends, and I think we understood them better now, and they understood us better as a result.

In 2000, the Orange Order hired a public relations firm and has retained professional media relations assistance since then. Philip, a media spokesperson for a district lodge, described the intention to diversify the Order's public image.

> We need to tell the good news story today rather than the bad news story that other ones
> are always telling, and we need to be a wee bit more in control of the type of message that
> we're putting down. That's why, as I say, within our district certainly, we have attempted
> to sort of open ourselves more to people and to say, "This is what we're about. Ask us the
> questions, and we'll try to answer them," and people can say, "Ah well, that's only a group
> trying to use their own propaganda to gain something in some way." All right, you can
> take that as an argument if you want, but as I say, for so many years of a negative type of
> a picture going out, I mean there was times I would really only have appeared on TV,
> either to defend something or to be blamed for something, and what we were sort of
> saying was…there's many other facets to Orangeism. Don't forget these other things
> exist. We're not denying that there's a problem with Garvaghy Road, but these other
> things exist as well, and you have to see the thing in the proper balance, and within the
> District itself there has been the desire to do that.

Philip is referring to his particular district, but his statement reflects many other comments collected from Orangemen in Belfast and at the Grand Orange Lodge.

Many of those in positions of leadership, especially among the officers of the Grand Lodge, who have embraced the importance of building public support and blunting the criticism of critics, intend to frame themselves as having relevance in Northern Ireland's civil society under the new dispensation. They hope to develop new roles for the Order that will attract popular legitimacy, and as one prominent Orangeman in the Belfast County lodge told me at an open house and children's art competition in a lodge on the Shankill Road, they are trying to "open the doors to the community."

Lobbying and Political Capital

One model, lobbying and community leadership, was articulated in a speech by Dr. David Hume, the director of services of the Grand Orange Lodge. He envisions the Orange Order standing between the unionist grassroots and the state, serving as an advocacy or interest group:

> The Orange Order is at the heart of lobbying at all levels over issues affecting us and our
> constituency, and we will continue to do so. We are working with the tourism authorities
> to progress the Twelfth and our cultural heritage as strong marketable elements for vis-
> itors. Our lodges are very involved in their communities, and we are encouraging civic
> leadership among our members. The Orange Order, part of the community since 1795,
> remains very much a part of it today.…We are, in short, not a force which is spent and
> on the decline, but an organization and a positive force which is at the heart of the
> Protestant community, and which will continue to be so.

The use of the term "lobbying" is interesting because it suggests a position or role outside of the state and situates the institution within the context of a working democracy, a frame that contrasts the Order's more familiar emphasis on themes of "defense" that have dominated official resolutions the Order ratifies on the Twelfth each year (Stevenson, Condor, and Abell 2007). Curtis, a Grand Lodge officer reiterated interest in a lobbying strategy in one of our conversations:

> So, I feel there's going to be more involvement in communities. We're going to be a lobby group into the future in terms of the political parties, unionist parties, and I think we're going to be very involved.... We have a unique network of people who are involved, and we want to use that to branch out into the communities and to play, you know, a very big role in terms of specific leadership where, in many areas, people are just not involved in their community. We have that basis that we can involve our people in the communities, and we should be looking at issues, whether it's, you know, roads issues or other issues, general issues with a small "p." I feel lodges have a role there to play.

Turning to civic service marks a substantial shift from the Order's traditional focus on religion and unionist politics toward building influence through organizing around ethnic identity at the grassroots. Again, Curtis explained:

> I suppose it would be worth maybe mentioning that in general terms, more people turn out for our 12th July processions than actually vote for unionist parties in elections and I think that sets things into context.... My view always is that, if as a cultural entity we are together, then that's the most important thing. The politics will come and go, but we must hold our identity, and the only way we do that is through the cultural side of things.... When you see four hundred thousand people turning out to the 12th of July, that's actually what they're saying, you know, they're saying "*We're part of this Protestant, Orange family, and this is our day.*" There might be political defeats and there might be political victories, but the bedrock of it all is the cultural side of it, and I believe from our context, the bedrock of it all for them is the Orange Order, because it is the umbrella that links them all, whatever political party they vote for, no matter what church they go to, that's what links them.

Consequently, the Order's leadership has turned more attention to parades as a tool of outreach, and they have found a potential partner in the tourism industry.

Tourism

Tourism has provided another particularly useful vehicle for promoting stronger public relations and raising the Orange Order's profile as a civic organization. Curtis described the lodge's engagement with tourism officials as "a civic thing." Both the Irish and Northern Irish governments have put cultural tourism in Protestant areas on the agendas of their tourism agencies. In 2007, Tourism Ireland began incorporating Ulster-Scots images into its materials. Organizations like the Orange Order or the Ulster Bands Association can point to the process of working with state agencies to legitimate their activities. The Orange Order in particular has made much of its consultations with the Northern Ireland Tourist Board and Tourism Ireland (Republic of Ireland) in establishing "Flagship Twelfths," parading events in selected towns that are organized to be tourist and family friendly. Representatives of the Northern Ireland Tourist Board began attending Twelfth parades in 2005. Eventually, they hope to have the events featured on the agencies' Web sites. In 2009, the Order collaborated with the Belfast Chamber of Trade and Commerce to open city-center stores for four hours between the Twelfth parade's departure and its return later in the day. Street entertainers were employed to help entertain shoppers and establish a festive atmosphere. Though some skepticism was expressed, the new initiative played well in the media and even several skeptical commentators were left appreciating the outcome and hoping that this was not an isolated moment of change.

A consortium led by the former director of the Ulster-Scots Agency, Lord Laird, has acquired a twenty-seven-acre portion of the Boyne battlefield site and it is working with the Orange Order and the Irish government, which has invested €30 million to develop 500 acres of the site, including an interpretive and educational center. The Grand Orange Lodge of Ireland has devised a "Williamite Trail" map that can be used to guide tourists to visit major sites associated with the movement of William's armies in the seventeenth century. According to Liam Clarke, writing in the *Sunday Times*, "The Irish government and Laird's consortium believe the battlefield will become one of the top 10 tourist attractions in Ireland. The OPW [Office of Public Works] estimates it will attract 100,000 visitors a year" (July 23, 2006). Working with the Irish government helps the Order shed its image of being allergic to all things Irish and has allowed Orangemen to show that they can be significant players in cross-border affairs.

Even further afield, the Order has proposed to attract tourists from the United States in a bid to replicate the enormous tourist industry that has grown up around Irish culture. A senior DUP MLA described the potential for Scots-Irish tourism when we met in the DUP's conference room in City Hall offices in 2007:

> Isn't it far better to sell Northern Ireland as unique in that we've got a cultural mix nobody else has? So that even Tourism Ireland now says the biggest potential growth area in America isn't Irish Americans, it's the Scotch Irish. And they're out targeting those states where you've got strong Scotch Irish presence, because they've played out Boston. The market in Boston—and Ireland and Boston—'til there's nothing left. If anybody doesn't know about [Ireland] now, they'll never know. Whereas all of those other [states], you know, Virginia, the Carolinas, Tennessee...all those areas where you have a significant Scotch Irish presence, particularly Virginia, they're concentrating on....We see huge potential growth there for tourism economically and job creation. And when people come here from America and want to see local culture, if you can employ the Irish dancers this night and later on you have the Highland dancers, everybody's gaining something. That's one of the key elements. It's about quality and diversity but yet, interdependence.

The visit of Orange Order representatives to the Smithsonian Festival in Washington, D.C., in 2007 has also been framed as an effort to develop international tourism in the interest of building the local economy. In a November 2007 press release anticipating an annual remembrance ceremony for Orangemen who were killed during the Troubles, Grand Master Robert Saulters declared the Smithsonian trip a successful contribution to the goal of building a new kind of cultural tourism:

> The highlight of the year was the visit to the Smithsonian Festival in Washington. I was proud to lead a strong Orange Order delegation and I believe we put the Institution firmly on the map in the United States. We hear constantly about the Irish-American lobby but no-one should ever under-estimate the Ulster-Scots/Orange or Protestant dimension that exists in the States and has made such a positive contribution to society there. The contacts we made there will be extremely beneficial to the Order and I believe that ultimately they will also be beneficial to Northern Ireland. We have been working very closely and successfully with the tourist authorities on both sides of the border in Ireland, and we all know that the American market is one that we can tap into. Great strides have been made in promoting the Twelfth and there is much more that can be done. Cultural tourism can be a major asset to our economy, and the Order is fully prepared to play its role. (GOLI press release, December 12, 2007)

Along similar lines, Grand Lodge officers and Niall Gibbons, director of corporate services for Tourism Ireland, hope that Orange lodge minute books can be used to assist tourists who come to Ireland while tracing their genealogies (*Orange Standard,* December 2007).

Recruitment and Institution Building

The long-term success or decline of any given organization is of less interest here than its potential to play a role in conflict transformation, but for the organizations themselves, recruitment and membership can be important motivating concerns. Curtis linked efforts to make Twelfth parades more festive with the institution's ability to maintain membership levels.

> It's a family day; you've got families there. It is not enough, in the twenty-first century, to use that phrase; it is not enough to have a platform there to have a small number of stalls round the field, mainly fish and chips stalls or whatever else, and nothing else to entertain people. That is not enough, and if that were to continue, my belief would be that today's children, the eight- and the ten- and the twelve-year-olds that you would take along today will not be going in twenty or thirty years' time, because they'll say, "*Well it was just boring; I don't want to be there.*" So, we want to make sure that we keep our community together, and we have to move forward, and we have to look at how we can do that and still preserve the best of the tradition of course....Nobody should assume the Orange Order is always going to be here, you know. I believe it will, from a positive point of view, but I think we have to act as if, well, we have to work to make sure this is the case. We can't just let things go.

As we discovered in chapter 5, the Orange Order has been in significant membership decline since the 1960s, though it remains the largest nonchurch voluntary association in Northern Ireland. Given the steady fall-off in its rolls (which the Grand Lodge rarely discusses), we could expect the institution to be motivated to adopt new frames and activities designed to welcome prospective members, especially youth.

Propaganda

Perhaps the most obvious rationale for employing public and media relations strategies through cultural activities is to engage in framing in ways that blunt criticism, improve public opinion, and mobilize support. Effective public and media relations strategies try to gain the moral high ground and deploy challenges to opponents. Grand Secretary Drew Nelson's speech to Orangemen from the platform in Bangor illustrates the way in which the Orange Order's public relations initiatives have afforded it some room to turn and criticize nationalist critics:

> Nationalist politicians, if they believe in a shared future for Northern Ireland, need to show some respect for the Orange Order. During the last few years, we have reached out to the Nationalist community as never before, meeting with the Department of Foreign Affairs of the Republic of Ireland, the SDLP and the leadership of the Roman Catholic Church. We did so in a spirit of openness and goodwill. But that spirit of goodwill is not being reciprocated by nationalist and republican political leaders. Perhaps we were naïve, when we believed their assertions that they wanted to see a shared future in Northern Ireland. (GOLI press release, July 13, 2009)

By seeking to improve its image in the public eye and among nationalists, the Order buys opportunities to demand recognition from their critics.

It is worth noting that the shift of attention among some Orange leaders to changing the institution's raison d'être to lobbying and improving public and media relations also constitutes a fault line within the Order. At the children's art competition award reception on the Shankill Road, one Orange leader told me that they are trying to reach out to the community, though some members prefer that the Order maintain a "traditional approach." He explained, "We are trying to go through a process of bringing those people along while trying some new things."

The Reverend Brian Kennaway (2006) has been outspoken in his book about the necessity of fundamental changes in the internal leadership and governance of the Order, not merely in its presentation to the wider world, a sentiment that was expressed in an interview with Nathan, a former member of the education committee.

> Yes, I think there is a greater awareness of public relations. There is a greater awareness of media. There is a greater awareness of the use of media consultants within the Order, and that has to be welcomed, but in saying that, to get the media strategy or the media presentation correct, they fail to recognize the unpalatable and the unacceptable face of Orangeism. It's still there, and very often when press interviews are given, press state-

ments are made, they are in direct contradiction to what actually happens on the ground, largely through the influence of paramilitaries, largely through the influence of unacceptable behavior, from whichever way it comes. So until that issue is addressed, and the huge issue of membership entry, where the terms and conditions of membership entry are certainly not met, they always have a problem in that [the institution] has traditionally gone for number as opposed to quality of the members. So until that core issue is addressed, PR and media presentation will be perceived by many as just pure spin.

The Orange Order Grand Lodge leadership has made strategic choices to improve its image, paying closer attention to public relations. However, as Nathan's comment indicates, projecting a new image creates expectations that the policy and practice of the institution align with the image. The tension and debate that is generated can lead to internal stability (as the Orange reformation group within the Order indicates) as, at the same time, it produces new and fundamental institutional identities. When these changes entail commitments to persuasive methods of pursuing political or social goals, we can say they contribute to conflict transformation, even when they are motivated by pragmatic concerns.

■ STRATEGY, PRAGMATISM, AND CONFLICT
TRANSFORMATION

Previous chapters focused on the important role that cultural expressions can play in reproducing and shaping the psychocultural landscape within and between groups. In this chapter, I have adopted a more functional approach in identifying the kinds of pragmatic motivations that can underpin cultural traditions activities that mitigate polarizing practices and provide opportunities for the reframing of ethnopolitical identities in less dogmatic ways.

What does all this mean for the claims I have made that there is such a thing as grassroots conflict transformation that includes the mitigation of symbolic practices, innovative heritage work, and the reframing of collective identities? Can new agendas that one might interpret as contributing to conflict transformation be driven by collective or self-interests? Is it antithetical or problematic for the reframing of relationships across the ethnopolitical divide to be in some way "bought" with incentives that are political, monetary, or otherwise? These questions can raise thorny ethical dilemmas. For those who consider themselves victims of discrimination, intimidation, or violence, proposals to merely incentivize *less* injustice or sectarianism can be difficult to accept. Some will perceive something inauthentic and opportunistic in the proposition that groups might benefit from removing intimidating murals. Surely moves to mitigate the most offensive expressions of collective identities should be offered out of a sincere interest in redressing injustice.

The problem, of course, is that, within those organizations, those moves are often considered sacrifices and risks taken for peace, not the righting of wrongs.

We need to also consider the perspective of those who do not necessarily embrace an ambitious peace agenda, see themselves as "peacemakers," or even fully approve of the details of the political peace process in Northern Ireland. Most people appreciate the end of violence, and regardless of the extent to which they identify with peacebuilding, they are nonetheless part of a society that is moving in new directions. The "rules of the game," so to speak, have been shifting, and yet, the world in which they live remains divided along the same old ethnic and political lines. Even teenagers are skeptical about the future of community relations and continue to disapprove of religious mixing. In fact, their rates of skepticism and disapproval surpass those of adults (Schubotz and Devine 2009).[9]

Most unionists and nationalists remain committed to the fundamentals of their political beliefs, and the primary challenge of peacemaking in Ireland has been a painstaking process of incrementally piecing together compromises that have allowed people to maintain fundamental beliefs but adopt new formal relations. Political negotiations have involved many carefully designed incentive structures, most of which are of course contentious from one perspective or the other, but their net effect has made power sharing governance possible. We should not be surprised that grassroots peacebuilding involves at least some of the same dynamics, especially in the most ideologically committed quarters. Groups' identity interests are particularly strong in conflict situations such as, Northern Ireland, but they coexist with other economic and social interests that offer opportunities to encourage change. Indeed, such an emerging pragmatism could be interpreted as a sign that ethnopolitical collective identities are losing some of the zero-sum qualities that made them such a potent catalyst of the Troubles.

One of the fundamental tenets of cultural traditions work holds that greater awareness of a sense of shared heritage can build confidence, replacing insecurities that fuel ethnopolitical conflict. However, those activities are not designed and executed in isolation from other social, political, and economic concerns, especially when we are talking about local grassroots organizations where many dimensions of residents' lives are shared, from local commerce to housing and education. Thus, it seems natural that concerns often associated with community development, such as, environmental ones, should overlap with cultural ones, like bonfires. Organizations' mobilization capacities reflect their abilities to plan and to organize cultural events and their abilities to understand and respond effectively to social and political challenges within their locales. The potential to improve quality of life and the promise of civic empowerment may provide important opportunities for local leaders to sell new agendas and encourage experimentation around long-held identities.

Collective identity and collective action are intimately intertwined with one another, as I described in chapter 2, and in the long run, new strategies require new identities. Luke, a community development officer in East Belfast, described the tensions between core identities and new conflict strategies:

LUKE: Orangeism reaches [a point where they say], "Okay, so let's celebrate." What you're actually doing is, your intention is to fight the conflict in a new way, with new tactics. "So we pull this Ulster-Scots thing, and we connect trans-atlantically, and we connect in other ways, you know, so that we can become more attractive," and at the same time that will corrupt you. The weapon that you are reaching for will also be aimed at your own heart, and in order to sustain that... the mere opening of yourself in that way, and the letting in of air will actually change you or transform you as well. And if you resist that, well you make no gains, and ultimately, you die.

LEE: So, do you think they might be willing to open themselves in that way?

LUKE: Well, I don't know. I wonder.

LEE: Is it important?

LUKE: Oh, I think it is, but the issue is, whether they see it as [transformative]. I mean, this is me talking off the top of my head. Did Republicanism see that actually internationalizing this process [of conflict] over thirty years was actually going to end up limiting the goals they could achieve in their timescales?

For republicans, adopting new strategies, such as, TUAS (Tactical Use of Armed Struggle) and later an international and cross-border constitutional political agenda based on the terms of the Belfast/Good Friday Agreement, meant abandoning the expediency and clarity of "driving the British out" militarily. In order for new political strategies to be sustained among republicans, they must be successfully framed as consonant with basic tenets of republicanism. Luke seems unsure that republicans fully appreciated the implications of adopting new strategies for the "heart" of republicanism, and they are surely not alone. To anticipate those kinds of ideological changes requires a high degree of reflexivity that is elusive but important for leaders to possess if they are to strategize in ways that contribute to the transformation of conflict away from violence and toward nonviolent contention.

Nothing suggests that unionists and loyalists are likely to be any more reflexive than republicans. Indeed, as defenders of the status quo, they are probably inclined to be less reflexive. However, there also seems to be a growing awareness among many that the future of their shared identity is contingent on their ability to be selective and revise it. Jordan, a loyalist ex-combatant, who spent more than a decade in prison and works with other ex-combatants and victims in reconciliation programs, believes there is a willingness among many Protestants to redefine their identities in ways that are less polarized:

I think, to a certain degree, coming out of any conflict situation, there's always a degree of revisionism that takes place on all sides. But generally speaking, I think, in the Protestant, unionist, and loyalist communities, there's a recognition that your culture has to continue to evolve and develop [with] the change in dispensations that takes place. And that if it doesn't, it's quite quickly forgotten about and disappears.... We need to look at what's good about it, and in some senses, it needs to be almost like the phoenix rising up out of the ashes, you know, in terms of the damage that was done to the culture and the tradition because of the conflict. [We need] to reclaim what it really stands for and to reclaim the positive side of it in terms of celebrating your culture, but not in a way that disrespects or diminishes someone else's culture. Being an Orangeman or being a loyalist or being a Protestant or being British [represented] a particular identity during the conflict that's no longer applicable in terms of the new dispensation. I think that is a positive thing. I mean, I suppose it's the difference between growing up in a culture where difference is something to be feared and growing up in a culture where difference is something that can be embraced.

Interestingly, Jordan uses a republican image of the phoenix rising from the ashes, and he attributes the "recognition that your culture has to continue to evolve and develop" more broadly than I might, but given his depth of experience in loyalism and reports from other interviewees, there does seem to be evidence of a growing willingness to acknowledge and strategically adapt to new social and political circumstances.

I have already noted the softening of attitudes regarding EU and IFI funding, and offers of support from the Irish government have, remarkably, been taken up by even the most staunchly unionist organizations. The Grand Orange Lodge of Ireland accepted €250,000 from the Irish government in 2008 for the improvement of Orange halls in border counties, a move that would have been unlikely in previous years, despite the Grand Lodge's long-standing all-Ireland jurisdiction (Orange Order press release, February 5, 2008). The Orange Order is not the only PUL organization to receive Irish funding. In 2007, the Irish government offered funds to a community group in the notoriously loyalist Mt. Vernon estate in North Belfast. According to a spokesperson for the *Taoiseach*, "The aim of the fund is to assist and encourage the development of local organisations. The Taoiseach approved a grant of €4,000 for a piece of artwork to commemorate the link between the 16th Irish and the 36th Ulster Divisions" (*Observer*, July 22, 2007). The linking of funds "for the development of local organizations" through a World War I art project is notable in itself. The fact that the funds were accepted from the Irish government is even more remarkable and signals a redefinition of identity boundaries from a time when loyalists believed the Irish government, operating on behalf of the Catholic Church, was bent on reincorporating Northern Ireland into a homogenized Gaelic nation.

■ CONCLUSION

Pragmatism and strategic thinking underpin many of the initiatives described in this book. Grassroots unionist and loyalist organizations that have focused on symbolic and heritage activities are becoming more interested in community development issues. Conversely, community development organizations recognize the depth of ethnic and political identification in "hard-to-reach" loyalist areas and often combine their work with cultural traditions work, as the Skainos project Web site demonstrates.

The emerging turn to both community development work and heritage work is of course taking place within a shifting political and economic context. Efforts to mitigate symbolic displays of ethnopolitical identity covered in preceding chapters are facilitated by changing political circumstances since the Belfast/Good Friday Agreement, including funding for programs that encourage the softening of the symbolic landscape. The Irish and British governments, the EU, the countries associated with the IFI, and district councils have contributed funds to cultural traditions work, and unionist and loyalist organizations have taken them up in a mounting departure from earlier policies of refusing funds that could in any way be seen as politically tainted.

General support for devolution has made political participation and efficacy imperative, especially for unionists, who have relied heavily on British state sponsorship and the ability of unionist parties to wield influence at Westminster. With the principle of consent enshrined in the Belfast/Good Friday Agreement, political realities have changed, and ensuring popular support for political agendas is increasingly important. The Orange Order, for example (having cut its formal ties with the Ulster Unionist Party), has prioritized lobbying and media and public relations work and has done so partly by launching heritage projects, such as, the Williamite Trail and the new Boyne battlefield site, and turning the Twelfth into a tourist-friendly festival. However, many of those I interviewed expressed frustration at their lack of preparation for grassroots mobilization and public relations work.

On the community development front, there is little consensus on how to address the problem of community empowerment and the development of social capital, but some feel that cultural traditions work can serve as a kind of training ground for basic grassroots organizing skills. Many find it easier to organize around cultural and historical traditions activities, with which they are already familiar and which can be supported through grants and funding schemes. In short, it is important to appreciate the structural context in which grassroots unionism is seeking to remain relevant. A range of pressures and incentives, political and economic, are helping to drive the shifts in strategy among many of the organizations I encountered. However, these new strategies should not be seen merely as efforts at resource accumulation. Changing the rules and norms with which many Protestants identify (such as, accepting external funding or meeting with republicans) or the symbolic displays that perform identity are a tenuous and sometimes delicate business. Social psychological needs for ontological security and the depth of identification with ethnic displays and rituals contend with the political and economic opportunity structures producing a time of uncertain transition for many Protestants. PUL organizations, such as, the Orange Order, have been encouraged to adopt more persuasive and public strategies by funding schemes and changing political and cultural circumstances. To the extent that new norms of civic and political engagement (even if contentious) are legitimized and internalized by unionists and loyalists, we can say that conflict transformation is under way even if the process is incomplete.

■ Notes

1. http://www.skainos.org/ (accessed March 31, 2009).

2. http://www.visitnorthernireland.com/opencontent/default.asp?itemid=154& section=Useful+Info (accessed June 12, 2009).

3. "The Marching Band Economy." *To the Beat of the Drum*, 2004, pp. 21–22. (See also Jarman 2000:169.)

4. Both Protestants and Catholics were equally (24 percent) likely to approve of the role of EU Peace II-funded community projects on their communities' socioeconomic development. However, 50 percent or more of both Protestants and Catholics indicated they were not aware of any impact (Byrne, Fissuh, Thiessen, and Irvin 2008).

5. Definitive comparative data on the distribution of community development funds is difficult to find, but Cairns, Van Til, and Williamson (2003) note some reports of higher levels of funding to Protestant areas of Belfast compared to Catholic areas (pp. 28–29; 36–37).

6. Brewer (2010) reminds us that civil society includes a range of voluntary organizations that may actively attempt to spoil peace and democracy and promote racism, sectarianism, and other dangerous ideologies (pp. 51–52).

7. Interestingly, in their survey, Cairns, Van Til, and Williamson (2003) found no overall difference between Protestants and Catholics with regard to social capital, and found that only rural Protestants differed significantly from urban Protestants by displaying greater appreciation for collectivist values over individualistic ones. However, in focus groups, they found, as I have, that leaders and community workers in loyalist areas report that Protestants tend to embrace a culture of individualism and a merit-based work ethic. Any acknowledgment of social problems or crises that would require social welfare intervention is avoided as it could be interpreted as a sign of weakness and the failure of the state. Thus, Protestants perceive that social problems have not been dealt with collectively but have been swept under the rug (p. 26).

8. In 1978, republicans held in the Maze Prison demanded political status and refused to don prison uniforms, leaving them with only the blankets in their cells to wear. The blanket strikes evolved into hunger strikes in 1980.

9. Schubotz and Devine (2009) report that sixteen-year-olds continue to harbor doubts about the future of community relations in Northern Ireland and religious mixing, though they are more open than adults to racial and ethnic mixing.

8   Conclusion

In 2006, Duncan Morrow (2006), the chief executive director of the Community Relations Council, wrote in the council's journal, *Shared Space*:

> There is no such thing as benign apartheid in Northern Ireland. There is deterrence and there is moving away from deterrence. The only apartheid that is benign is one that removes the threat. For that to happen, Northern Ireland would have to be "ethnically cleansed" in toto, and internationally patrolled borders erected in contradiction of everything which the European Union stands for. The building of bridging capital and the slow erosion of the need for deterrence is the only other sustainable model. In the interim is a slow and sullen peace, in which people are glad to emerge from the past but deeply sceptical of the future. Political parties which exist to deter one another will find this dilemma difficult to resolve. But the predictable result of a refusal to invest in real bridging [capital] is a return to deterrence and the collapse of any possibility of internal government. The result, provided the British-Irish consensus remains, will be a holding operation awaiting the further outbreak of a commitment to building bridging social capital. The degree of our commitment to trust-building will be the single most important factor in determining the social, economic and political life of Northern Ireland over the next few years. (p. 74)

Gesturing to Frank Wright's (1992) work on "communal deterrence," Morrow understands that sustainable peace is ultimately a social problem, not merely a political problem. "Moving away from deterrence" means relinquishing a perpetual state of vigilance and building trust and relationships across the ethnic divide that, so far, has persisted alongside the establishment of power sharing governance. The process is facilitated through working politics, but it is fundamentally social. Only as people with deeply socialized collective identities, who live in a society that is both culturally and institutionally divided and who harbor traumatic memories of thirty years of violent conflict, come to accept less exclusive definitions of the situation can the constitutional issue be settled in a sustainable way.

A conflict transformation model of sustainable peacebuilding requires changes in collective subjective orientations or attitudes so that relationships can be built among groups of people that have developed mutually polarized identities. The transformation of "hearts and minds" has been the subject of much important community relations work in Northern Ireland and deserves ongoing attention alongside the considerable progress in establishing a power sharing government at Stormont and implementing the terms of the Belfast/Good Friday Agreement. Understanding how such change might occur from *within* local organizations and communities, based around preexisting sources of legitimacy, deserves close attention.

The involvement of those segments of the population that have cultivated the most exclusive identities, or those for whom inclusion is highly conditional, is crucial. I have chosen in this project to focus on those who are involved, through a range of organizations and activities, in the reproduction of unionist and loyalist ideology and identity. Muralists, Orangemen, bands, paramilitaries, and community development organizations feature prominently.

The fundamental motivation for the project has been to assess the potential for what Morrow calls "real bridging." We should ask if there is any potential for the easing of ethnopolitical exclusion from within, especially as some groups and communities have often been called "hard to reach" by community relations experts. As Liechty and Clegg (2001) and others have argued, calls for fundamental realignments are more credible when they come from recognized figures drawing on shared ideological resources (Cochrane and Dunn 2002; Brewer 2003; Gormley-Heenan and Robinson 2003). As Morrow points out, short of complete ethnic cleansing, a process of collective reevaluation, redefinition, and cooperation will be necessary. The full participation of unionists and loyalists will be important, and it will have to be, to a significant extent, on their terms. How can they arrive at such a point?

Liechty and Clegg (2001) have proposed that some of the most polarizing beliefs that make improving community relations difficult can be modified while maintaining the essence of group identity. "What cannot be negotiated can sometimes be mitigated" (Liechty and Clegg 2001:229). I have taken the concept of mitigation, applied it to Protestant/unionist/loyalist (PUL) cultural expressions, and documented a movement by grassroots organizations to innovate and choreograph traditional expressions of ethnopolitical identity, such as parades, murals, bonfires, and memorials. This kind of cultural experimentation allows participants to maintain a sense of ontological security or confidence while moderating expressions that can generate fear or discomfort for Catholic or other communities. The process can serve a particularly important function in providing space and sources of legitimacy for leaders to introduce ideas or proposals that might otherwise be dismissed with insufficient consideration (Brewer 2003; Gormley-Heenan and Robinson 2003). Organizations that have modified cultural expressions have, for example, developed cross-community and cross-border history projects, interface management schemes, and dialogue over parading conflicts, to name a few promising initiatives.

This bending of traditional practices causes ripples at the borders of collective identities, not precipitating wholesale switches in identities but changing their content. Orangemen become lobbyists who contend with others on behalf of their membership or the communities where their lodges are, as opposed to "defenders" whose purpose is to dogmatically assert, as a matter of sovereign privilege, their British citizenship. Loyalist bands become historical enthusiasts and civic youth organizations. Paramilitaries begin to think of themselves as community organizers. Each of these incremental transformations deserves both encouragement and scrutiny and ideally will feed into a dialogue about the past and the future in Northern Ireland as these organizations engage more fully in civic life and seek to persuade others, and crucially, they must also be open to persuasion.

Intra-communal cultural and historical work does not offer a panacea for eth-nopolitical polarization but it can help to create a more conducive physical and mental environment for better relations. At the same time, it presents a number of dangerous pitfalls. Attitudinal change is bound to be incremental and may not keep pace with expectations outside of working-class Protestant/unionist/loyalist communities for the memories and the trappings of the Troubles to be safely stowed away. This may reflect both unrealistic expectations and a reluctance by some local leaders to give up the influence that association with intimidating or sectarian symbols and practices has provided them in the past. Furthermore, if the mitigation of offensive cultural practices does not go far enough, and old forms of symbolic exclusion are replaced with new ones under the cover of "heritage," little progress will be made in improving community relations.

Finally, as we consider the potentials and pitfalls of cultural and historical iden-tity work for improving community relations, we should avoid seeing the process as one of pacification in which Protestant/unionist/loyalist organizations are expected, as a matter of course, to abandon heritage work. Instead, if developing cultural projects builds social capital and civic organizing capacity and prepares people to engage in cross-community work and constructive conflict, such as, engaging with political representatives or developing grassroots campaigns, and if it leads to more sophisticated understandings of intertwined histories, then it serves an important role in authentic conflict transformation.

This brings us to a central problematic that has provoked much debate. How can the development of activities that are designed to celebrate narratives particular to one community contribute to a shared future? Surely reinscribing difference is counterproductive to building bridging capital, undermining distrust, and devel-oping cooperative attitudes (Cochrane and Dunn 2002:170). This would be the case if the composition of ethnic identities were static and if ethnic boundaries were sharp, rigid, and clearly defined. However, we are becoming increasingly aware of the malleability of ethnic identities and the modularity of their compo-nents (narratives, activities, symbols) whereby some can be foregrounded while others recede into the background. In this manner, the makeup of identities can change, making them less impenetrable without rejecting them altogether, as Ross (2001) explains:

> How can we incorporate identity dynamics into efforts to manage ethnic conflict con-structively? To do so, we must begin with the parties' frames of reference, and recognize that cognitive approaches that try to persuade parties that they are wrong or efforts to change the ethnic categories groups use (governments try to do this all the time) almost always fail. A more productive approach acknowledges groups' perceptions of threats to their identity and seeks to diminish them. For example, recognition and acceptance of

the power of a group's narratives can create new possibilities for cooperation. Linking identity (and threats to identity) to new metaphors or rearranging the content of old ones in culturally acceptable ways, is another possibility for creating new patterns of group interaction. (p. 174)

The reconfiguration of collective identities may occur more easily when adherents feel that the process does not threaten the fundamental integrity of their world-view. Foregrounding or developing new ways of expressing collective identity can create space for relinquishing other practices or principles. In other words, identities are strong but reconfigurable. In some cases, symbols can become shared across ethnic boundaries, signaling a softening of group boundaries, such as, the appropriation of St. Patrick by both Protestants and Catholics.

The opportunity structure for reconfiguring collective identities is more amenable in the absence of violence or high levels of inequality and can be incentivized, as we discussed in chapter 7. Changes in leadership can prove crucial. The interaction of conducive opportunity structures and incentives and creative leadership lies at the heart of peacebuilding. The process involves a rich mixture of political, cultural, and psychological factors that might be considered the deep realpolitik of conflict transformation. The complexity and sensitivity of these processes of cultural change are often underestimated. The process of reconfiguration within groups can be contentious, and the rate of change will often fail to conform to what many, especially in middle and upper classes, would prefer.

■ SOCIAL JUSTICE

The model of conflict transformation I have presented is not without its philosophical and ethical challenges. Some will argue that while Northern Ireland may have largely left political violence behind, it continues to struggle with class division and ethnic, gender, and racial intolerance. Anti-patriarchal discourses were sidelined over the course of the Troubles and are now being overshadowed by ethnic identity politics. O'Reilly (2004) articulates this position concisely:

The debate over the political and cultural shape of a future Northern Ireland is now being played out in large part through the language of culture, heritage and traditions, squeezing out other alternative approaches—including attempts to increase the profile of class-based and feminist-influenced politics. The politics of culture is the new hegemony, and there is as yet, no unified, effective discourse to oppose it. (p. 186)

O'Reilly's critique is provocative, and this book is somewhat limited with respect to women's or immigrants' voices. I have focused on organizations and activities that primarily involve men. Politics remains highly masculine in Northern Ireland, though some advances have been made by unionists and loyalists. The Progressive Unionist Party (PUP) has taken deliberate steps to prioritize the involvement of women and has endorsed supportive positions on gay and lesbian rights, urban regeneration, and the environment, among others (McAuley 2002:111, 2004b:86).

On the other hand, a comprehensive model of conflict transformation that is as inclusive as possible and includes a vision of Northern Ireland with a wider global engagement, where any number of progressive agendas could take root, is arguably one with feminist underpinnings. It seeks to encourage and make space for as wide a range of participation as possible while recognizing that ethnic divisions and sectarianism are deeply rooted, enough that they cannot be simply bypassed for many in Northern Ireland.

The question of justice in Northern Ireland is a thorny one that is nowhere near resolution or consensus. Many register discomfort when incentives for heritage or social work are offered to organizations that have been either directly involved in violence or that have contributed to sectarian division and fear. However, as Shirlow and Murtagh (2006) point out, "The conflict that is Northern Ireland will only be resolved when the central protagonists shift in a forward and inclusive direction. At present they do so, but with caution and complex irony" (p. 173). That irony is too much for many, especially when it comes to paramilitary organizations, and while victims of paramilitary violence have often demonstrated incredible generosity and forgiveness, latitude cannot necessarily be expected of them. Victims' grief can never be fully assuaged, but all quarters have a responsibility to move as swiftly as possible to mitigate or abandon practices that exacerbate their discomfort.

■ COMMUNITY RELATIONS

One of the ultimate tests of unionists' and loyalists' efforts to mitigate offensive public displays and the reconfiguration of ethnic identities is the extent to which they actually help improve relations with nationalists. There is no doubt that activities such as, the hanging of flags, frequent band parades, and bonfires go unappreciated among most nationalists. For many, these activities symbolize inequality and domination, and it may take considerable time and further effort to sufficiently influence nationalist attitudes toward grassroots unionist and loyalist organizations. When David Scott, Grand Lodge's education officer met with Limavady councillors in February 2009, he was essentially rebuffed, told by Sinn Féin Councilor Cathal O'hOisin, "Sort out your own house and then come back to us" (*Derry Journal*, February 13, 2009).

Bonfires and band parades may never become popular with nationalists, but the question is whether, in the medium term, moves to abandon offensive aspects of these expressions can improve the prospects of bridge building. There is evidence that some thawing is under way. Fionnuala O'Connor, a journalist for the nationalist-leaning *Irish Times,* wrote of the July parading season in 2005: "At this time of year the very air incites to hatred, filled as it too often is with the sound of marching bands commemorating the ancient triumph of Protestants over Catholics, and the crack of petrol-bombs" (*Irish Times*, July 1, 2005). O'Connor continued to criticize the Orange Order in a story published shortly before the

Twelfth in 2009, but she also acknowledged that an unclear and incomplete transition is under way (*Irish News*, July 7, 2009). A fellow journalist at the *Irish News*, Allison Morris, reported on downsized Eleventh Night bonfires in 2009 in Tigers Bay and Woodvale Park:

> What most struck me, as a nationalist from west Belfast, was that I was not in the slightest bit apprehensive. In fact, I totally related to the event as it was very similar to my memories of the early days of the west Belfast Féile an Phobail before that became the slick operation it is today. (*Irish News*, July 13, 2009)

We need not revise the historical record on Drumcree and other contentious parades or pretend that bonfires are not intentionally built at interfaces and desecrate Catholic and nationalist symbols to acknowledge a growing number of initiatives by grassroots unionists to mitigate these practices. At the same time, remarks such as, Grand Master Robert Saulters's blanket reference in an editorial to the "Roman Catholic IRA" can counteract mitigation efforts (*Orange Standard*, October 2010).

The centrality of the symbolic construction of ethnic boundaries in the intractability of many ethnopolitical conflicts has been well established. As we continue to learn more about the recursive relationships between collective identity and collective action and the malleability of ethnic identity change within and between categories, we should be able to extend the tools of cultural analysis to conflict transformation and the unwinding of polarized ethnopolitical relations. Writing in the *Independent* in 2008, Maurice Hayes, a long-time civil servant, the first chairperson of the Northern Ireland Community Relations Commission, and a former Irish senator, noted that "apparently impenetrable" symbolic barriers continue to be breached at the grassroots.

> A feature of the process is that whatever rapprochement, real or simulated, has been achieved between party leaders at the top, it has taken a long time for this to trickle down the chain where there is not only fear, insecurity and the memory of recent hurts and historic animosity, but also a deep-seated sectarianism. The celebration at the Boyne, the mock sword play between Bertie and Paisley, was highly symbolic in its way and very important for the future, but unless and until some of the same degree of mutual respect begins to manifest itself in the dreary terraces of North Belfast and the Drumlins of North Armagh and East Tyrone, not only will the problems rumble on for another generation or two but an opportunity to eradicate the virus of sectarianism will have been lost. It is in this context that the meeting of Gerry Adams with Portadown Orangemen, under the chairmanship of a local businessman, is both groundbreaking and significant. Significant too is the fact that after the first disclosure by way of leak, it caused hardly a ripple in the media. Normality takes strange shapes. Another apparently impenetrable barrier has been pierced, indicative of a general, if slow, metamorphosis in society. It can only be a good thing that people are reaching out across political and cultural divides in an attempt to understand each other. It is, of course, at street or community level that

these things will be sorted out, to enable parades to take place in a way which is acceptable to all, which can indeed be celebrated as the Boyne itself is now celebrated and to enable the removal of the "peace walls" which survive as a monument to fear and insecurity. The most lasting barriers are in the minds of men and it requires dialogue, interchange, the beginning of understanding and a development of trust to secure their removal. That senior members of the Orange Order in Portadown should have met with Gerry Adams is an important milestone in this process. (*Independent*, June 30, 2008)

The kind of incremental cultural and psychological change that Hayes perceives lies at the heart of conflict transformation. Grassroots ownership of change is necessary, and as many quarters as possible should be encouraged to figure out how to evolve with the new dispensation, whether motivated by pragmatic concerns for organizational survival or out of a genuine desire to participate in a multicultural public life that was long impossible during decades of violent conflict. Often both motivations are at play. This book has attempted to document what these important internally negotiated processes look like, even as they may take longer than many would like.

■ REFERENCES

Ackerman, Peter and Christopher Kruegler. 1994. *Strategic Nonviolent Conflict: The Dynamics of People Power in the Twentieth Century*. Westport, Conn.: Praeger.

Adamson, Ian. [1982] 1987. *The Identity of Ulster: The Land, the Language, and the People*. Belfast: Pretani Press.

Adamson, Ian. 1991. *The Ulster People: Ancient, Medieval and Modern*. Ireland: Pretani Press.

Adamson, Ian. [1974] 1995. *The Cruthin: The Ancient Kindred*. Newtownards: Nosmada Books.

Alexander, Jeffrey C. 2004. "Cultural Pragmatics: Social Performance between Ritual and Strategy." *Sociological Theory* 22(4):527–573.

Amir, Yehuda. 1969. "Contact Hypothesis in Ethnic Relations." *Psychological Bulletin* 71:319–342.

Anderson, Benedict R. O. G. 1991. *Imagined Communities: Reflections on the Origin and Spread of Nationalism*. London: Verso.

Aretxaga, Begoña. 1997. *Shattering Silence: Women, Nationalism, and Political Subjectivity in Northern Ireland*. Princeton, N.J.: Princeton University Press.

ARK. 1998–2008. *Northern Ireland Life and Times Survey* [MRDF]. Belfast: ARK [producer]. Belfast: ARK www.ark.ac.uk/nilt [distributor].

ARK. 1999. *Northern Ireland Life and Times Survey* [MRDF]. Belfast: ARK [producer]. Belfast: ARK. www.ark.ac.uk/nilt [distributor].

ARK. 2000–2005. *Northern Ireland Life and Times Survey* [MRDF]. Belfast: ARK [producer]. Belfast: ARK. www.ark.ac.uk/nilt [distributor].

ARK. 2000–2008. *Northern Ireland Life and Times Survey* [MRDF]. Belfast: ARK [producer]. Belfast: ARK. www.ark.ac.uk/nilt [distributor].

ARK. 2001. *Northern Ireland Life and Times Survey* [MRDF]. Belfast: ARK [producer]. Belfast: ARK. www.ark.ac.uk/nilt [distributor].

ARK. 2003. *Northern Ireland Life and Times Survey* [MRDF]. Belfast: ARK [producer]. Belfast: ARK. www.ark.ac.uk/nilt [distributor].

ARK. 2007. *Northern Ireland Life and Times Survey* [MRDF]. Belfast: ARK [producer]. Belfast: ARK. www.ark.ac.uk/nilt [distributor].

ARK. 2008a. *Northern Ireland Life and Times Survey* [MRDF]. Belfast: ARK [producer]. Belfast: ARK. www.ark.ac.uk/nilt [distributor].

ARK. 2008b. *Young Life and Times Survey* [MRDF]. Belfast: ARK [producer]. Belfast: ARK. www.ark.ac.uk/ylt [distributor].

ARK. 2009a. *Northern Ireland Life and Times Survey* [MRDF]. Belfast: ARK [producer]. Belfast: ARK. www.ark.ac.uk/nilt [distributor].

ARK. 2009b. *Young Life and Times Survey* [MRDF]. Belfast: ARK [producer]. Belfast: ARK. www.ark.ac.uk/ylt [distributor].

Ascherson, Neal. 2004. "'Better Off without Them'? Politics and Ethnicity in the Twenty-First Century." *International Affairs* 80(1):99–106.

Aughey, Arthur. 1989. *Under Siege: Ulster Unionism and the Anglo-Irish Agreement*. Belfast: Blackstaff Press.

Aughey, Arthur. 1997. "The Character of Ulster Unionism." In *Who Are the People? Unionism, Protestantism and Loyalism in Northern Ireland*, edited by P. Shirlow and M. McGovern, p. 16–33. London: Pluto Press.

Ballymacarrett Arts and Cultural Society. 2000. *Prods Can't Act, Sing or Dance*. Belfast: Ballymacarrett Arts and Cultural Society.

Bardon, Jonathan. 1992. *A History of Ulster*. Belfast: Blackstaff Press.

Barnes, Barry. 2000. *Understanding Agency: Social Theory and Responsible Action*. Thousand Oaks, Calif.: Sage.

Barth, Fredrik. 1969. *Ethnic Groups and Boundaries: The Social Organization of Culture Difference*. Boston: Little, Brown.

Barthel, Diane L. 1996. *Historic Preservation: Collective Memory and Historical Identity*. New Brunswick, N.J.: Rutgers University Press.

Becker, Gary S. 1964. *Human Capital: A Theoretical and Empirical Analysis, with Special Reference to Education*. New York: National Bureau of Economic Research.

Bell, Desmond. 1990. *Acts of Union: Youth Culture and Sectarianism in Northern Ireland*. Basingstoke, Hampshire: Macmillan.

Berbrier, Mitch. 2000. "Ethnicity in the Making: Ethnicity Work, the Ethnicity Industry, and a Constructionist Framework for Research." *Perspectives on Social Problems* 12:69–88.

Blackbourn, Jessie and Kacper Rekawek. 2007. *Ten Years On: Who Are the Winners and Losers from the Belfast Agreement?* More 4, Belfast. (http://cain.ulst.ac.uk/events/peace/docs/blackbourn_rekawek_08.htm).

Bloomer, Stephen. 2008. "Bridging the Militarist-Politico Divide: The Progressive Unionist Party and the Politics of Conflict Transformation." In *Transforming the Peace Process in Northern Ireland: From Terrorism to Democratic Politics*, edited by A. Edwards and S. Bloomer, pp. 97–113. Dublin: Irish Academic Press.

Bond, Doug. 1992. "Introduction." *Transforming Struggle: Strategy and the Global Experience of Nonviolent Direct Action*, pp. 1–6. Cambridge, Mass.: Program on Nonviolent Sanctions in Conflict and Defense, Center for International Affairs, Harvard University.

Boulding, Elise. 2000. *Cultures of Peace: The Hidden Side of History*. Syracuse: Syracuse University Press.

Boulding, Kenneth Ewart. 1989. *Three Faces of Power*. Newbury Park, Calif.: Sage.

Bourdieu, Pierre. 1986. "The Forms of Capital." In *Handbook of Theory and Research for the Sociology of Education*, edited by J. G. Richardson, pp. 241–258. New York: Greenwood Press.

Bourdieu, Pierre. 1991. *Language and Symbolic Power*, edited by J. B. Thompson. Cambridge, Mass.: Harvard University Press.

Bourdieu, Pierre and Loïc J. D. Wacquant. 1992. *An Invitation to Reflexive Sociology*. Chicago: University of Chicago Press.

Brewer, John D. 2003. *C. Wright Mills and the Ending of Violence*. New York: Palgrave Macmillan.

Brewer, John D. 2010. *Peace Processes: A Sociological Approach*. Cambridge: Polity.

Brewer, John D. and Gareth I. Higgins. 1998. *Anti-Catholicism in Northern Ireland, 1600–1998: The Mote and the Beam*. London: Macmillan.

Brown, Paul. 2002. "Peace but No Love as Northern Ireland Divide Grows Ever Wider." *The Guardian*, January 4, p. 3.

Brown, William. 2003. *An Army with Banners: The Real Face of Orangeism*. Belfast: Beyond the Pale.

Bruce, Steve. 1994a. "Cultural Traditions: A Double-Edged Sword?" *Causeway* (Autumn):21–24.

Bruce, Steve. 1994b. *The Edge of the Union: The Ulster Loyalist Political Vision*. Oxford: Oxford University Press.

Bruce, Steve. 2007. *Paisley: Religion and Politics in Northern Ireland*. Oxford: Oxford University Press.

Bryan, Dominic. 2000. *Orange Parades: The Politics of Ritual, Tradition, and Control*. London: Pluto Press.

Bryan, Dominic. 2004. "Drumcree: Marching Towards Peace in Northern Ireland?" In *Peace at Last? The Impact of the Good Friday Agreement on Northern Ireland*, edited by J. Neuheiser and S. Wolff, pp. 94–110. New York: Berghahn Books.

Bryan, Dominic, T. G. Fraser, and Seamus Dunn. 1995. *Political Rituals: Loyalist Parades in Portadown*. Coleraine: Centre for the Study of Conflict, University of Ulster.

Bryan, Dominic and Gordon Gillespie. 2005. *Transforming Conflict: Flags and Emblems*. Belfast: Institute for Irish Studies, Queen's University of Belfast. http://www.research. ofmdfmni.gov.uk/flags.pdf.

Bryan, Dominic and Gordon Gillespie. 2006. "Flags and Emblems." In *Sharing over Separation: Actions Towards a Shared Future*, pp. 41–66. Belfast, Northern Ireland: Northern Ireland Community Relations Council.

Bryan, Dominic and Gillian McIntosh. 2005. "Symbols: Sites of Creation and Contest in Northern Ireland." *SAIS Review* 25(2):127–137.

Bryan, Dominic and Clifford Stevenson. 2006. *Flags Monitoring Project 2006: Preliminary Findings*. Belfast: Institute for Irish Studies, Queen's University of Belfast.

Bryan, Dominic and Clifford Stevenson. 2009. "Flagging Peace: Struggles over Symbolic Landscapes in the New Northern Ireland." In *Culture and Belonging in Divided Societies: Contestation and Symbolic Landscapes*, edited by M. Ross, pp. 68–84. Philadelphia: University of Pennsylvania Press.

Bryan, Dominic, Clifford Stevenson, and Gordon Gillespie. 2007. "Flagging Identities: Assessing the Display and Regulation of Political Symbols across Northern Ireland in 2006." *Shared Space* (4):49–71.

Bryan, Dominic, Clifford Sevenson, and Gordon Gillespie. 2008. *Flags Monitoring Project: 2007 Report*. Belfast: Institute for Irish Studies, Queen's University of Belfast.

Bryan, Dominic, Clifford Stevenson, and Gordon Gillespie. 2009. *Flags Monitoring Project 2008/09: Interim Report Covering 2008 with Comparative Figures from 2007 and 2006*. Belfast: Institute for Irish Studies, Queen's University of Belfast.

Bryson, Lucy and Clem McCartney. 1994. *Clashing Symbols: A Report on the Use of Flags, Anthems and Other National Symbols in Northern Ireland*. Belfast: Institute of Irish Studies for the Community Relations Council.

Buckley, Anthony. 1989. "'We're Trying to Find Our Identity': Uses of History among Ulster Protestants." In *History and Ethnicity*, edited by E. Tonkin, M. Chapman, and M. McDonald, pp. 183–197. New York: Routledge.

Buckley, Anthony D. 1985–1986. "Chosen Few: Biblical Texts in the Regalia of an Ulster Secret Society." *Folk Life* 24.

Buckley, Anthony D., ed. 1998. *Symbols in Northern Ireland*. Belfast: Institute of Irish Studies, Queen's University of Belfast.

Buckley, Anthony G. and Mary Catherine Kenney. 1995. *Negotiating Identity: Rhetoric, Metaphor, and Social Drama*. Washington, D.C.: Smithsonian Institution Press.

Byrne, Jonny. 2008. "Bonfire Management Programme." *CRC e-Bulletin* (3):12–13.

Byrne, Jonny and Caroline Wilson. 2007. "Eleventh Night Bonfires: Managing and Exploring Issues around Cultural Diversity and Good Relations." *Shared Space* (4):37–47.

Byrne, Sean. 1995. "Conflict Regulation or Conflict Resolution: Third Party Intervention in the Northern Ireland Conflict: Prospects for Peace." *Journal of Terrorism and Political Violence* 7(2):1–24.

Byrne, Sean and Michael J Ayulo. 1998. "External Economic Aid in Ethno-Political Conflict: A View from Northern Ireland." *Security Dialogue* 29:421–434.

Byrne, Sean and Neal Carter. 1996. "Social Cubism: Six Social Forces of Ethnoterritorial Politics in Northern Ireland and Québec." *Peace and Conflict Studies* 3(2):52–71.

Byrne, Sean, Eyob Fissuh, Chuck Thiessen, and Cynthia Irvin. 2008. "The Role of the International Fund for Ireland and the European Union Peace II Fund in Promoting Peace and Reducing Violence in Northern Ireland." Paper presented at the International Studies Association, March 26–29, 2008, San Francisco, California.

Byrne, Sean and Cynthia Irvin. 2001. "Economic Aid and Policy Making: Building the Peace Dividend in Northern Ireland." *Policy and Politics* 29(4):413–429.

Byrne, Sean and Cynthia Irvin. 2002. "A Shared Common Sense: Perceptions of the Material Effects and Impacts of Economic Growth in Northern Ireland." *Civil Wars* 5(1):55–86.

Cairns, Ed. 1994. *A Welling Up of Deep Unconscious Forces: Psychology and the Northern Ireland Conflict*. Coleraine: Centre for the Study of Conflict.

Cairns, Ed, Jon Van Til, and Arthur Williamson. 2003. *Social Capital, Collectivism-Individualism and Community Background in Northern Ireland*. Belfast: Northern Ireland Executive.

"Catholic Face in Loyalist Estate." 2003. *BBC News*, August 13, 2005. Retrieved November 5, 2006, http://news.bbc.co.uk/2/hi/uk_news/northern_ireland/4259524.stm.

Central Statistics Office Ireland. 2007. *Census 2006: Religion*. Dublin: Stationery Office. Retrieved December 11, 2009, http://www.cso.ie/census/census2006results/volume_13/volume_13_religion.pdf.

Chaiken, Shelly L., Deborah H. Gruenfeld, and Charles M. Judd. 2000. "Persuasion in Negotiations and Conflict Situations." In *The Handbook of Conflict Resolution: Theory and Practice*, edited by M. Deutsch and P. T. Coleman, pp. 144–165. San Francisco: Jossey-Bass.

Claval, Paul. 2007. "Changing Conceptions of Heritage and Landscape." In *Heritage, Memory and the Politics of Identity: New Perspectives on the Cultural Landscape*, edited by N. Moore and Y. Whelan, pp. 85–93. Burlington, Vt.: Ashgate.

Cochrane, Feargal. 2001. *Unionist Politics and the Politics of Unionism since the Anglo-Irish Agreement*. Cork: Cork University Press.

Cochrane, Feargal and Seamus Dunn. 2002. *People Power? The Role of the Voluntary and Community Sector in the Northern Ireland Conflict*. Cork, Ireland: Cork University Press.

Coleman, James S. 1988. "Social Capital in the Creation of Human Capital." *American Journal of Sociology* 94:S95–S120.

Coleraine Borough Council. 2003. *Equality Impact Assessment: Bonfires*. Coleraine, Northern Ireland: Coleraine Borough Council.

Connor, Walker. 1994. *Ethnonationalism: The Quest for Understanding*. Princeton, N.J.: Princeton University Press.

Coser, Lewis A. 1956. *The Functions of Social Conflict*. Glencoe, Ill.: Free Press.

Coulter, Colin. 1997. "The Culture of Contentment: The Political Beliefs and Practice of the Unionist Middle Classes." In *Who Are the People? Unionism, Protestantism and Loyalism in Northern Ireland*, edited by P. Shirlow and M. McGovern, pp. 114–139. London: Pluto Press.

Coy, Patrick G. and Lynne M. Woehrle, eds. 2000. *Social Conflicts and Collective Identities*. Lanham, Md.: Rowman & Littlefield.

Crocker, Chester A., Fen Osler Hampson, and Pamela R. Aall, eds. 2005. *Grasping the Nettle: Analyzing Cases of Intractable Conflict*. Washington, D.C.: United States Institute of Peace Press.

Cultural Traditions Group. 1995. *Giving Voices: The Work of the Cultural Traditions Group 1990–1994*. Belfast: Cultural Traditions Group of the Northern Ireland Community Relations Council.

Dangerfield, George. 1976. *The Damnable Question: A Study in Anglo-Irish Relations*. Boston: Little, Brown.

Darby, John. 1986. *Intimidation and the Control of Conflict in Northern Ireland*. Dublin: Gill and Macmillan.

de Tocqueville, Alexis and Arthur Goldhammer. 2004 [1835]. *Democracy in America*. New York: Library of America.

Deutsch, Morton. 1973. *The Resolution of Conflict: Constructive and Destructive Processes*. New Haven: Yale University Press.

Deutsch, Morton. 1991. "Subjective Features of Conflict Resolution: Psychological, Social and Cultural Influences." In *New Directions in Conflict Theory: Conflict Resolution and Conflict Transformation*, edited by R. Väyrynen, pp. 26–56. Newbury Park, Calif.: Sage.

Deutsch, Morton. 1998. "Constructive Conflict Resolution: Principles, Training, and Research." In *The Handbook of Interethnic Coexistence*, edited by E. Weiner, pp. 199– 216. New York: Continuum.

Deutsch, Morton and Peter T. Coleman, eds. 2000. *The Handbook of Conflict Resolution: Theory and Practice*. San Francisco: Jossey-Bass.

Devine, Paula and Dirk Schubotz. 2004. *Us and Them?* ARK Northern Ireland Social and Political Archive. Retrieved September 16, 2008, http://www.ark.ac.uk/publications/updates/update28.pdf.

Dunn, Seamus. 1995. "The Conflict as a Set of Problems." In *Facets of the Conflict in Northern Ireland*, edited by S. Dunn, pp. 3–14. New York: St. Martin's Press.

Dunn, Seamus and Valerie Morgan. 1994. *Protestant Alienation in Northern Ireland*. Coleraine: Centre for the Study of Conflict.

Durkheim, Emile. 1915. *The Elementary Forms of the Religious Life, a Study in Religious Sociology*. New York: Macmillan.

East Belfast Historical and Cultural Society. 2006. "Thorndyke Street Murals." Belfast: East Belfast Historical and Cultural Society.

Edwards, Ruth Dudley. 1999. *The Faithful Tribe: An Intimate Portrait of the Loyal Institutions*. London: Harper Collins.

Eller, Jack and Reed Coughlin. 1993. "The Poverty of Primordialism: The Demystification of Ethnic Attachments." *Ethnic and Racial Studies* 16(2):183–202.

Elliott, Sydney and W.D. Flackes. 1999. *Northern Ireland: A Political Directory 1968–1999.* Belfast: Blackstaff Press.

English, Richard. 2002. "The Growth of New Unionism." In *Changing Shades of Orange and Green: Redefining the Union and the Nation in Contemporary Ireland*, edited by J. Coakley, pp. 95–105. Dublin: University College Dublin Press.

Evans, Jocelyn A. J. and Jonathan Tonge. 2007. "Unionist Party Competition and the Orange Order Vote in Northern Ireland." *Electoral Studies* 26(1):156–167.

Eyben, Karin, Duncan Morrow, and Derick Wilson. 1997. *A Worthwhile Venture? Practically Investing in Equity Diversity and Interdependence in Northern Ireland*: Ulster: University of Ulster.

Farrington, Christopher. 2006. *Ulster Unionism and the Peace Process in Northern Ireland.* New York: Palgrave Macmillan.

Farrington, Christopher. 2008. "Loyalists and Unionists: Explaining the Internal Dynamics of an Ethnic Group." In *Transforming the Peace Process in Northern Ireland: From Terrorism to Democratic Politics*, edited by A. Edwards and S. Bloomer, pp. 28–43. Dublin: Irish Academic Press.

Farry, Stephen. 2006. "Northern Ireland: Prospects for Progress in 2006?" *United States Institute of Peace: Special Report*, September 2006, pp. 1–20.

Finlayson, Alan. 1997. "The Problem of 'Culture' in Northern Ireland: A Critique of the Cultural Traditions Group." *Irish Review* (20):76–88.

Fitzduff, Mari. 1991. *Approaches to Community Relations Work.* Northern Ireland Community Relations Council, Belfast. Retrieved July 14, 2008, http://cain.ulst.ac.uk/issues/community/fitzduff.htm.

Fitzduff, Mari. 2002. *Beyond Violence: Conflict Resolution Process in Northern Ireland.* New York: United Nations University Press.

FitzGerald, Garret. 1988. *Thoughts on Two Cultures: Learning to Live Together.* London: David Davies Memorial Institute of International Studies.

Flanagan, R. 1999. *Report of the Chief Constable 1998/99.* Royal Ulster Constabulary, Belfast.

Foster, R. F. 1983. "History and the Irish Question." *Transactions of the Royal Historical Society* 33:169–192.

Fraser, T. G. 2000. *The Irish Parading Tradition: Following the Drum.* Houndmills, Basingstoke, Hampshire: Macmillan.

Fulkerson, Gregory M. and Gretchen H. Thompson. 2008. "The Evolution of a Contested Concept: A Meta-Analysis of Social Capital Definitions and Trends." *Sociological Inquiry* 78(4):536–557.

Gallagher, Frankie. 2007. *A Danger to No One, an Opportunity for Everyone: Report on the Background and Work of the CTI—Loyalism in Transition Project.* Conflict Transformation Initiative.

Gallaher, Carolyn. 2007. *After the Peace: Loyalist Paramilitaries in Post-Accord Northern Ireland.* Ithaca: Cornell University Press.

Galtung, Johan. 1975. *Essays in Peace Research.* Copenhagen: Ejlers.

Galtung, Johan. 1995. "Conflict Resolution as Conflict Transformation: The First Law of Thermodynamics Revisited." In *Conflict Transformation*, edited by K. Rupesinghe, pp. 51–64. New York: St. Martin's Press.

Gamson, William A. 1968. *Power and Discontent*. Homewood, Ill.: Dorsey Press.

Gandhi, Mohandas K. (1945) 1967. *The Mind of Mahatma Gandhi*, edited by R. K. Prabhu and U. R. Rao. Ahmedabad: Navajivan.

Ganiel, Gladys. 2006. "Ulster Says Maybe: The Restructuring of Evangelical Politics in Northern Ireland." *Irish Political Studies* 21(2):137–155.

Ganiel, Gladys. 2008a. *Evangelicalism and Conflict in Northern Ireland*. New York: Palgrave Macmillan.

Ganiel, Gladys. 2008b. "A Framework for Understanding Religion in Northern Irish Civil Society." In *Global Change, Civil Society and the Northern Ireland Peace Process: Implementing the Political Settlement*, edited by C. Farrington, pp. 159–179. New York Palgrave Macmillan.

Ganiel, Gladys and Paul Dixon. 2008. "Religion, Pragmatic Fundamentalism and the Transformation of the Northern Ireland Conflict." *Journal of Peace Research* 45(3):419–436.

Gecas, Viktor. 2000. "Value Identities, Self-Motives, and Social Movements." In *Self, Identity, and Social Movements*, vol. 13, edited by S. Stryker, T. J. Owens, and R. W. White, pp. 93–109. New York: Aldine de Gruyter.

Geertz, Clifford. 1963. "The Integrative Revolution." In *Old Societies and New States: The Quest for Modernity in Asia and Africa*, edited by C. Geertz, pp. 108–113. New York: Free Press of Glencoe.

Gidron, Benjamin, Stanley Nider Katz, and Yeheskel Hasenfeld. 2002. *Mobilizing for Peace: Conflict Resolution in Northern Ireland, Israel/Palestine, and South Africa*. New York: Oxford University Press.

Goffman, Erving. 1959. *The Presentation of Self in Everyday Life*. Garden City, N.Y.: Doubleday.

Goffman, Erving. 1963. *Stigma: Notes on the Management of Spoiled Identity*. New York: Simon & Schuster.

Gormley-Heenan, Cathy and Gillian Robinson. 2003. "Political Leadership: Protagonists and Pragmatists in Northern Ireland." In *Researching the Troubles: Social Science Perspectives on the Northern Ireland Conflict*, edited by O. Hargie and D. Dickson, pp. 259–272. Edinburgh: Mainstream.

Graff-McRae, Rebecca Lynn. 2009. "Popular Memory in Northern Ireland." In *War Memory and Popular Culture: Essays on Modes of Remembrance and Commemoration*, edited by M. Keren and H. H. Herwig, pp. 41–56. Jefferson, N.C.: McFarland.

Gribbin, Vincent, Roisin Kelly, and Claire Mitchell. 2005. *Loyalist Conflict Transformation Initiatives*. Belfast: Northern Ireland Executive.

Grosby, Steven. 1994. "The Verdict of History: The Inexpungeable Tie of Primordiality—a Response to Eller and Coughland." *Ethnic and Racial Studies* 17(2):164–171.

Haddick-Flynn, Kevin. 1999. *Orangeism: The Making of a Tradition*. Dublin: Wolfhound Press.

Halbwachs, Maurice. 1980. *The Collective Memory*. New York: Harper & Row.

Hall, Michael. 1986. *Ulster: The Hidden History*. Belfast: Pretani.

Hall, Michael. 1993. *Ulster's Shared Heritage*. Newtownabbey, Co Antrim: Island Publications.

Hall, Michael. 1994a. *The Cruthin Controversy*. Belfast: Regency Press.

Hall, Michael. 1994b. *Ulster's Protestant Working Class*. Belfast: Farset Community Think Tanks Project.

Hall, Michael. 2006. *Conflict Transformation Initiative: Loyalism in Transition: A New Reality?* Vol. 1. Belfast: Farset Community Think Tanks Project.

Hall, Michael. 2007. *Is There a Shared Ulster Heritage?* Vol. 83. Belfast: Island Publications/ Farset Community Think Tanks Project.

Hamilton, Jennifer, Ulf Hansson, John Bell, and Sarah Toucas. 2008. *Segregated Lives: Social Division, Sectarianism and Everyday Life in Northern Ireland.* Belfast: Institute for Conflict Research.

Hawthorne, James. 1989. "Cultural Pluralism, or Plain Sectarianism." *Fortnight* (278):28–30.

Hayes, Bernadette C. and Ian McAllister. 2009. "Religion, Identity and Community Relations among Adults and Young Adults in Northern Ireland." *Journal of Youth Studies* 12(4):385–403.

Hayes, Maurice. 1990. "Whither Cultural Diversity?" Paper presented at MSSc Irish Studies Forum November 29, Queen's University of Belfast.

Hennessey, Thomas. 1996. "Ulster Unionism and Loyalty to the Crown of the United Kingdom, 1912–74." In *Unionism in Modern Ireland: New Perspectives on Politics and Culture,* edited by R. English and G. Walker. New York: St. Martin's Press.

Hennessey, Thomas. 1997. *A History of Northern Ireland 1920–1996.* London: Macmillan.

Herbison, Ivan. 1992. "Language, Literature, and Cultural Identity: An Ulster-Scots Perspective." In *Styles of Belonging: The Cultural Identities of Ulster,* edited by J. Lundy and A. M. Póilin, pp. 54–62. Belfast: Lagan Press.

Higgins, Gareth I. 2000. "Great Expectations: The Myth of Antichrist in Northern Ireland." Ph.D. Dissertation, School of Sociology and Social Policy, Queen's University, Belfast.

Hillyard, Paddy, Bill Rolston, and Mike Tomlinson. 2005. *Poverty and Conflict in Ireland: An International Perspective.* Dublin: Institute of Public Administration (Ireland), Combat Poverty Agency.

Hoppen, K. Theodore. 1989. *Ireland since 1800: Conflict and Conformity.* New York: Longman.

Hughes, Joanne. 1998. "Community Relations in Northern Ireland: Lessons from Drumcree." *Journal of Ethnic and Migration Studies* 24(3):433–450.

Hughes, Joanne and Caitlin Donnelly. 2003. "Community Relations in Northern Ireland: A Shift in Attitudes?" *Journal of Ethnic and Migration Studies* 29(4):643–661.

Hughes, Joanne, Caitlin Donnelly, Gillian Robinson, and Lizanne Dowds. 2003. *Community Relations in Northern Ireland: The Long View.* ARK Northern Ireland Social and Political Archive. Retrieved October 31, 2006,http://www.ark.ac.uk/publications/ occasional/occpaper2.PDF.

Hume, David. 2007. "Gathering Memories after Fifteen Years…" *Broadisland Journal* 31–35.

Interagency Working Group on Bonfires. 2006. *Bonfires: A Report by the Interagency Working Group on Bonfires.* Belfast, Northern Ireland: Environment and Heritage Service.

International Fund for Ireland. 2005. *Sharing This Space: A Strategic Framework for Action* 2006–2010. International Fund for Ireland. http://www.internationalfundforireland. com/publications/IFIstrategy.pdf.

International Fund for Ireland. 2008. *Annual Report and Accounts.* International Fund for Ireland. http://www.internationalfundforireland.com/publications/IFI%20Annual%20 Report%2008.pdf.

Irish Parades Emergency Committee & Brehon Law Society. 2004. *Marching and Disorder: Conflict in Northern Ireland: Summer 2003 International Observers' Report*. New York: Irish Parades Emergency Committee & Brehon Law Society.

Irish Parades Emergency Committee & Brehon Law Society. 2005. *Law and Lawlessness: Summer 2004 International Observers' Report*. New York: Irish Parades Emergency Committee & Brehon Law Society.

Irish Parades Emergency Committee & Brehon Law Society. 2006. *Sectarianism on Parade: Orange Parades in Northern Ireland: Summer 2005 International Observers' Report*. New York: Irish Parades Emergency Committee & Brehon Law Society.

Irish Parades Emergency Committee & Brehon Law Society. 2007. *Make Sectarianism History: International Observers' Report, Northern Ireland 2006*. New York: Irish Parades Emergency Committee & Brehon Law Society.

Irish Parades Emergency Committee & Brehon Law Society. 2008. *11 Years On: Orange Marches and Nationalist Resistance, 1997–2007: International Observers' Report, Northern Ireland 2007*. New York: Irish Parades Emergency Committee & Brehon Law Society.

Irvin, Cynthia L. 1999. *Militant Nationalism: Between Movement and Party in Ireland and the Basque Country*. Minneapolis: University of Minnesota Press.

Jarman, Neil. 1992. "Troubled Images: The Iconography of Loyalism." *Critique of Anthropology* 12(2):133–165.

Jarman, Neil. 1997. *Material Conflicts: Parades and Visual Displays in Northern Ireland*. New York: Berg.

Jarman, Neil. 2000. "For God and Ulster: Blood and Thunder Bands and Loyalist Political Culture." In *The Irish Parading Tradition, Ethnic and Intercommunity Conflict Series*, edited by T. G. Fraser, pp. 158–172. New York: St. Martin's Press.

Jarman, Neil 2004. "Shrouded Signs and Obscured Symbols." In *All over Again*, edited by E. McTigue, N. Jarman, and A. Kelly. Belfast: Belfast Exposed Photography.

Jarman, Neil. 2005. "Painting Landscapes: The Place of Murals in the Symbolic Construction of Urban Space." In *National Symbols, Fractured Identities: Contesting the National Narrative*, edited by M. E. Geisler, pp. 172–191. Middlebury, Vt.: Middlebury College Press.

Jarman, Neil. 2007. "Pride and Possession, Display and Destruction." In *Flag, Nation, and Symbolism in Europe and America*, edited by T. H. Eriksen and R. Jenkins, pp. 88–101. New York: Routledge.

Jarman, Neil and Dominic Bryan. 1996. *Parade and Protest: A Discussion of Parading Disputes in Northern Ireland*. Coleraine: Centre for the Study of Conflict, University of Ulster.

Jarman, Neil and Dominic Bryan. 1998. *From Riots to Rights: Nationalist Parades in the North of Ireland*. Coleraine: Centre for the Study of Conflict, University of Ulster.

Jasper, James M. 1997. *The Art of Moral Protest: Culture, Biography, and Creativity in Social Movements*. Chicago: University of Chicago Press.

Jenkins, Richard. 2008. *Rethinking Ethnicity*. Thousand Oaks, CA: Sage.

Jones, Charles. 1997. *The Edinburgh History of the Scots Language*. Edinburgh: Edinburgh University Press.

Jordan, Glenn. 2001. *Not of This World? Evangelical Protestants in Northern Ireland*. Belfast: Blackstaff Press.

Kane, Anne. 2000. "Narratives of Nationalism: Constructing Irish National Identity during the Land War, 1879–82." *National Identities* 2(3):245–264.

Kaufmann, Eric P. 2007. *The Orange Order: A Contemporary Northern Irish History*. Oxford: Oxford University Press.

Kee, Robert. 1972. *The Green Flag: The Turbulent History of the Irish National Movement*. New York: Delacorte Press.

Kelly, Aaron. 2004. "Walled Communities." In *All over Again*, edited by E. McTigue, N. Jarman, and A. Kelly. Belfast: Belfast Exposed Photography.

Kennaway, Brian. 2006. *The Orange Order: A Tradition Betrayed*. London: Methuen.

Kertzer, David I. 1988. *Ritual, Politics, and Power*. New Haven: Yale University Press.

King, Anthony. 2004. *The Structure of Social Theory*. New York: Routledge.

Kirk, John M. 1998. "Ulster Scots: Realities and Myths." *Ulster Folklife* 44:69–93.

Kriesberg, Louis. 1998a. *Constructive Conflicts: From Escalation to Resolution*. Lanham, Md.: Rowman & Littlefield.

Kriesberg, Louis. 1998b. "Intractable Conflicts." In *The Handbook of Interethnic Coexistence*, edited by E. Weiner, pp. 332–342. New York: Continuum.

Kriesberg, Louis. 2007. *Constructive Conflicts: From Escalation to Resolution*. Lanham, Md.: Rowman & Littlefield.

Kriesberg, Louis, Terrell A. Northrup, and Stuart J. Thorson. 1989. *Intractable Conflicts and Their Transformation*. Syracuse, N.Y.: Syracuse University Press.

Kurtz, Lester R. 1983. "The Politics of Heresy." *American Journal of Sociology* 88:1085–1115.

Lederach, John Paul. 1995. "Conflict Transformation in Protracted Internal Conflicts: The Case for a Comprehensive Framework." In *Conflict Transformation*, edited by K. Rupesinghe, pp. 201–222. New York: St. Martin's Press.

Lederach, John Paul. 1997. *Building Peace: Sustainable Reconciliation in Divided Societies*. Washington, D.C.: United States Institute of Peace Press.

Lederach, John Paul. 2005. *The Moral Imagination: The Art and Soul of Building Peace*. Oxford: Oxford University Press.

Leonard, Madeleine. 2008. "Building, Bolstering and Bridging Boundaries: Teenagers' Negotiations of Interface Areas in Belfast." *Journal of Ethnic and Migration Studies* 34(3):471–489.

Liechty, Joseph. 1993. *Roots of Sectarianism in Ireland*. Belfast: Joseph Liechty.

Liechty, Joseph. 1995. "The Nature of Sectarianism Today." In *Papers of the 1994 Corrymeela Ecumenical Conference*, edited by T. Williams and A. Falconer, pp. 9-29. Dublin: Dominican Publications in assoc. with the Irish School of Ecumenics.

Liechty, Joseph and Cecelia Clegg. 2001. *Moving beyond Sectarianism: Religion, Conflict, and Reconciliation in Northern Ireland*. Blackrock, Co. Dublin: Columba Press.

Lisle, Debbie. 2006. "Local Symbols, Global Networks: Rereading the Murals of Belfast." *Alternatives* 31(1):27–52.

Loftus, Belinda. 1994. *Mirrors: Orange & Green*. Dundrum, Co. Down: Picture Press.

Longley, Edna. 1987. "Opening Up: A New Pluralism." *Fortnight* (256):24–25.

Loughlin, James. 2000. "Parades and Politics: Liberal Governments and the Orange Order, 1880-86." In *The Irish Parading Tradition: Following the Drum*, edited by T. G. Fraser, pp. 27–43. London: Macmillan.

Mac Ginty, Roger and Pierre du Toit. 2007. "A Disparity of Esteem: Relative Group Status in Northern Ireland after the Belfast Agreement." *Political Psychology* 28(1):13–31.

Mac Ginty, Roger, Orla T. Muldoon, and Neil Ferguson. 2007. "No War, No Peace: Northern Ireland after the Agreement." *Political Psychology* 28(1):1–11.

Mach, Zdzislaw. 1993. *Symbols, Conflict, and Identity: Essays in Political Anthropology.* Albany: State University of New York Press.

McAuley, James. 1997. "'Flying the One-Winged Bird': Ulster Unionism and the Peace Process." In *Who Are the People? Unionism, Protestantism and Loyalism in Northern Ireland*, edited by P. Shirlow and M. McGovern, pp. 158–175. London: Pluto Press.

McAuley, James. 2008. "Constructing Unionist and Loyalist Identities." In *Transforming the Peace Process in Northern Ireland: From Terrorism to Democratic Politics*, edited by A. Edwards and S. Bloomer, pp. 15–27. Dublin: Irish Academic Press.

McAuley, James W. 2002. "The Emergence of New Loyalism." In *Changing Shades of Orange and Green: Redefining the Union and the Nation in Contemporary Ireland*, edited by J. Coakley, pp. 106–122. Dublin: University College Dublin Press.

McAuley, James W. 2004a. "Peace and Progress? Political and Social Change among Young Loyalists in Northern Ireland." *Journal of Social Issues* 60(3):541–562.

McAuley, James W. 2004b. "Ulster Unionism after the Peace." In *Peace at Last? The Impact of the Good Friday Agreement on Northern Ireland*, edited by J. Neuheiser and S. Wolff, pp. 76–93. New York: Berghahn Books.

McAuley, James W. 2008. "Two traditions in unionist political culture: a commentary." In *Irish Political Studies Reader: Key Contributions*, edited by Conor McGrath and Eoin O'Malley, pp. 128–135. London: Routledge.

McAuley, James W. and Jonathan Tonge. 2007. "For God and for the Crown: Contemporary Political and Social Attitudes among Orange Order Members in Northern Ireland." *Political Psychology* 28(1):33–54.

McCall, Cathal. 2002. "Political Transformation and the Reinvention of the Ulster-Scots Identity and Culture." *Identities: Global Studies in Culture and Power* 9:197–218.

McCauley, Clark. 2002. "Head-First Versus Feet-First in Peace Education." In *Peace Education: The Concept, Principles, and Practices around the World*, edited by G. Salomon and B. Nevo, pp. 63–71. Mahwah, N.J.: Lawrence Erlbaum Associates.

McGarry, John and Brendan O'Leary. 1995. *Explaining Northern Ireland: Broken Images.* Oxford: Blackwell.

McKittrick, David and David McVea. 2002. *Making Sense of the Troubles: The Story of the Conflict in Northern Ireland.* Chicago: New Amsterdam Books.

McVeigh, Robbie. 1995. "Cherishing the Children of the Nation Unequally: Sectarianism in Ireland." In *Journal: A Quarterly Journal for Community Relations Trainers and Practitioners*, edited by P. Clancy, S. Drudy, K. Lynch, and L. O'Dowd, pp. 620–651. Dublin: Institute of Public Administration.

McVeigh, Robbie. 1997. "Symmetry and Assymetry in Sectarian Identity and Division." *Journal: A Quarterly Journal for Community Relations Trainers and Practitioners* (16):3–5.

Mead, George Herbert. 1934. *Mind, Self & Society from the Standpoint of a Social Behaviorist*, edited by C. W. Morris. Chicago: University of Chicago Press.

Melaugh, Martin. 2009, "Draft List of Deaths Related to the Conflict 2002–2009." http://cain.ulst.ac.uk/issues/violence/deaths.htm.

Melaugh, Martin. 2010, "Political Party Support in Northern Ireland, 1969 to the Present." Retrieved July 8, 2010, http://cain.ulst.ac.uk/issues/politics/election/electsum.htm.

Melucci, Alberto. 1995. "The Process of Collective Identity." In *Social Movements and Culture*, edited by H. Johnston and B. Klandermans, pp. 41–63. Minneapolis: University of Minnesota Press.

Miall, Hugh. 2004. *Conflict Transformation: A Multi-Dimensional Task*. Berghof Research Center for Constructive Conflict Management, Berlin. Retrieved July 15, 2010,http://berghof-handbook.net/documents/publications/miall_handbook. pdf.

Miller, David W. 1978. *Queen's Rebels: Ulster Loyalism in Historical Perspective*. Dublin: Gill and Macmillan.

Mills, C. Wright. 1959. *The Sociological Imagination*. New York: Oxford University Press.

Mitchell, Claire. 2003. "Protestant Identification and Political Change in Northern Ireland." *Ethnic and Racial Studies* 26(4):612–631.

Mitchell, Claire. 2006. *Religion, Identity and Politics in Northern Ireland: Boundaries of Belonging and Belief*. Aldershot, Hants, England: Ashgate.

Mitchell, Claire. 2008a. "For God and…Conflict Transformation? The Churches' Dis/ Engagement with Contemporary Loyalism." In *Transforming the Peace Process in Northern Ireland: From Terrorism to Democratic Politics*, edited by A. Edwards and S. Bloomer, pp. 148–162. Dublin: Irish Academic Press.

Mitchell, Claire. 2008b. "The Limits of Legitimacy: Former Loyalist Combatants and Peace-Building in Northern Ireland." *Irish Political Studies* 23(1):1–19.

Modood, Tariq. 1999. "New Forms of Britishness: Post-Immigration Ethnicity and Hybridity in Britain." In *The Expanding Nation: Towards a Multi-Ethnic Ireland*, edited by R. Lentin, pp. 34–40. Dublin: Trinity College Dublin.

Moore, Niamh and Yvonne Whelan. 2007. *Heritage, Memory and the Politics of Identity: New Perspectives on the Cultural Landscape*. Burlington, Vt.: Ashgate.

Morgan, Valerie. 1995. *Peacekeepers? Peacemakers? Women in Northern Ireland* 1969–1995. INCORE, Coleraine: INCORE. Retrieved October 5, 2010, http://cain.ulst.ac.uk/ issues/women/paper3.htm.

Morgan, Valerie. 2004. "Women and a 'New' Northern Ireland." In *Peace at Last? The Impact of the Good Friday Agreement on Northern Ireland*, edited by J. Neuheiser and S. Wolff, pp. 153–167. New York: Berghahn Books.

Morrissey, Mike, Pat McGinn, and Brendan McDonnell. 2002. *Report on Research into Evaluating Community-Based and Voluntary Activity in Northern Ireland*. Belfast: The Voluntary & Community Unit, DSD.

Morrow, Duncan. 2006. "Sustainability in a Divided Society: Applying Social Capital Theory to Northern Ireland." *Shared Space* (2):63–77.

Morrow, Duncan, Derek Birrell, John Greer, and Terry O'Keeffe. 1994. *The Churches and Inter-Community Relationships*. Coleraine: Centre for the Study of Conflict, University of Ulster.

Muldoon, Orla T., Karen Trew, Jennifer Todd, Nathalie Rougier, and Katrina McLaughlin. 2007. "Religious and National Identity after the Belfast Good Friday Agreement." *Political Psychology* 28(1):89–103.

Mulholland, Peter. 1999. "Drumcree: A Struggle for Recognition." *Irish Journal of Sociology* 9:5–30.

Neilands, Colin. 1997. "Building Better Communities: Community Development and Community Relations Initiatives in Northern Ireland." *Journal: A Journal for CR Trainers & Practitioners* (16):10–12.

Newton, Michael. 2006. "Hitting below the Belt: A Review Essay of *Born Fighting*." *History Scotland* 6(5):46–49.

Nic Craith, Máiréad. 2001. "Politicised Linguistic Consciousness: The Case of Ulster-Scots." *Nations and Nationalism* 7(1):21–37.

Nic Craith, Máiréad. 2002. *Plural Identities—Singular Narratives: The Case of Northern Ireland*. New York: Berghahn Books.

Nic Craith, Máiréad. 2003. *Culture and Identity Politics in Northern Ireland*. New York: Palgrave Macmillan.

Nordstrom, Carolyn. 1995. "Contested Identities/Essentially Contested Powers." In *Conflict Transformation*, edited by K. Rupesinghe, pp. 93–113. New York: St. Martin's Press.

Northern Ireland Community Relations Council. 2007. *Moving Forward: Steps beyond Division. 17th Annual Report* 2006–2007. Belfast: Northern Ireland Community Relations Council.

Northern Ireland Statistics and Research Agency. 2001. *Northern Ireland Census* 2001 *Key Statistics*. Northern Ireland Statistics and Research Agency. Retrieved October 5, 2010, http://www.nisranew.nisra.gov.uk/Census/Census2001Output/KeyStatistics/keystats.html#Ward%20Level.

Northrup, Terrell A. 1989. "The Dynamic of Identity in Personal and Social Conflict." In *Intractable Conflicts and Their Transformation*, edited by L. Kriesberg, T. A. Northrup, and S. J. Thorson, pp. 55–82. Syracuse, New York: Syracuse University Press.

Northrup, Terrell A. 1992. "The Collusion of Enemies: Identity and Conflict in Northern Ireland." Program on the Analysis and Resolution of Conflict, Maxwell School of Citizenship and Public Affairs, Syracuse University.

Northrup, Terrell A. 1997. "Identity Theory." In *Protest, Power, and Change: An Encyclopedia of Nonviolent Action from Act-up to Women's Suffrage*, edited by R. S. Powers, W. B. Vogele, C. Kruegler, and R. M. McCarthy, pp. 239–241. New York: Garland.

O'Hearn, Denis. 1983. "Catholic Grievances, Catholic Nationalism: A Comment." *British Journal of Sociology* 34(3):438–445.

O'Keeffe, Tadhg. 2007. "Landscape and Memory: Historiography, Theory, Methodology." In *Heritage, Memory and the Politics of Identity: New Perspectives on the Cultural Landscape*, edited by N. Moore and Y. Whelan, pp. 3–18. Burlington, Vt.: Ashgate.

"Old Masters Change Murals." 2005. *BBC*, August 13, 2003. Retrieved November 5, 2006, http://news.bbc.co.uk/go/pr/fr/-/2/hi/uk_news/northern_ireland/4562793.stm.

Olick, Jeffrey K. 1999. "Collective Memory: The Two Cultures." *Sociological Theory* 17(3):333–348.

Olick, Jeffrey K. and Joyce Robbins. 1998. "Social Memory Studies: From 'Collective Memory' to the Historical Sociology of Mnemonic Practices." *Annual Review of Sociology* 24:105–140.

O'Reilly, Camille. 2004. "The Politics of Culture in Northern Ireland. In *Peace at Last? The Impact of the Good Friday Agreement on Northern Ireland*, edited by J. Neuheiser and S. Wolff, pp. 168–187. New York: Berghahn Books.

P/U/L Working Group. 2000. *Engaging Protestant/Unionists/Loyalists in Community Relations*. Newcastle, Co. Down, Northern Ireland: P/U/L Working Group.

Parades Commission for Northern Ireland. 2007. *Annual Report and Financial Statements for the Year Ended March 31, 2007*. Belfast: Parades Commission for Northern Ireland.

Parkinson, Alan F. 1998. *Ulster Loyalism and the British Media*. Dublin, Ireland: Four Courts Press.

Patterson, Henry and Erick Kaufmann. 2007a. "From Deference to Defiance: Popular Unionism and the Decline of Elite Accommodation in Northern Ireland." In *Devolution and Constitutional Change in Northern Ireland*, edited by P. Carmichael, C. Knox, and R. D. Osborne, pp. 83–95. Manchester: Manchester University Press.

Patterson, Henry and Eric Kaufmann. 2007b. *Unionism and Orangeism in Northern Ireland since 1945: The Decline of the Loyal Family*. Manchester: Manchester University Press.

Pettigrew, Thomas F. 1998. "Intergroup Contact Theory." *Annual Review of Psychology* 49:65–85.

"Portadown Orangemen: We Haven't Gone Away, You Know." 2008. *Belfast Telegraph*, July 4.Retrieved July 5, 2008, http://www.belfasttelegraph.co.uk/news/local-national/portadown-orangemen-we-haven8217t-gone-away-you-know-13896981.html.

Porter, Norman. 1996. *Rethinking Unionism: An Alternative Vision for Northern Ireland*. Belfast: Blackstaff Press.

Potter, Michael. 2008. "Women, Civil Society and Peace-Building in Northern Ireland: Paths to Peace through Women's Empowerment." In *Global Change, Civil Society and the Northern Ireland Peace Process: Implementing the Political Settlement*, edited by C. Farrington, pp. 142–158. New York: Palgrave Macmillan.

"Protestant Marching Bands." 2005. Thinking Allowed, August 17, 2005. Retrieved October 13, 2007, http://www. bbc.co.uk/radio4/factual/thinkingallowed_20050817. shtml.

Putnam, Robert D. 1995. "Bowling Alone: America's Declining Social Capital." *Journal of Democracy* 6(1):65–78.

Putnam, Robert D. 2000. *Bowling Alone: The Collapse and Revival of American Community*. New York: Simon & Schuster.

Putnam, Robert D. 2001. "Civic Disengagement in Contemporary America." *Government and Opposition* 36(2):135–156.

Putnam, Robert D., Robert Leonardi, and Raffaella Nanetti. 1993. *Making Democracy Work: Civic Traditions in Modern Italy*. Princeton, N.J.: Princeton University Press.

Radford, Katie. 2001. "Creating an Ulster Scots Revival." *Peace Review* 13(1):51–57.

Reid, Whitelaw. [1912] 2005. *The Scot in America and the Ulster Scot*. Bangor, Co. Down, Northern Ireland: Books Ulster.

Reimann, Cordula. 2004. *Assessing the State-of-the-Art in Conflict Transformation*. Berlin: Berghof Research Center for Constructive Conflict Management. Retrieved July 15, 2010, http://berghof-handbook.net/documents/publications/reimann_handbook.pdf.

Rolston, Bill. 1987. "Politics, Painting and Popular Culture: The Political Wall Murals of Northern Ireland." *Media, Culture, and Society* 9(1):5–28.

Rolston, Bill. 1991. *Politics and Painting: Murals and Conflict in Northern Ireland*. Rutherford, N.J.: Associated University Presses.

Rolston, Bill. 1992. *Drawing Support: Murals in the North of Ireland*. Belfast: Beyond the Pale Publications.

Rolston, Bill. 1998. "What's Wrong with Multiculturalism?" In *Rethinking Northern Ireland: Culture, Ideology, and Colonialism*, edited by D. Miller, pp. 253–274. Harlow: Longman.

Rose, Richard. 1971. *Governing without Consensus: An Irish Perspective*. Boston: Beacon Press.

Ross, Marc Howard. 1993. *The Culture of Conflict: Interpretations and Interests in Comparative Perspective*. New Haven: Yale University Press.

Ross, Marc Howard. 2001. "Psychocultural Interpretations and Dramas: Identity Dynamics in Ethnic Conflict." *Political Psychology* 22(1):157–178.

Ross, Marc Howard. 2007. *Cultural Contestation in Ethnic Conflict*. Cambridge: Cambridge University Press.

Ross, Marc Howard, ed. 2009. *Culture and Belonging in Divided Societies: Contestation and Symbolic Landscapes*. Philadelphia: University of Pennsylvania Press.

Ruane, Joseph and Jennifer Todd. 1996. *The Dynamics of Conflict in Northern Ireland: Power, Conflict, and Emancipation*. New York: Cambridge University Press.

Ruane, Joseph and Jennifer Todd. 2004. "The Roots of Intense Ethnic Conflict May Not in Fact Be Ethnic: Categories, Communities and Path Dependence." *Archives européennes de sociologie* 45(2):209–232.

Ruddy, Brid. undated. *Drama and Arts across Borders*. Belfast: Ballymacarrett Arts and Cultural Society.

Rupesinghe, Kumar. 1995a. *Conflict Transformation*. New York: St. Martin's Press.

Rupesinghe, Kumar. 1995b. "Conflict Transformation." In *Conflict Transformation*, edited by K. Rupesinghe, pp. 65–92. New York: St. Martin's Press.

Ryan, Stephen. 1995. "Transforming Violent Intercommunal Conflict." In *Conflict Transformation*, edited by K. Rupesinghe, pp. 223–265. New York: St. Martin's Press.

Ryan, Stephen. 2007. *The Transformation of Violent Intercommunal Conflict*. Burlington, Vt.: Ashgate.

Ryder, Chris and Vincent Kearney. 2001. *Drumcree: The Orange Order's Last Stand*. London: Methuen.

Sandy Row Project Team. 2004. *Addressing the Needs of Working Class Protestant Communities*. Belfast: Department of Social Development.

Santino, Jack. 2001. *Signs of War and Peace: Social Conflict and the Use of Public Symbols in Northern Ireland*. New York: Palgrave.

A Shared Future—Policy and Strategic Framework for Good Relations in Northern Ireland [Consultation Document]. 2003. Belfast: Northern Ireland Executive. Retrieved August 27, 2009, http://www.asharedfutureni.gov.uk/2003_consultation_paper.pdf.

A Shared Future—Policy and Strategic Framework for Good Relations in Northern Ireland. 2005. Belfast: Northern Ireland Executive. Retrieved August 27, 2009, http://www.ofmdfmni.gov.uk/asharedfuturepolicy2005.pdf.

Schelling, Thomas C. 1976. *Arms and Influence*. Westport, Conn.: Greenwood Press.

Scherrer, Christian P. 2008. "Violent Conflict: Contemporary Warfare, Mass Violence and Genocide—Dataset 1985–2005, Typologies, and Trends." In *Encyclopedia of Violence, Peace and Conflict*, edited by L. R. Kurtz, pp. 2331–2382. Amsterdam: Elsevier.

Schirch, Lisa. 2001. "Ritual Reconciliation: Transforming Identity/Reframing Conflict." In *Reconciliation, Justice, and Coexistence: Theory and Practice*, edited by M. Abu-Nimer, pp. 145–161. Lanham: Lexington Books.

Schubotz, Dirk. 2008. "Is There a Protestant Brain Drain from Northern Ireland?" *Shared Space* (6):5–19.

Schubotz, Dirk and Paula Devine. 2009. "Update on Attitudes to Community Relations in Northern Ireland." *CRC e-Bulletin* (5):1–5.

Schubotz, Dirk and Gillian Robinson. 2006. *Cross-Community Integration and Mixing: Does It Make a Difference?* ARK Northern Ireland Social and Political Archive. Retrieved May 27, 2008, http://www.ark.ac.uk/publications/updates/update43.pdf.

Schwartz, Barry. 1996. "Introduction: The Expanding Past." *Qualitative Sociology* 19(3):275–282.

Sharp, Gene. 1973. *The Politics of Nonviolent Action*, Vols. 1–3. Boston: Porter Sargent.

Shirlow, Peter. 2003. "Ethno-Sectarianism and the Reproduction of Fear in Belfast." *Capital & Class* 80:77–93.

Shirlow, Peter, Brian Graham, Kieran McEvoy, Félim Ó hAdhmaill, and Dawn Purvis. 2005. *Politically Motivated Former Prisoner Groups: Community Activism and Conflict Transformation*. Belfast: Northern Ireland Community Relations Council.

Shirlow, Peter, Brian Graham, Amanda McMullan, Brendan Murtaugh, Gillian Robinson, and Neil Southern. 2006. "Population Change and Social Inclusion Study, Derry/ Londonderry." *Shared Space* (3):59–72.

Shirlow, Peter and Mark McGovern. 1997a. "Introduction." In *Who Are the People? Unionism, Protestantism and Loyalism in Northern Ireland*, edited by P. Shirlow and M. McGovern, pp. 1–15. London: Pluto Press.

Shirlow, Peter and Mark McGovern. 1997b. *Who Are the People? Unionism, Protestantism and Loyalism in Northern Ireland*. London: Pluto Press.

Shirlow, Peter and Mark McGovern. 1998. "Language, Discourse and Dialogue: Sinn Fein and the Irish Peace Process." *Political Geography* 17(2):171–186.

Shirlow, Peter and Brendan Murtagh. 2006. *Belfast: Segregation, Violence and the City*. London: Pluto Press.

Shirlow, Peter, Gillian Robinson, Brian Graham, Neil Southern, Amanda McMullan, and Brendan Murtagh. 2005. *Population Change and Social Inclusion Study Derry/ Londonderry*. University of Ulster and Queens University in association with St. Columb's Park House Reconciliation Centre.

Shuttleworth, Ian and Chris Lloyd. 2006. "Are Northern Ireland's Two Communities Dividing? Evidence from the Census of Population 1971–2001." *Shared Space* (2):5–13.

Sillito, David. 2003. "Picture Politics." *BBC News*, August 13. Retrieved November 5, 2006, http://news.bbc.co.uk/2/hi/programmes/newsnight/3147185.stm.

Simmel, Georg. 1971. "Conflict." In *On Individuality and Social Forms: Selected Writings*, edited by D. N. Levine, pp. 70–95. Chicago: University of Chicago Press.

Sluka, Jeffrey A. 1992. "The Politics of Painting: Political Murals in Northern Ireland." In *The Paths to Domination, Resistance, and Terror*, edited by C. Nordstrom and J. Martin, pp. 190–216. Berkeley: University of California Press.

Smithey, Lee A. 2002. "Strategic Collective Action and Collective Identity Reconstruction: Parading Disputes and Two Northern Ireland Towns." Dissertation, Department of Sociology, University of Texas at Austin.

Smithey, Lee A. 2008. "Grassroots Unionism and Conflict Transformation." *Shared Space* (6):51–68.

Smithey, Lee A. 2009a. "Social Movement Strategy, Tactics, and Collective Identity." *Sociology Compass* 3:658–671.

Smithey, Lee A. 2009b. "Conflict Transformation, Cultural Innovation, and Loyalist Identity in Northern Ireland." In *Culture and Belonging in Divided Societies: Contestation and Symbolic Landscapes*, edited by M. Ross, pp. 85–106. Philadelphia: University of Pennsylvania Press.

Smithey, Lee A. and Lester R. Kurtz. 2003. "Parading Persuasion: Nonviolent Collective Action as Discourse in Northern Ireland." *Research in Social Movements, Conflicts and Change* 24:319–359.

Smithey, Lee A. and Michael P. Young. 2010. "Parading Protest: Orange Parades in Northern Ireland and Temperance Parades in Antebellum America." *Social Movement Studies* 9(4):393–410.

Smithey, Lee and Lester R. Kurtz. 1999. "We Have Bare Hands: Nonviolent Social Movements in the Soviet Bloc." In *Nonviolent Social Movements*, edited by S. Zunes, L. Kurtz, and S. B. Asher, pp. 96–124. Malden, Mass.: Blackwell.

Smyth, Marie and Jennifer Hamilton. 2003. "The Human Costs of the Troubles." In *Researching the Troubles: Social Science Perspectives on the Northern Ireland Conflict*, edited by O. Hargie and D. Dickson, pp. 15–36. Edinburgh: Mainstream.

Special EU Programmes Body. 2007. *Peace [Three] Operational Programme.* European Union Programme for Territorial Co-operation, Belfast: Special EU Programmes Body.

Stevenson, Clifford, Susan Condor, and Jackie Abell. 2007. "The Minority-Majority Conundrum in Northern Ireland: An Orange Order Perspective." *Political Psychology* 28(1):105–125.

Sullivan, Paul and John McCarthy. 2004. "Toward a Dialogical Perspective on Agency." *Journal for the Theory of Social Behavior* 34(3):291–309.

Tajfel, Henri. 1981. *Human Groups and Social Categories: Studies in Social Psychology.* Cambridge: Cambridge University Press.

Tajfel, Henri. 1982. *Social Identity and Intergroup Relations.* New York: Cambridge University Press.

Tajfel, Henri and John C. Turner. 1986. "The Social Identity Theory of Intergroup Behavior." In *Psychology of Intergroup Relations*, edited by S. Worchel and W. G. Austin, pp. 7–24. Chicago: Nelson-Hall.

Taylor, Peter. 1998. *Provos: The IRA and Sinn Fein.* London: Bloomsbury.

Taylor, Peter. 1999. *Loyalists.* London: Bloomsbury.

Teixeira, Bryan. 1999. "Nonviolence Theory and Practice." In *Encyclopedia of Violence, Peace, and Conflict*, edited by L. R. Kurtz, pp. 555–565. San Diego: Academic Press.

"£3.3m Going to Replacing Murals." July 10, 2006. Retrieved November 5, 2006, http://news.bbc.co.uk/go/pr/fr/-/2/hi/uk_news/northern_ireland/5163170.stm.

de Tocqueville, Alexis and Arthur Goldhammer. 2004 [1835]. *Democracy in America.* New York: Library of America.

Todd, Jennifer. 1987. "Two Traditions in Unionist Political Culture." *Irish Political Studies* 2(1):1–26.

Todd, Jennifer. 1988. "The Limits of Britishness." *Irish Review* 5:11–16.

Todd, Jennifer. 2005. "Social Transformation, Collective Categories, and Identity Change." *Theory and Society* 34:429–463.

Todd, Jennifer, Theresa O'Keefe, Nathalie Rougier, and Lorenzo Cañás Bottos. 2006. "Fluid or Frozen? Choice and Change in Ethno-National Identification in Contemporary Northern Ireland." *Nationalism and Ethnic Politics* 12:323–346.

Tonge, Jon, Jocelyn Evans, Robert Jeffery, and James W. McAuley. Forthcoming. "New Order: Political Change and the Protestant Orange Tradition in Northern Ireland." *British Journal of Politics and International Relations.*

Tonge, Jonathan. 2005. *The New Northern Irish Politics?* New York: Palgrave Macmillan.

Tonge, Jonathan and James W. McAuley. 2008. "The Contemporary Orange Order in Northern Ireland." In *Protestant Identities in Ireland*, edited by M. Busteed, F. Neal, and J. Tonge, pp. 289–302. Manchester: Manchester University Press.

Väyrynen, Raimo, ed. 1991a. *New Directions in Conflict Theory: Conflict Resolution and Conflict Transformation.* Newbury Park, Calif.: Sage.

Väyrynen, Raimo. 1991b. "To Settle or to Transform? Perspectives on the Resolution of National and International Conflicts." In *New Directions in Conflict Theory: Conflict Resolution and Conflict Transformation*, edited by R. Väyrynen, pp. 1–25. Newbury Park, Calif.: Sage.

Volkan, Vamik D. 1997. *Bloodlines: From Ethnic Pride to Ethnic Terrorism.* New York: Farrar, Straus and Giroux.

Waddell, Neil and Ed Cairns. 1986. "Situational Perspectives on Social Identity in Northern Ireland." *British Journal of Social Psychology* 25:25–31.

Wagner-Pacifici, Robin. 1996. "Memories in the Making: The Shapes of Things That Went." *Qualitative Sociology* 19(3):301–322.

Walker, Brian Mercer. 1996. *Dancing to History's Tune: History, Myth, and Politics in Ireland.* Belfast: Institute of Irish Studies at Queen's University of Belfast.

Walker, Brian Mercer. 2000. *Past and Present: History, Identity, and Politics in Ireland.* Belfast: Institute of Irish Studies, Queen's University of Belfast.

Walker, Graham. 2004. *A History of the Ulster Unionist Party: Protest, Pragmatism and Pessimism.* Manchester: Manchester University Press.

Wallensteen, Peter. 1991. "The Resolution and Transformation of International Conflicts: A Structural Perspective." In *New Directions in Conflict Theory: Conflict Resolution and Conflict Transformation*, edited by R. Väyrynen, pp. 129–152. Newbury Park, Calif.: Sage.

Walsh, Brendan M. 1970. *Religion and Demographic Behaviour in Ireland.* Dublin: Economic and Social Research Institute.

Ward, Peter and Donal McDade. 1997. *Public Attitudes to Parades and Marches in Northern Ireland.* Belfast: Research and Evaluation Services (RES) for the Independent Review of Parades and Marches.

Ward, Rachel. 2006. *Women, Unionism and Loyalism in Northern Ireland: From "Tea-Makers" to Political Actors.* Dublin: Irish Academic Press.

Webb, James H. 2004. *Born Fighting: How the Scots-Irish Shaped America.* New York: Broadway Books.

Weber, Max. [1920] 1978. *Economy and Society: An Outline of Interpretive Sociology*, edited by G. Roth and C. Wittich. Los Angeles: University of California Press.

Weiner, Eugene, ed. 1998. *The Handbook of Interethnic Coexistence.* New York: Continuum.

Wheeler, Eleanor. 2007. *Art for Arterial Routes: Connecting the Communities of Belfast.* Belfast: Belfast City Council Development Department.

Whyte, John. 1983. "How Much Discrimination Was There under the Unionist Regime, 1921–1968?" In *Contemporary Irish Studies*, edited by T. Gallagher and J. O'Connell. Manchester: Manchester University Press.

Whyte, John. 1990. *Interpreting Northern Ireland.* Oxford: Oxford University Press.

Wimmer, Andreas. 2005. "Ethnic Boundary Making Revisited. A Field Theoretic Approach." *IMIS-Beitrage* 27:53–70.

Wimmer, Andreas. 2008. "The Making and Unmaking of Ethnic Boundaries: A Multilevel Process Theory." *American Journal of Sociology* 113(4):970–1022.

Woehrle, Lynne M., Patrick G. Coy, and Gregory M. Maney. 2008. *Contesting Patriotism: Culture, Power, and Strategy in the Peace Movement.* Lanham, Md.: Rowman & Littlefield.

Wright, Frank. 1992. *Northern Ireland: A Comparative Analysis.* Dublin: Gill and Macmillan.

Young, James Edward. 1993. *The Texture of Memory: Holocaust Memorials and Meaning.* New Haven: Yale University Press.

Zerubavel, Eviatar. 1996. "Social Memories: Steps to a Sociology of the Past." *Qualitative Sociology* 19(3):283–299.

Zito, Salena. 2008. "Wooing the Scots-Irish." *Tribune-Review,* March 2.

■ INDEX